Location Privacy in Wireless Sensor Networks

SERIES IN SECURITY, PRIVACY, AND TRUST
Series Editors: Pierangela Samarati and Jianying Zhou

Location Privacy in Wireless Sensor Networks
Ruben Rios, Javier Lopez, and Jorge Cuellar (2016)

Touchless Fingerprint Biometrics
Ruggero Donida Labati, Vincenzo Piuri, and Fabio Scotti (2015)

Location Privacy in Wireless Sensor Networks

Ruben Rios • Javier Lopez • Jorge Cuellar

CRC Press
Taylor & Francis Group
Boca Raton London New York

CRC Press is an imprint of the
Taylor & Francis Group, an **Informa** business

CRC Press
Taylor & Francis Group
6000 Broken Sound Parkway NW, Suite 300
Boca Raton, FL 33487-2742

Printed on acid-free paper
Version Date: 20160609

International Standard Book Number-13: 978-1-4987-7633-2 (Hardback)

Library of Congress Cataloging-in-Publication Data

Names: Rios, Ruben, 1983- author. | López, Javier, author. | Cuellar, Jorge, author.
Title: Location privacy in wireless sensor networks / authors, Ruben Rios, Javier López, and Jorge Cuellar.
Description: Boca Raton : Taylor & Francis, a CRC title, part of the Taylor & Francis imprint, a member of the Taylor & Francis Group, the academic division of T&F Informa, plc, 2016. | Series: Series in security, privacy, and trust | Includes bibliographical references and index.
Identifiers: LCCN 2016017470 | ISBN 9781498776332 (alk. paper)
Subjects: LCSH: Location-based services--Security measures. | Internet of things--Security measures. | Wireless sensor networks--Security measures.
Classification: LCC TK5105.65 .R56 2016 | DDC 621.3841/92--dc23
LC record available at https://lccn.loc.gov/2016017470

Visit the Taylor & Francis Web site at
http://www.taylorandfrancis.com

and the CRC Press Web site at
http://www.crcpress.com

Printed and bound in the United States of America by Publishers Graphics, LLC on sustainably sourced paper.

Contents

1 **Introduction** 1
  1.1 Wireless Sensor Networks 2
  1.2 Overview of Security in Wireless Sensor Networks 6
  1.3 Privacy in Wireless Sensor Networks 9
      1.3.1 User-Centric Privacy 10
      1.3.2 Network-Centric Privacy 12
            1.3.2.1 Content-Oriented Privacy 12
            1.3.2.2 Context-Oriented Privacy 15
  1.4 Location Privacy in Wireless Sensor Networks 16
      1.4.1 Motivating Scenario 17
      1.4.2 Source-Location Privacy 18
      1.4.3 Receiver-Location Privacy 20
  1.5 Book Outline 22

2 **Suitability of Computer-Based Anonymity Systems** 25
  2.1 Anonymous Communications Systems 26
      2.1.1 Anonymity Terminology 27
      2.1.2 Anonymity Properties in Wireless Sensor Network 29
      2.1.3 Classification of Solutions 31
  2.2 Centralized Schemes 33
      2.2.1 Single-Proxy 33
      2.2.2 Mixes 35
      2.2.3 Onion Routing and Tor 38
  2.3 Decentralized Schemes 40
      2.3.1 Crowds and Hordes 41
      2.3.2 GNUnet Anonymity Protocol 43
      2.3.3 DC-nets and Herbivore 45
  2.4 Evaluation 48

3 **Analysis of Location Privacy Solutions in WSNs** 53
  3.1 Node Identity Protection 54

3.1.1 Pool of Pseudonyms 55
3.1.2 Cryptographic Pseudonyms 56
3.2 Source Protection 59
3.2.1 Local Adversaries 59
3.2.1.1 Undirected Random Paths 60
3.2.1.2 Directed Random Paths 64
3.2.1.3 Network Loop Methods.............................. 68
3.2.1.4 Fake Data Sources 71
3.2.2 Global Adversaries 73
3.2.2.1 Dummy Traffic Injection 74
3.2.2.2 Energy-Aware Approaches 75
3.2.3 Internal Adversaries 80
3.3 Receiver Protection 83
3.3.1 Local Adversaries 83
3.3.1.1 Basic Countermeasures.............................. 84
3.3.1.2 Biased Random Walks................................ 85
3.3.1.3 Fake Traffic Injection.............................. 86
3.3.1.4 Sink Simulation..................................... 87
3.3.2 Global Adversaries 89
3.3.2.1 Traffic Homogenization............................. 90
3.3.2.2 Sink Simulation..................................... 92
3.3.2.3 Relocation and Disguise............................ 94
3.4 Summary.. 96

4 Context-Aware Source-Location Privacy 99
4.1 Problem Statement... 100
4.1.1 Network Model... 100
4.1.2 Threat Model... 101
4.2 Context-Aware Location Privacy...................................... 102
4.2.1 Overview... 102
4.2.2 Software Integration... 102
4.2.3 Adversary Detection... 103
4.2.4 Route Updating Process...................................... 105
4.2.5 Data Forwarding Process..................................... 106
4.3 Shortest-Path CALP Routing... 108
4.3.1 Shortest-Path Routing....................................... 108
4.3.2 Combination with CALP...................................... 109
4.4 Protocol Evaluation... 112
4.4.1 Simulation Scenario... 112
4.4.2 Privacy Protection Level.................................... 113
4.4.3 Protocol Overhead... 115
4.4.4 Safety Distance Impact...................................... 118
4.5 Summary and Improvements.. 121

5 Probabilistic Receiver-Location Privacy **123**
  5.1 Problem Statement 124
    5.1.1 Network Model 124
    5.1.2 Threat Model 125
      5.1.2.1 Traffic Analysis Attacks 125
      5.1.2.2 Routing Tables Inspection 127
  5.2 Homogeneous Injection for Sink Privacy 128
    5.2.1 Overview 128
    5.2.2 Routing Tables Creation 130
    5.2.3 Desired Properties 131
    5.2.4 Transmission Protocol 132
  5.3 Node Compromise Protection 134
    5.3.1 Overview 134
    5.3.2 Basic Countermeasures 134
    5.3.3 Perturbation Requirements 135
    5.3.4 Perturbation Algorithm 139
  5.4 Protocol Evaluation 142
    5.4.1 Network Topology 142
    5.4.2 Message Delivery Time 145
    5.4.3 Fake Traffic Overhead 148
    5.4.4 Privacy Protection 149
  5.5 Summary and Improvements 153

6 Conclusion **155**
  6.1 Summary 155
  6.2 Future Challenges 157
    6.2.1 Cost-Effective Location Privacy Solutions 158
    6.2.2 Complete Privacy Solutions 158
    6.2.3 Realistic Adversaries 159
    6.2.4 Interoperable Evaluation Framework 160
    6.2.5 Future Sensor Networks 161

References **165**
Index **177**

Chapter 1

Introduction

The Internet as we know it is rapidly evolving and is expected to remove the digital barrier that covers the physical world. In the near future, not only traditional computing devices will be connected to the Internet, but also almost any everyday object, such as cars, lampposts, and even people, will have a representation in the digital world. Everyday objects will be equipped with tiny processors, radio transceivers, sensors, and actuators and will be addressable and queriable from anywhere and at anytime. The world will be covered with billions of smart interacting objects offering all sorts of services and bringing economic growth and comfort to industries, governments, and final users. This evolution of the Internet is already known as the Internet of Things.

The Internet of Things is an evolving paradigm that was originally expected to be realized by equipping physical objects with costless radio identification tags. Over time, this paradigm has embraced other technologies, and the original vision has been augmented with sensing and data mining capabilities. In this new vision of the Internet of Things, sensing technologies play a crucial role as they enable computers to understand, reason, and act upon the physical world. Wireless sensor network (WSN) is one of such technologies and a key component of the Internet of Things, feeding backend servers with vast amounts of information for further processing and analysis, which enables the discovery of new knowledge and the provision of innovative services. The benefits that these technologies will bring about are undeniable; however, they may come at the cost of an unprecedented privacy loss.

This chapter introduces the concept of WSNs and identifies the privacy problems that come with it. This is the core technology around which all the privacy discussions raised in this book revolve. As such, this chapter pays special attention to highlighting the most distinguishing features of WSNs, which differentiate them from other computing paradigms and make them attractive for countless application scenarios. This chapter also shows how these particular features affect, to a considerable extent, the security and privacy of these networks and the environment where they are deployed. Moreover, it identifies some typical attacker models and describes various types of common attacks to these networks.

Subsequently, this chapter deals with the problem of privacy preservation in WSNs and presents the two main categories of privacy issues arising from the deployment and operation of these networks in diverse scenarios, namely, user-centric and network-centric privacy problems. After briefly analyzing the causes of user-centric privacy issues, the chapter dives into network-centric privacy. At this point, the main problem addressed in this book, namely, location privacy, is considered. The importance of this problem is motivated with a critical scenario where safeguarding location information is essential for the safety and survivability of both the network and the entities being monitored in the field. Finally, the chapter ends with a brief description of the organization of the following chapters.

1.1 Wireless Sensor Networks

WSNs [54] are highly distributed systems consisting of two types of devices, namely, the sensor nodes and the base stations. The sensor nodes (or motes) are matchbox-sized computers that have the ability to monitor the physical phenomena occurring in their vicinity and to wirelessly communicate with devices nearby. Frequently, sensor nodes are densely deployed around a phenomenon of interest. On the contrary, the base station (or sink) is a powerful device, usually a single computer, that gathers and processes all the information collected by the sensor nodes. The base station serves as an interface between the sensor nodes and the users. In some sense, sensor nodes are to computers what sensory cells are to living organisms, the wireless channels can be regarded as the nerves since they are used to connect and transmit information to the central nervous system, and the base station behaves as the brain.

Sensor nodes can be fitted with a large variety of physical sensors (e.g., temperature, humidity, pressure, vibration, radiation), which make WSNs a highly customizable technology capable of performing many diverse tasks. The versatility of the devices combined with their small size permits sensor networks to be unobtrusively embedded into systems for the purpose of monitoring and controlling very diverse environments and assets. In fact, WSNs have been successfully applied to precision agriculture and farming [72,90], habitat and environmental monitoring [86,93,95], e-health and assisted-living control [34,146], industrial control and critical infrastructure protection [19,49], structural health monitoring [24,71], and homeland security and military applications [52,57], among many others.

One of the most distinguishing features of WSNs is the severe hardware limitations of sensor nodes. From an architectural point of view, these tiny devices consist of four essential components [2]: the sensing unit, the processing unit, the transceiver, and the power unit (see Figure 1.1). The sensing unit consists of a series

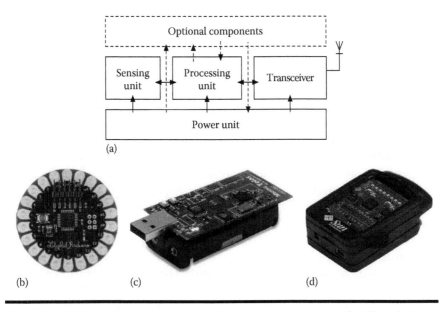

Figure 1.1 **Wireless sensor nodes. (a) Hardware components. (b) LilyPad. (From Arduino, Lilypad arduino, Online, November 2014, http://arduino.cc/en/pmwiki. php?n=Main/ArduinoBoardLilyPad.) (c) TelosB. (From MEMSIC, TelosB platform, Online, November 2014, http://www.memsic.com/ wireless-sensor-networks/ TPR2420.) (d) SunSPOT. (From Oracle Labs, Sun spot world, Online, November 2014, http://www.sunspotworld. com/.)**

of physical sensors that provides the node with the ability to measure different environmental conditions, as previously stated. The processing unit consists of a simple microcontroller whose computational capabilities and memory space are limited to a few megahertz (typically between 8 and 16 MHz) and a few kilobytes (typically between 4 and 10 kB for RAM memory and between 48 and 128 kB for instruction memory), respectively. Although this is the most typical configuration for sensor nodes, these values may vary depending on the application scenario they are intended for. Therefore, we can distinguish three classes of sensor nodes [119]: extremely constrained sensor nodes, typical sensor nodes, and high-performance sensor nodes. Figure 1.1 shows one example of a sensor node for each of these categories.

The radio interface or transceiver allows the sensor node to send and receive messages wirelessly at a low data rate (between 70 and 250 kB/s) usually in the 2.4 GHz unlicensed ISM band of the radio spectrum. Some sensor nodes, especially legacy devices like Mica2Dot [37], operate at frequencies under 1 GHz. Choosing between one band or another really depends on the application scenario. Communications in higher frequency bands have a longer range but find it difficult to overcome obstacles. Normally, the maximum communication range outdoors is around 100 m for low-power configurations [54], although some manufactures claim they can transmit data at distances over 20 km in open spaces with high-sensitivity sub-GHz transceivers [82]. Notwithstanding, this is quite unusual and impractical for battery-powered devices due to the high-energy waste involved in the transmissions of messages over such long distances.

Additionally, some sensor node might be fitted with optional components depending on the application's requirements. These components include, but are not limited to, localization systems (e.g., GPS chips), power scavengers (e.g., solar panels), mobilizers, and external flash memories. Finally, the power unit is in charge of supplying energy to all the components and, as aforementioned, the operation of sensor networks is extremely influenced by this component.

The power unit is, in fact, the most limiting factor in sensor nodes because all other components depend on it to operate. Since the power unit usually consists of two AA batteries (i.e., 3 V), which cannot be replaced or recharged once the network has been deployed, all other components must use energy responsibly. This issue has several important implications, for example, in the operating speed of the nodes. The most common built-in microcontrollers can operate at different speeds [13,132], but due to the limited voltage supplied by the batteries, by default, the operating system* of the sensor nodes reduces the speed to the minimum. Also, it is well known that the energy consumed by the transceiver is far greater than the energy consumed by the microcontroller, and therefore it is advisable to favor computation over transmissions [129]. Although the analysis is based on a particular sensor platform,[†] the results may be extrapolated to other platforms.

The communication model in WSNs is clearly affected by the previous features. Although the data reporting methods in WSNs can be time driven, query driven, event driven, or hybrid [3], the event-driven approach is the most usual one. This is mainly due to the fact that it is suitable for time-critical applications while being energy efficient. In the event-driven model, a sensor node starts reporting data to the base station immediately after an event of interest (i.e., a [sudden] change to the properties of a particular phenomenon) has been detected in its vicinity and stays silent otherwise. Consequently, if there are no events to be reported, the energy consumption of the nodes is moderately low. Moreover, since the transmission power of the nodes is usually not sufficient (or too energy consuming) to establish a direct communication with the base station, the data source uses multihop communications to deliver the sensed data. This means that to reach their destination, the packets sent by remote nodes go through multiple intermediate nodes, which act as data relays.

---

* Some renowned operating systems for sensor networks are TinyOS [77] and Contiki [47].
† The analysis is focused on the Mica2 platform, which uses an Atmel128L microcontroller and a CC1100 chip transceiver. When active, the microcontroller consumes 8 mA while the radio consumes 7 mA in listening mode and up to 21.5 mA for maximum transmission power (+10 dB).

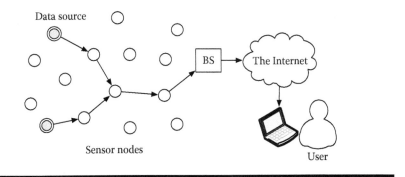

Figure 1.2   Single-path routing in WSNs.

Many routing protocols have been devised to allow remote sensor data to reach the base station [3]. However, there are two main approaches that stand out from the others, namely, flooding-based and single-path routing protocols. A baseline flooding is a simple routing algorithm in which every message received by a node is forwarded to all its neighbors except to the one that sent it.* Recipient nodes repeat the process, thereby making the packet eventually visit all the nodes in the network. This approach is very reliable because it provides a lot of redundancy, but it is also very energy inefficient because it involves all the nodes in the transmission of a single message that is intended to a single node, typically the base station. This family of protocols have other disadvantages such as packet duplicates at the destination and packet collisions especially when the number of simultaneous data sources is high. On the contrary, a single-path (or shortest-path) routing protocol is intended to minimize the number of relaying nodes to reach the destination of the message. In a single-path routing, whenever a node has event data to transmit, it sends a message to a neighboring node that is closer† to the base station than itself. This operation is repeated for each of the nodes in the communication path until the data are eventually delivered. The process is depicted in Figure 1.2, where data sources, colored in gray, rely on nodes closer to the base station to deliver their messages. All future messages from the same source node will follow the same path unless a topology change (e.g., due to the death of a node) occurs.

Additionally, some sensor networks may take advantage of data-aggregation protocols [51] to further reduce network traffic on its way to the base station. Data aggregation consists of a set of operations (e.g., counting, average, maximum, minimum) that are performed at some intermediate points of the network to combine

---

* Actually, every neighbor receives the message because of the broadcast nature of the communication channel but the original sender discards the message.

† The distance is usually measured in terms of the number of hops (i.e., intermediaries) that are
necessary to reach a particular node.

the data originating from different sources. Processing data at intermediate nodes results in a more energy-efficient data communication, thereby increasing the overall lifetime of the network.

1.2 Overview of Security in Wireless Sensor Networks

Despite the unprecedented benefits that WSNs may bring to our society, there are many relevant issues that demand meticulous attention. Sensor networks are inherently insecure, and due to the severe hardware limitation of sensor nodes, most well-founded security solutions, which can effectively protect traditional computer systems and networks, have to be adapted or they simply do not work on these devices. Additionally, these networks are typically unattended, which means that once deployed in remote or hostile environments, no network maintenance is done. This not only affects the lifetime of the sensor nodes whose batteries cannot be replaced but also provides attackers physical access to the devices, which are rarely tamper resistant* due to the implications in the overall cost of the network. Furthermore, the broadcast nature of the transmission medium gives access to the packets exchanged by the sensor nodes to anyone within the communication range.

Consequently, adversaries may take advantage of the distinguishing features of WSNs in order to launch different types of attacks against the network. Sensor networks are particularly vulnerable to attackers who may hinder the correct operation of the network and thus annul all the potential benefits of this technology. More precisely, adversaries can be classified based on their capabilities as follows [141]:

- *Internal vs. external*: The distinction between an internal and an external attacker lies in whether the attacker is a member of the network or an outsider. External attacks are performed by entities that do not belong to the network, while internal attacks are performed by legitimate nodes that behave in an unintended or malicious way.
- *Passive vs. active*: The distinguishing feature between these attackers resides in their ability to disrupt the normal network operation. A passive attacker is an eavesdropper and limits his or her actions to merely observing the messages exchanged by the sensor nodes. In contrast, the active attacker does not only listen but may introduce new packets, modify or block packets in transit, tamper with the devices, or a combination of these.
- *Mote class vs. laptop class*: The main difference between these attackers is on their hardware resources. A mote-class adversary has capabilities similar to an ordinary sensor node, while the laptop-class adversary has access to more

---

* A tamper-resistant module is a piece of hardware (e.g., a smart card) that holds the cryptographic material, program, and sensitive application data of the device. These modules cannot be cloned or physically manipulated.

powerful devices with greater transmission range, processing power, memory storage, and energy budget than typical sensor nodes. A similar distinction is made when referring to the ability of the attacker to control or monitor only a part or the whole network. In this case, it is usual to talk about local or global adversaries.

Note that these categories are not mutually exclusive and an adversary can simultaneously be categorized as an external, passive, and mote-class attacker. This is, in fact, the most usual type of adversary found in the literature when considering privacy issues in sensor networks as it will be shown in the following sections.

The most challenging security-related task in WSNs is to maintain the availability of the network due to the constrained and unattended nature of the nodes, which cannot do much to protect themselves from powerful and not so powerful adversaries. A powerful adversary can easily target the devices themselves, the batteries, or the communication channels in order to disrupt the network operation. Nonetheless, there are some other threats that do not necessarily affect the availability but rather the confidentiality and integrity of the communications or the system as a whole. Some of these attacks may affect several security properties at once. In the following, we provide a nonexhaustive list of potential threats affecting WSNs [138]:

- *Denial of service (DoS) attacks* are any action that reduces or neutralizes the ability of a device, system, or network to perform as expected. A standard DoS attack is jamming the communication channel, which consists of the transmission of a signal that interferes with and affects the frequency spectrum used by the sensor nodes. Similar attacks may also be launched at the link layer by generating collisions, at the routing layer by dropping packets, or at the application layer by flooding a sensor node with so many requests that it eventually runs out of memory or battery.
- *Information flow attacks* target the communication channels in order to compromise the confidentiality and/or the integrity of the transmissions. An attacker may simply observe the communications but he or she may also intercept, modify, replay, or fabricate messages. The first type of attack is intended to retrieve valuable information from the packets traversing the network, while the remaining attacks mainly focus on deceiving the base station to accept a false data value or are part of a more sophisticated attack.
- *Physical attacks* are actions targeting the hardware components of the sensor nodes. In this type of attacks, the adversary has physical access to the sensor node and may access any information contained in it, such as the event data, the program binaries, or the cryptographic material. Additionally, the attacker may modify information within the sensor node in order to create a compromised version that is under the control of the adversary. This is usually the first

step in performing the identity attacks described in the following. Furthermore, the attacker may change the topology of the network by moving some sensor nodes to a different network position, removing them or destroying the devices.

■ *Identity attacks* concentrate on spoofing or replicating the identities of legitimate nodes of the network. The Sybil attack is a form of identity attack where a single node uses multiple (new or stolen) identities. In contrast, a node replication attack consists of having several nodes in the network using the same identity. The final goal of these attacks depends on the application but they are usually effective in obstructing routing algorithms, intrusion detection, and any voting-based mechanisms.

■ *Protocol attacks* concentrate on disrupting routing protocols, data-aggregation mechanisms, and other platform-specific operations. Attacks on the routing layer include attracting or deviating network traffic from particular regions, increasing latency, or dropping messages. In a selective forwarding attack, a malicious node drops some of the packets it receives based on a given criteria. A sinkhole attack aims to attract network traffic toward a particular node controlled by the adversary. In a wormhole attack, a compromised node receives packets and tunnels them (e.g., using a directional wireless link) to another point of the network and then replays them back into the network. This behavior may disrupt some topology discovery mechanisms. Additional attacks include the injection of fake control packets (i.e., hello flood and acknowledgment spoofing attacks).

Consequently, the need for security mechanisms in WSNs is undeniable and many different techniques have been devised to counter these types of attacks. A summary of typical attacks and their countermeasures is provided in Table 1.1. Many of these attacks can be countered by techniques that require the establishment and use of secrets, and thus, key management schemes are essential to provide security in sensor networks. The goal of key management schemes [157] is to generate, distribute, update, and revoke the key material necessary to establish secure (i.e., confidential, unforgeable, and authenticated) communication channels between nodes. However, implementing robust and efficient security primitives in WSNs, especially public-key cryptography, is very challenging given the resource constraints of sensor nodes.

Nonetheless, the use of cryptography is not enough to protect the nodes from physical attacks. To that end, the hardware layer could integrate some protection mechanisms, like tamper-resistant modules, but these would significantly increase the cost of each individual node. A more affordable solution is to use code obfuscation and data scrambling mechanisms [5,89], which would slow down and possibly prevent the analysis of the internals of the nodes. Additionally, the sensor network may incorporate trust management systems [88] and intrusion detection systems [8] to further protect the network.

Table 1.1 Typical Attacks and Countermeasures in a WSN

Category	Subtype	Countermeasures
Denial of service	Channel jamming, packet dropping, packet flooding	Spread spectrum, frame size limitation, redundancy, client puzzles
Information flow	Interception modification, replay, fabrication	Encryption, message authentication codes, timestamping
Physical	Sensor tampering, node destruction	Trusted platform modules, program obfuscation
Identity	Node replication, spoofing, Sybil attacks	Radio fingerprinting, code attestation, random key predistribution, location verification
Protocol	Selective forwarding, sinkhole, wormhole, hello flood, acknowledgment spoofing	Traffic monitoring, multi path routing, packet leashes, authentication

1.3 Privacy in Wireless Sensor Networks

Extensive work has been done on the protection of WSNs from the hardware to the application layer; however, privacy preservation has not received that much attention in these scenarios. Before sensor networks are pushed to the forefront, it is absolutely necessary to consider and address all potential privacy risks that may arise from the adoption of this technology. As a matter of fact, advances in technology* have always revolutionized the way in which privacy is violated and protected.

We distinguish two major categories of privacy problems due to the deployment of WSNs. This taxonomy is based on the entity that is aiming to breach privacy and the entity whose privacy is violated. In the first group, *user-centric privacy*, the privacy perpetrator is the network (owner) itself, while, in the second group, *network-centric privacy*, an entity takes advantage of the network to obtain sensitive information. In either case, the information obtained by the privacy perpetrator may be related to individuals or critical assets. As shown in Figure 1.3, the classification can be broken down into further categories for specialized problems. This book concentrates on the part of the tree colored in gray.

---

* A very good paper by Jan Holvast [59] compiles a history of privacy. The author shows how the birth of new inventions and technologies (e.g., the printing press, automatic photography, the Internet) have influenced and invaded the privacy of individuals and organizations.

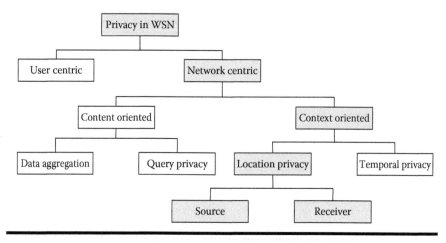

Figure 1.3 Classification of privacy problems in WSN.

1.3.1 User-Centric Privacy

The most obvious privacy risk introduced by WSNs is due to the unobtrusiveness and ubiquity of sensor nodes, which allows them to inadvertently spy on anyone or anything within the reach of the network. Moreover, the reduced cost and size of sensor nodes favor the deployment of large-scale surveillance networks, which may go unnoticed by unaware individuals. Prior to sensing technologies, users needed to take an active role in communications in order to put their privacy at stake. Unfortunately, with the advent of tiny sensor nodes, privacy can be breached at anytime regardless of being an active user of the system, and these invasions to personal privacy may appear in all sorts of everyday situations. Furthermore, the ability of sensor networks to collaboratively analyze and automatically correlate data at different periods of time can result in highly accurate tracking and profiling applications.

As far back as 1991, Mark Weiser [144] warned about the importance of privacy protection in ubiquitous computing scenarios, where sensing technologies are one of the cornerstones of these environments:

> hundreds of computers in every room, all capable of sensing people near them and linked by high-speed networks, have the potential to make totalitarianism up to now seem like sheerest anarchy.

In this Orwellian* scenario, privacy-friendly engineering approaches [131] are off topic because the owner or administrator of the network is a malicious entity

---

* This adjective is used to negatively describe the situation of the society in the novel *1984* by George Orwell, where the authorities (i.e., thought police) are constantly monitoring the population to detect improper thoughts and behavior.

(e.g., a governmental agency) and is therefore unwilling to admit that the network is used for surveillance activities. Besides, this type of threat cannot be easily tackled by technological means alone; rather, severe laws, regulations, audits, and sanctions are also absolutely necessary as data-hungry businesses and organizations are interested in gathering as much information as possible about current and potential consumers in order to offer value-added services but also share and sell this information to third parties for various purposes. In fact, Camenisch [20] describes personal information as the "new currency on the Internet" due to the change on the business model over the last few years. Now services are offered in exchange of personal information instead of money.

Otherwise, legitimate networks may opt to apply a privacy-by-policy approach, thereby informing the user of the collection of personally identifiable information* and the application of fair information practices (FIPs) to these data. FIPs establish a number of principles including user awareness, consent, access and control, purpose specification, data minimization, and secure storage. In other words, users must be aware of being subject to data collection and they must explicitly allow the collection, processing, storage, and dissemination of data about themselves. Also, the data collector must clearly specify the purpose of data collection and use the data for no other purposes. Moreover, the collection of personal information must be minimized and retained only for as long as it is necessary to fulfil the original purpose specified to the user. Finally, the collected data must be secure and accessible to the user at all times, being the data collector responsible for any privacy breaches.

Nonetheless, making the sensor network responsible for presenting privacy policies to the user in a meaningful and unobtrusive way is not a trivial task, especially due to a lack of adequate interfaces. Another option is to let the user define his or her own privacy preferences in order to illustrate how much privacy he or she is willing to give up when interacting with the network. Some approaches [73] have concentrated on these policy-agreement protocols to protect users, privacy, but in most cases, if the policies do not agree, the user cannot access the service. Another limitation to these approaches is on how to ensure that the policies are correctly defined and suitable for each user's privacy expectations.

A more suitable approach is to follow the privacy-by-architecture (or privacy-by-design) principle, which not only minimizes the collection of personally identifiable information but also promotes client-side data storage and processing. The idea is that personal data only leaves the user's domain after sufficient care has been taken to correctly anonymize and reduce the quality of the data (e.g., by adding noise, reducing the precision) in such a way that it is still useful for the provision of the service but it does not leak private information. For example, an extensive body of research has concentrated on the disassociation of identity and location information [16,21,35,55] because of the criticality of these data. Knowing the location of

---

* Personally identifiable information [96] is any information that (1) can be used to distinguish or trace an individual's identity and (2) is linkable to an individual.

a person at a particular moment reveals a lot of information, especially if these data are periodically accessible. Therefore, if one observes that an individual is at a particular location at 3 a.m., this might indicate that this individual is at home, but after continuous observations of the same location, the initial hypothesis becomes much more plausible.

1.3.2 Network-Centric Privacy

Although the most obvious privacy risk associated with sensor networks is due to their ability to collect massive amounts of fine-grained data about the entities in their vicinity, there are also a number of equally relevant privacy issues that may affect not only the network itself but also the individuals, businesses, and assets being monitored by the network. And more importantly, these new privacy problems are still present despite the application of fair information principles.

Unlike user-centric privacy problems where the privacy invader is the sensor network, in network-centric privacy, the privacy perpetrator is an external entity who benefits from a legitimate sensor network to compromise privacy. Therefore, privacy issues go beyond mass surveillance and, even if a network does not surreptitiously gather information, it can be used as a mechanism to invade individual privacy.

A number of network-centric privacy problems have been identified. These can be classified as content-oriented and context-oriented privacy threats [108]. The categorization is based on the type of data the adversary is interested in or is capable of retrieving from the sensor network.

1.3.2.1 Content-Oriented Privacy

Content-oriented privacy threats are mainly due to the ability of an adversary to observe or in some way manipulate the actual contents of the packets traversing the network. A clear example scenario is the Smart Grid [50], where smart meters (i.e., household embedded devices used for measuring utility consumption) use adjacent meters to relay consumption data to a readings collection device, which in turn transmits the readings to the utility company for the purpose of billing. Although the Smart Grid scenario is far more complex [61], as it also includes the generation, transmission, distribution, operation, and market domains, the edge network has many similarities to a typical WSN as it can be seen in Figure 1.4. The smart meters behave as sensor nodes and the collection device is like a base station that processes the readings.

A first line of defense to protect content-oriented privacy in sensor networks is to apply secure encryption schemes in order to provide confidentiality* and integrity to

---

* Confidentiality and privacy are different yet related properties. Data confidentiality does not necessarily imply privacy; it only prevents unauthorized access to data. Consequently, if the original data are personally sensitive, confidentiality helps to enforce privacy, while this is not the case the other way around.

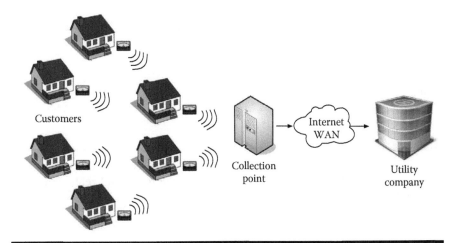

Figure 1.4 Simplified smart metering scenario.

the data in transit. However, this straightforward countermeasure can only provide protection from a subset of potential adversaries, that is, external observers.

An internal attacker (i.e., a legitimate sensor node controlled by a malicious entity) can still intercept, store, and analyze the data being broadcast by its neighbors since it owns legitimate decryption keys. To prevent intermediaries from peeking at the data of other nodes (e.g., the electricity consumption from a neighbor), it is possible to apply end-to-end encryption between the data source and the sink. This is a simple and effective solution but it presents at least two problems: (1) the need for additional key material to allow the destination to decrypt the messages, possibly without even knowing the original sender, and (2) the disruption of some common operations performed by the network. In particular, end-to-end encryption precludes the use of data-aggregation protocols because intermediate aggregator nodes are unable to combine their own data with that contained in the packets they receive and forward.

Therefore, the research community has struggled to develop *privacy-aware data aggregation*-mechanisms capable of preventing insider attacks. The main idea behind most of these solutions is to perturb the original data in such a way that an aggregator cannot obtain the contribution of a single source node even though the aggregated result remains correct. Some solutions are based on the addition of noise to the contributions of the sensor nodes in the form of random values that can later be removed by the aggregator [58]. Some other approaches leverage on the properties of homomorphic encryption schemes in order to allow intermediate nodes to aggregate their own data to received packets without the need to decrypt them. To allow decryption of aggregated data, each node shares a secret key with the base station [23] or uses multiple random keys from a network-wide key pool shared (or not) with the base station [158]. Additionally, some authors have provided solutions to some specific

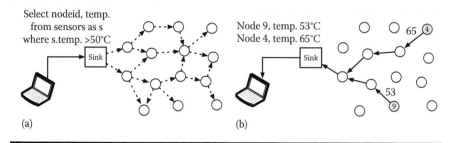

Figure 1.5   Query response in WSN. (a) User asks for sensor nodes whose temperature is over 50°C. (b) Nodes 4 and 9 match the query and reply with their temperature readings.

aggregation functions such as additive [58] and histogram [60,159] operations. The former proposes slicing the data into chunks and distributing them to some neighbors, which finally add (i.e., aggregate) the shares received from all its neighbors before submitting the result to the base station. The latter uses a histogram of a particular granularity and each of the sensor nodes informs to the base station of not the real value but rather the histogram interval where its readings lie.

Finally, some research on protecting *query privacy* in WSNs has also been conducted. The goal is to reduce the risk of data exposure when issuing queries to a sensor network. For example, an oil company may learn the interest of a competitor for petroleum exploration in a particular area based on the queries issued to the network (see Figure 1.5). Therefore, it is important to conceal the (identities of) nodes that respond to a particular query. The trivial solution to the problem is to make all sensor nodes reply to queries even if the user is not interested in them. After receiving the readings, the base station (or the user) keeps the relevant data and discards the rest. This approach is very simple and provides perfect privacy, but it is also extremely inefficient, especially when the network is densely populated. Consequently, several research efforts have been done to find a balance between privacy and efficiency. Di Pietro and Viejo [44] benefit from data aggregation to reduce the amount of traffic generated in the network if all sensor nodes respond to queries. A different approach is to hide the actual target node by issuing bogus queries to the network [22]. A similar approach [39] is to issue a query following a particular path in the network such that the target node is potentially any node in the path. However, this requires additional knowledge about the topology of the network. To overcome this problem, the scheme proposed in [45] leverages on data replication at a number of random locations in the network, thus unlinking the data from their sources. When the user sends a query, it is forwarded to several random destinations, hoping to hit one of the replicas. Also, some authors [56] have explored the minimum necessary communication overhead to achieve a certain level of privacy when issuing queries to a sensor network.

1.3.2.2 Context-Oriented Privacy

Context-oriented privacy concerns the protection of the data associated with the operation of the network. These data are not part of the actual packet contents exchanged by the sensor nodes; they are instead metadata* related to the measurement and transmission of the sensed data. Therefore, even if the payloads are suitably protected from eavesdropping, an adversary could obtain other sensitive information that might compromise the privacy of the network itself and the privacy of the events being monitored. In fact, the mere presence of messages traversing the network is usually indicative that some kind of event is taking place.

Traffic analysis [115] is a very powerful set of mechanisms that helps to determine information about the entities exchanging information by observing the attributes of the communications. These mechanisms can be used to extract and infer much sensitive information about the network from apparently innocuous metadata generated during the operation of the network. A number of features were analyzed by Pai et al. [109]:

■ The *frequency spectrum* used for the communication might reveal the sensor platform being used. Recent technologies like micaz, IRIS, and Imote2 can be easily distinguished from older ones like cricket and Mica2 because the former performs at the 2.4 GHz spectrum, while the latter performs at sub-GHz frequencies. Being able to distinguish the types of sensor nodes in use may allow an attacker to exploit platform-specific vulnerabilities. Also, by using a spectrum analyzer, an attacker might be able to determine the owner of the network since different frequency bands are assigned and licensed for different purposes and to distinct organizations in different countries. For example, the 300–420 MHz band is reserved for governmental use in the United States.

■ The *transmission rate* at which messages are generated and delivered to the base station is a good indicator of the quantity and nature of the events being monitored. In event-driven sensor networks, the mere transmission of messages reveals the presence of events in the network to an observer. Similarly, the absence of messages might be an indicator of sensitive information. Consider, for example, a sensor network deployed to monitor the heartbeat of a patient. A high transmission rate might indicate that the patient is in a stressful situation, while a low or a complete lack of messages may imply that the patient is sleeping, has fainted, or has suffered a cardiac arrest.

■ The *message size* provides information about the type and precision of the data being collected. When a sensor network is used to monitor phenomena of different granularities, like presence (Boolean) or radiation (double), the attacker can easily distinguish which type of event data is contained in each

---

* Metadata are data that are used to describe or to provide additional information about other data.

message based on its size. Additionally, the adversary can guess the purpose of the network given the deployment scenario and the message length because a coarse-grained data collection is used for slow-varying phenomena, while a fine-grained data collection is suitable for fast-varying phenomena. Moreover, some data-aggregation protocols might introduce privacy issues because as the nodes incorporate their own data to received messages, the messages might increase in size. This feature can help the adversary determine the proximity to the base station since a lengthy packet is more likely to have traversed many nodes.

■ The *communication pattern* reveals information about the network topology. Any solution for WSNs is especially tailored to preserve the limited battery of sensor nodes in order to extend the lifetime of the network. In particular, the event-driven data reporting model and the use of shortest-path routing protocols are intended to reduce the high cost associated with wireless communications. These features can be exploited by an adversary to discover the location of important network nodes, generally the data sources and the base station, as they are associated with individuals or relevant assets.

An additional contextual privacy consideration is made by Kamat et al. [67], who suggest that it is also important to hide the time of occurrence of events because this information may allow an adversary to predict future behaviors of the phenomena being monitored by the network. This privacy problem, known as "temporal privacy," is particularly relevant in mobile asset monitoring applications since the adversary may guess the pattern of movement of these assets.

Admittedly, some of the problems introduced by these features can be circumvented by implementing simple countermeasures, like a fixed message size regardless of the length of the contents. However, concealing the information associated with some other features is less straightforward. Preventing the disclosure of location information about relevant network nodes is a particularly challenging and safety-critical task.

1.4 Location Privacy in Wireless Sensor Networks

Based on the original privacy definition by Alan F. Westin [4], location privacy can be defined as the desire to determine under what circumstances and to what extent location information is exposed to other entities. Therefore, location privacy in WSNs aims to preserve the location of relevant nodes in the network. More precisely, it focuses on preventing an adversary from determining the location of the data sources and the base station. These are called, respectively, the source- and the receiver-location privacy problems.

Although this problem has been extensively studied in other domains, especially those involving the use of handheld devices to access location-based services

[10,11,38,130], the location privacy problem in WSNs presents new features and nuances that pose challenging problems that need to be tackled from a different perspective.

1.4.1 Motivating Scenario

In order to illustrate the importance of location privacy problems in WSNs and to facilitate future analysis and discussion, we present a motivating scenario that captures the most distinguishing features of both source-location and receiver-location privacy. The criticality of the scenario highlights the importance of the problem and the need to develop solutions to protect from adversaries.

Consider a military environment like the one depicted in Figure 1.6, where a large number of sensor nodes are deployed in a vast area for the purpose of monitoring the movements and whereabouts of the troops and assets (e.g., armaments, tanks, drones) belonging to a military force. The goal of the network is to better coordinate and control the troops during attack and reconnaissance missions. Doubtlessly, the deployment of a monitoring sensor network can mean a significant advantage over the enemy.

Given the critical nature of the scenario, information must be processed and analyzed in real time. Therefore, immediately after the detection of an event of interest (e.g., the presence of troops) in the area controlled by a sensor node, the collected information is transmitted toward the base station on a multihop basis. Typically, single-path or flooding-based routing algorithms are used. As long as the

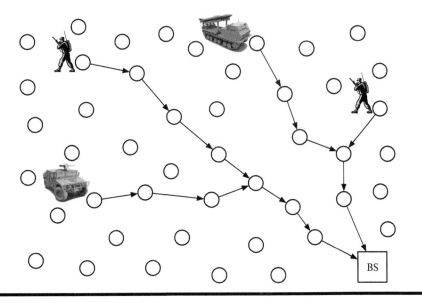

Figure 1.6   Sensor network deployment for military operations.

event persists, the corresponding sensor node will continue to generate new traffic, which is expected to reach the sink in the shortest time possible. In the meantime, an adversary (i.e., the enemy) will try to exploit the deployed infrastructure for his or her own benefit.

The importance of source-location privacy is not the protection of the hardware itself but on the need to hide to presence of events in the field. Especially sensitive scenarios are those involving individuals and valuable assets, like the military scenario depicted in Figure 1.6. An adversary who knows the location of a data source can determine with sufficient precision the area where an event has been detected, meaning that the enemy is capable of uncovering the location of targets in order to attack them. Moreover, protecting the location of the base station is extremely important because if it is compromised or even destroyed, the whole system is rendered useless. Besides the physical protection of the network, the location of the base station is strategically sensitive because this key device is most likely housed in a highly relevant facility. In the military scenario under consideration, the attacker can accomplish a more devastating attack by targeting the base station, which is located within the headquarters of its enemy.

Despite the criticality of the military scenario, the location privacy problems are extensible to any conceivable scenario due to the singular communication pattern of WSNs. The attacker may exploit these properties to find the base station or data sources. To better understand the threat we must confront, it is necessary to know the general features of the adversarial model. The adversary is assumed to be aware of the methods and protocols being used by the network or he or she can eventually deduce them after sufficient observation of the network behavior. In other words, the adversary is assumed to be *informed*. Normally, he or she does not interfere with the normal operation of the network so as not to be detected because the network may implement intrusion detection mechanisms [8] that alert of abnormal situations. This would hinder the plans of the adversary or it could result in unwanted consequences (e.g., being attacked). Therefore, the attacker is usually considered to be *passive*. Additionally, the adversary has no control over the sensor network but in certain scenarios he or she may be able to capture and compromise some nodes to help him or her determine the location of particular nodes. So, the adversary is generally assumed to be *external*. Finally, depending on the power of the adversary, he or she may need to move in the field in order to find the target or he or she can remotely determine its location based on the analysis of the traffic captured by an adversarial network deployed for the purpose of eavesdropping the communications of the legitimate network. With respect to the hearing range of the adversaries, they can be considered either local or global.

1.4.2 Source-Location Privacy

The source-location privacy problem was first introduced and analyzed by Ozturk et al. [108]. The authors show how the operation of various routing protocols widely

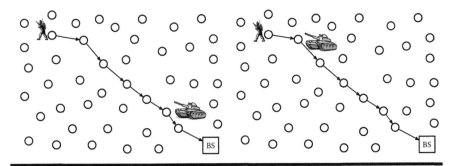

Figure 1.7   Source-location privacy problem in a military scenario.

used in WSNs (i.e., single-path and flooding algorithms) leak information about the nodes reporting event data to the base station.

An adversary with a local vision of the network communications, namely, a mote-class adversary, can act in the following way to find the source of event messages. Starting at any point of the network* and moving around, the attacker eventually stumbles upon a communication path originating from a remote sensor node. The adversary, who is equipped with a device capable of measuring the angle of arrival of received signals (i.e., a directional antenna), can estimate the sensor node that transmitted a message. This node is a mere intermediary in the communication path but by moving toward it and repeating the same process over and over again, the adversary can finally reach the original data source. This process is depicted in Figure 1.7, where the enemy (i.e., the tank) follows the communication path in reverse in order to find the soldiers. Thus, this strategy is usually referred to as traceback attack.

Note that the situation is not any better when there are multiple source nodes reporting event data to the base station. The reason is that the adversary is usually not interested in reaching a particular data source since all events are equally important to him or her.[†] In the military scenario considered here, any data source guides the enemy to a target. Similarly, in an endangered animal monitoring scenario, the location of a source node leads to an animal. In a cargo tracking application, data sources are directly related to the location of the cargo.

Some adversaries can achieve a global vision of the sensor network by deploying their own adversarial network. Therefore, the adversary does not need to move in the field; instead, he or she can simply analyze the data collected by his or her

---

* Usually the attacker is assumed to start in the vicinity of the base station from where he or she can observe any incoming communication.

† Most sensor networks only monitor a particular type of event. In a multievent sensor network, if the adversary wants to discern between different types of events, he or she might turn to the analysis of other features like those presented in Section 1.3.2.2.

network remotely. In this case, each adversarial node monitors the transmissions in its vicinity, and based on the number of packets overhead by each node, the adversary deduces the location of the data sources. In particular, the adversary can spot the area where a data source is located because sensor nodes only initiate a transmission in the presence of events. Moreover, the time at which a transmission takes place helps to determine the location of the source node. Clearly, the attacker can spot data sources by comparing the time at which any pair of adversarial nodes first observed a sequence of messages.

Additionally, some adversaries might also compromise a small portion of the sensor nodes in the network in an attempt to obtain information about the data sources. Since data are transmitted using multihop routing mechanisms, an adversary compromising a portion of the network has a certain probability that some of the nodes he or she controls is involved in the routing of the data to the base station. As compromised nodes are part of the network, they have access to any secrets shared with neighboring nodes, and thus, they could access the contents of the messages it forwards. Having access to the packet contents may allow en route nodes to retrieve the original data sender because this information must be contained somewhere in the packets to allow the base station recognize the data source.

1.4.3 Receiver-Location Privacy

The base station is the most precious element in a WSN and, as such, its location must be thoroughly protected from potential attackers. Deng et al. [41] started to investigate along this line by presenting a set of mechanisms that included the use of hashing functions to obfuscate the addressing fields in the packet headers. However, it was only later that they realized that this type of countermeasure was insufficient protection from adversaries performing both content analysis and more sophisticated traffic analysis attacks.

Local adversaries are interested in finding the base station and thus traceback attacks are no longer useful. Instead, the adversary must determine the direction of the communications flow. To that end, he or she might first turn to time correlation attacks, where the idea is to determine the next node in the communication path by observing the time difference between the transmission of a node and its neighbors. Based on the assumption that a node transmits a message immediately after it is received, the attacker can determine the next node in the path by observing the neighboring node that transmitted in the shortest space of time. Since event data are always addressed to the base station, by moving to the forwarding node, the attacker is capable of reducing the distance to the sink. This process is then repeated at each intermediate node until finally the attacker finds his or her target. Additionally, the adversary can opt to use a rate-monitoring attack to reach the base station. This attack is based on the fact that the transmission rate in the vicinity of the base station is higher than in remote areas because of the use of multihop communications (see Figure 1.8a). A sensor node close to the sink must serve as an intermediary for remote

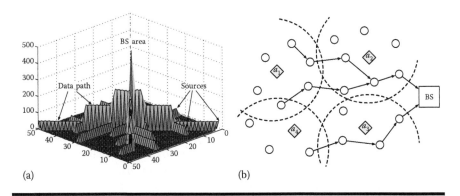

Figure 1.8 **Traffic rate monitoring in a typical WSN. (a) Number of transmissions in a WSN implementing single-path routing with 15 data sources and a single base station. (b) Adversarial network (a_i) deployed to monitor the transmissions of the legitimate network.**

nodes, thus increasing the number of packets it transmits. Consequently, before making a decision on his or her next move, the adversary observes the number of transmissions of a node and its neighbors. After a sufficient number of observations, the attacker can deduce the neighbor that is most likely to be closer to the base station and move accordingly.

Similarly, a global adversary uses rate-monitoring attacks to infer the location of the base station. The use of an adversarial network allows him or her to compare the number of packets observed in each area without having to move around in the field. The adversarial nodes recording a higher number of packets reveal to the attacker which areas are close to the base station. In Figure 1.8b, we illustrate the deployment of an adversarial network $\{a_1, \ldots, a_4\}$ observing the communications within its hearing range, which is represented by dashed semicircles. As the adversarial nodes a_2 and a_3 overhear a higher number of transmissions,* they are more likely to be close to the base station.

Finally, note that we are addressing homogenous sensor networks, where all the sensor nodes have the same role, that is, sensing, reporting, and relaying data. However, in heterogeneous sensor networks, the communication pattern may differ slightly depending on the configuration of the network. For example, in a hierarchical configuration, sensor nodes are organized into clusters controlled by a cluster head that makes all organizational decisions, like routing the data sensed by the cluster members to the base station. Therefore, the adversary might be interested in finding nodes with a particular functionality, like the cluster head.

---

* The use of data-aggregation algorithms may reduce the number of transmissions in the vicinity of the base station but the traffic pattern would still be pronounced in the presence of numerous data sources.

This book concentrates on the first type of network configuration although some of the approaches and solutions discussed hereafter may also be applicable to the second type of network.

1.5 Book Outline

WSNs bring tremendous benefits to our society due to their ability to link the virtual world and the real world. Unfortunately, the deployment of such context-aware technologies may also involve a number of risks and threats that need to be carefully assessed before they are socially accepted. A major impediment to social acceptance is the potential risk of privacy violations that WSNs entail. This is precisely the main focus of this book: *facilitating a privacy-aware integration of* WSNs in our daily lives.

In this first chapter, the concept of WSNs has been introduced and their main features have been illustrated, including hardware limitations, communication model, and routing protocols. A quick overview of security threats and countermeasures in this paradigm has also been provided. In addition, this chapter introduces the two main privacy research areas in WSNs and special attention is paid to context-oriented privacy. Then, the chapter delves into the location privacy problem, which have been extensively explained and motivated.

Before devising new tailored solutions to a given problem, it is necessary to analyze whether these new solutions are strictly necessary. This is especially important when there is a well-founded area with a number of solutions to problems that are closely related to the one being tackled. This is precisely the motivation of Chapter 2. Since location privacy problems in WSNs are caused by their particular communication pattern, these problems may be countered by traditional traffic analysis protection mechanisms devised for computer networks. This hypothesis has been rejected by several authors by simply claiming that sensor nodes cannot withstand the heavy computational overhead imposed by these solutions. However, this reason alone is insufficient to exclude them from the WSN domain as new sensor nodes with more capacity can be built. Therefore, this chapter studies which anonymity properties are most suitable to fit the particular features and requirements of location privacy in WSN, and on top of that, it analyzes some well-known computer-based anonymity solutions in order to give insight into their overhead and possible limitations to the application of the network.

Chapter 3 provides a literature review and analysis of the existing solutions for location privacy in WSNs. The presentation of this chapter is guided by several criteria that allow us to classify solutions according to the assets that demand protection, the capabilities of the adversary, and their most distinguishing features. First, we analyze a set of solutions that have been devised to protect the identity of the nodes during data transmission. Next, we concentrate on solutions aimed at hiding the location of the data sources and the base station by changing the normal communication pattern of the network. These solutions are further divided depending on the capabilities of the adversary under consideration: local or global eavesdropper and internal adversaries. For each individual solution, we present some advantages and limitations. This has helped to identify pitfalls, open problems, and possible lines for pushing forward the state of the art. As a result, we present a complete taxonomy of solutions and discuss some possible lines of actuation that are exploited in the following chapters.

The Context-Aware Location Privacy (CALP) is presented in Chapter 4. This mechanism benefits from the intrinsic nature of sensor nodes of being able to feel their environment to detect the presence of a mobile adversary in the network deployment area. The idea is to anticipate the movements of the adversary and modify the routing paths in order to minimize the number of packets he or she is able to capture. The scheme has been successfully applied to protect source-location privacy in the presence of local adversaries with different moving strategies. In particular, we have developed two versions of the CALP scheme, which differ on the penalty imposed on paths traversing the area where the adversary is located. Since the proposed scheme is only triggered in the presence of the adversary, it considerably reduces the overhead imposed on the network compared to previous solutions.

Chapter 5 describes a receiver-location privacy solution called the Homogeneous Injection for Sink Privacy with Node Compromise protection (HISP-NC) scheme. The proposed solution consists of two complementary schemes that deal with adversaries capable of observing the communications in a limited area of the network as well as inspecting the routing tables of a portion of the nodes. The first scheme injects controlled amounts of fake traffic to probabilistically hide the flow of real messages toward the base station. This scheme on its own provides an adequate protection level against local eavesdroppers but is useless if the adversary is capable of gaining the information contained in the routing tables of a few nodes. The second scheme provides, for the first time, some means of protection against this type of threat by perturbing the routing tables of the nodes in such a way that inspection attacks are not trivial but real messages reach the base station within a reasonable time frame.

Chapter 2

Suitability of Computer-Based Anonymity Systems

Anonymity networks are communications systems that allow individuals to interact with each other without revealing their identity or other sensitive information about themselves, like their habits or preferences. These systems have been around, at least theoretically, for several decades now since David Chaum first proposed a scheme for the transmission of untraceable e-mails through the Internet. This work pioneered many others and nowadays research in anonymous communications is a very prolific and solid field of study with a number of leading conferences and with real-world solutions, like the Tor network, which are used by millions of people on a daily basis.*

These systems are capable of providing some privacy guarantees by employing a number of techniques that are intended to obfuscate the traffic pattern. Since the location privacy problem is basically due to the pronounced communication pattern in sensor networks, it seems reasonable to study whether existing solutions are able to provide an adequate protection level in the sensors' domain before devising new ones. Therefore, this chapter analyzes the suitability of computer-based anonymous communications systems for the protection of location privacy in WSNs.

Several authors [102,139] have established that computer-based anonymous communications systems are not applicable to the sensor domain with vague

---

* See https://metrics.torproject.org/.

arguments about the prohibitive hardware requirements of such systems. Notwithstanding, given the extensive literature on anonymous communications systems and the maturity of research in the field, we believe that excluding the solid protection mechanisms provided by these systems without proper analysis would be a serious mistake, especially considering that the capabilities of sensor nodes can improve considerably in the future.

To decide whether or not anonymous communications systems are truly unsuitable for WSNs, it is necessary to strictly analyze the requirements, goals, and techniques proposed by these systems, as well as the particular features and requirements imposed by the new scenario. First, this chapter presents an analysis of anonymity properties and how they suit the location privacy problem in WSNs given the capabilities and strategies of the adversary. Next, it examines both centralized and decentralized anonymous communications systems in order to determine their limitations and imposed overhead. The chapter finishes with a brief discussion on the factors that may limit the application of the analyzed solutions in the realm of sensor networks.

2.1 Anonymous Communications Systems

Data communication networks allow us to establish online transactions with remote entities. These networks rely on a series of mechanisms and protocols that use addressing information to identify the parties that are intended to receive or route messages on their way to the destination.

Even when application-layer data are properly secured using end-to-end encryption, the addressing information (e.g., IP and MAC addresses) is sent in clear text in order to enable data routing at intermediate nodes. These addresses seldom change and appear in every single packet, which allows anyone observing the communication flow to correlate all the transactions belonging to a single user. Moreover, some addresses are unique to a specific device, which can be ultimately linked to a particular individual, thus severely compromising his or her privacy. Additionally, an ambitious adversary can perform more sophisticated traffic analysis attacks, such as monitoring the volume of packets being sent or received, in order to obtain more detailed information about a particular user.

Anonymous communications systems were devised precisely to protect users' privacy in the presence of highly motivated adversaries performing traffic analysis attacks. These systems are based on a number of mechanisms, usually built on top of cryptographic primitives, which are intended to conceal the addresses of the users as well as any other information associated with their identity that can be extracted by observing the traffic generated from their interactions with other users or systems.

Usually, anonymous communications systems consider a scenario like the one depicted in Figure 2.1. In this setting, a set of senders use a data communication network (e.g., the Internet) to send messages to a group of recipients and the goal is

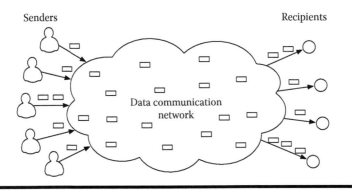

Senders   Recipients

Data communication
network

Figure 2.1 Communications setting.

to ensure that an attacker cannot retrieve sensitive information about the communicating parties from the observation of a portion of the network or the system as a whole. The attacker may be interested in determining different types of information from the set of potential senders and recipients, and the anonymous communications systems struggles to offer some anonymity-related properties that are intended to prevent that disclosure of sensitive information.

Pfitzmann and Hansen [110] provide a comprehensive and widely accepted terminology for describing privacy-related concepts. We adopt and review these definitions for our analysis, as having a complete understanding of anonymity properties is essential for a detailed analysis of any anonymity solution.

2.1.1 Anonymity Terminology

Defining privacy is usually difficult because of the subjectivity of the term. This concept has different interpretations and nuances depending on many different factors such as socioeconomical condition, level of educational, and religious beliefs. A simple yet renowned definition considers privacy as the right to be left alone [142]; however, new definitions have appeared as new ways of invading privacy have emerged. In the area of information technology, privacy can be defined as the right of individuals (or entities) to control the disclosure, processing, and dissemination of information about themselves. Therefore, privacy is closely related to anonymity because it describes the desire of an individual to remain unidentified when performing some action. However, anonymity is not the only useful property to accomplish privacy. Next, we review the most relevant privacy-related properties based on the terminology from Pfitzmann and Hansen [110].

Anonymity can be defined as the state of being not sufficiently identifiable within a set of subjects (i.e., the anonymity set) with potentially the same attributes as the original subject. In other words, anonymity mechanisms prevent the disclosure of the identity of the individual who performed a particular action (i.e., the attribute) by having a set of potential actors. Clearly, if all the members in the anonymity set are equally likely to be the author of the action, the anonymity becomes stronger as the size of the anonymity set grows. Ideally, the probability that an adversary can successfully determine the actual entity who performed the action is one over the size of the anonymity set. However, in practice, not all members in the anonymity set are equally likely to be the actual author. In the landscape of anonymous communications systems, the action usually refers to the transmission or reception of messages. Therefore, a sender may be anonymous within a set of potential senders, and similarly, a recipient may be anonymous within a set of potential recipients. These properties are known as sender and receiver anonymity, respectively.

Another important property for the protection of individual privacy is *unlinkability*. Unlinkability of two (or more) items of interest means that an adversary cannot sufficiently distinguish whether these items are related or not. By definition, the items of interest may be any element of the system, such as entities or messages. Therefore, we may encounter different types of unlinkability. Commonly, anonymous communications systems strive for the unlinkability of the sender and the receiver,* which provides the communicating parties with the ability to hide with whom they communicate. This is usually known as relationship unlinkability and it is useful in the presence of external observers trying to infer information about the preferences of an individual. When a user accesses an online service (e.g., websites) regularly, this reveals information about his or her interests. For example, daily visits to a particular online newspaper might reveal a right- or left-wing ideology. Besides, relationship unlinkability suggests that even when the sender and the receiver can each be identified as participants in a communication, they cannot be recognized as communicating with each other. This implies that the unlinkability property is stronger than anonymity.

Finally, undetectability and unobservability are properties that aim to protect the items of interest themselves. *Undetectability* of an item of interest means that the attacker cannot sufficiently determine whether a particular item exists or not. Similarly, *unobservability* means undetectability of the item against all external entities and, additionally, anonymity even against other subjects involved in the item of interest. In anonymous communications systems, the cited properties usually refer to messages as the objects of interest. Therefore, undetectability aims to prevent an attacker from determining whether (real) messages are being transmitted. On the other hand, unobservability not only implies that an external attacker cannot detect the presence of messages but also that other senders/receivers cannot sufficiently determine who is sending/receiving the messages. A sender is unobservable when the attacker is not able to determine whether any of the senders is transmitting real

---

* The attacker model determines the sort of unlinkability required. For example, message unlinkability is important for preventing a server from linking multiple requests from the same data source in order to avoid user profiling.

messages. Likewise, the recipient is unobservable if the adversary cannot conclude whether it is receiving real data messages.

2.1.2 Anonymity Properties in Wireless Sensor Network

Prior to the analysis of traditional anonymous communications systems, here we discuss the need for and suitability of the anonymity properties described in Section 2.1.1 with reference to the location privacy problem in WSNs. Among the various pieces of sensitive information that might be gathered by an observer of the communications, we concentrate on the location of the nodes reporting or receiving event messages since their location can be determined by means of traffic analysis.

Since the main focus of anonymous communications systems is hindering traffic analysis, in principle, these systems might also be ideal for protecting the location of the data sources and the base station in WSNs. However, there are several limitations to the application of traditional solutions in the sensors, domain. Here, we concentrate on discussing which of the design principles that have guided the development of computer-based anonymity systems are meaningful for the protection of location privacy in sensor networks.

First, anonymity is only necessary in certain circumstances in WSNs, even being detrimental to the correct operation of the network in some cases. In most application scenarios, source anonymity with respect to the recipient is not beneficial for the operation of the network. The reason is that the base station (i.e., the recipient) needs to know the identifier of the original data sender for the management and control of the environment being monitored. Not having this information implies that the base station cannot identify the location where the data were originally sensed, and thus, it is unable to provide the network administrator with relevant information about the sensor field. Notwithstanding, sender anonymity is useful to prevent external observers from determining the location of the data source. An adversary in possession of a map of the network, which can be created by patiently eavesdropping on every single network node, can easily correlate source identifiers in the packets to geographical locations in the field, thus compromising source-location privacy. By occasionally changing the nodes' IDs for pseudonyms,* the network can prevent such attack since the map of the attacker is only valid for a short period of time as long as the identifiers of the nodes remain unchanged. There are already several approaches that consider the use of dynamically changing pseudonyms for WSNs [100,107]. In these solutions, the pseudonyms are known to the base station, and it is, therefore, able to spot the occurrence of events in the field. Finally, it might be useful to prevent compromised sensor nodes (i.e., nodes controlled by the attacker) to gain access to the real source ID. Since remote sensor nodes rely on intermediate nodes to forward their data, if any of these en route nodes are compromised, they might get access to the source ID. This problem has also been considered

---

* A pseudonym is an identifier used instead of the original ID.

by some authors [111]. Therefore, source anonymity in WSNs is only necessary in certain circumstances.

Moreover, given the existing communications model in sensor networks, the sender–receiver unlinkability property does not make much sense. Typically, the network uses a many-to-one communication model, where any sensor node is a potential sender and the base station is the only receiver. Therefore, the property of relationship unlinkability is lost because, in any event data transmission, the base station is one of the participants. In traditional anonymous communications systems, relationship unlinkability is important in terms of the identity of the sender and the recipient because it gives away information about the behavior and preferences of users. On the contrary, in the case of location privacy in WSNs, all sensor nodes transmit to a single base station and therefore there is no such information gain. Here, the important issue is to determine the location of these nodes and this cannot be done by simply analyzing packets in transit unless this information is given either in the headers or in the payload. However, the attacker is assumed not to have access to the payload because it is cryptographically protected, but the header might provide some information on the source. This issue becomes problematic only in the case that the adversary already knows the network topology but, as aforementioned, this problem is related to source anonymity, not to unlinkability. Similarly, in the case of the receiver, since we are focusing on flat and homogeneous sensor networks with a single base station, which is in charge of collecting all the data, there is actually no need to indicate in the packets which node is the final recipient of the data. Finally, message unlinkability is also unnecessary and counterproductive for the same reasons as source anonymity.

As a matter of fact, the most natural property for the protection of location privacy is unobservability rather than unlinkability. By hiding the presence of the nodes reporting event data or receiving it, we can prevent the attacker from determining the location of events in the field and the location of the base station. More precisely, the attacker will be unable to obtain the location of the communicating nodes if he or she is unable to sufficiently detect the presence of event messages in the network. Clearly, if the attacker is not able to ascertain the existence of messages containing event data, he or she will not be able to determine which node is the sender or the recipient of that message under the assumption that he or she has no information other than the observed traffic. Note that the attacker could benefit from other sources of information, such as visual recognition of the event or previous knowledge about the nature of events being monitored, to aid him or her in the search. However, this is beyond the scope of this book and we assume that the adversary has no prior knowledge about the deployment of the network or visual information about the events taking place in the field.

In summary, some anonymity properties are not suitable or necessary for the protection of location privacy in WSNs. Notwithstanding, the following sections will delve into each specific solution regardless of their main design goal in order to have a clearer understanding of the particular features, the imposed overhead, and the techniques proposed by renowned computer-based anonymous communications systems originally devised for the Internet. This not only gives insight into how and which techniques can be applied to counter particular privacy problems but also enables us to finally assess the real limitations or potential applicability of these systems to preserve location privacy in the domain of WSNs.

2.1.3 Classification of Solutions

Many outstanding anonymous communications systems have been devised to hinder traffic analysis and thus improve the privacy protection in online communications. These systems have been designed with different goals in mind, and so, they pursue different anonymity properties. We propose a taxonomy of solutions that takes into consideration three major features, namely, (1) the main desired goal in the design of the anonymous communications systems, (2) the architectural design, and (3) the principal techniques used to reach the goals. This taxonomy is presented in Table 2.1 but, for the sake of simplicity, only the most commonly used techniques have been represented.

Among the multitude of anonymous communications systems designs, we have selected several eminent solutions that introduce various distinguishing features and countermeasures that are addressed for different adversarial models. From an architectural point of view, these solutions can be categorized as either centralized or decentralized. Centralized solutions are those in which the communicating parties are not an active part of the anonymity system, namely, there is a set of devices in between senders and recipients, which are responsible for forwarding and anonymizing the communications. Contrarily, in decentralized solutions each user collaborates in the forwarding process to conceal his or her own communications and the communications of other participants. Some of the analyzed solutions are partially decentralized because they rely on a central server that is in charge of providing all the information necessary to communicate with other members of the system or external entities, while other solutions are fully decentralized and not dependent on a central authority. Also, in these solutions, data recipients might be part of the anonymous communication network or external entities.

The proposed classification also takes into consideration the main goals pursued by these solutions. It is worth mentioning that some of these solutions might have been designed with several goals in mind but only the most relevant ones are included in the table for the sake of simplicity. For example, mix-net approaches aim to provide sender–receiver unlinkability although they might also ensure sender anonymity. Note that when we refer to sender anonymity, we usually refer to anonymity with respect to the data recipient. In many situations, a client is willing to gain access to a particular service but is reluctant to provide his or her real identity to a potentially untrustworthy service provider because of the concern of being tracked or profiled for illegitimate purposes, such as price discrimination.

Table 2.1   Classification of Anonymous Communications Systems

	Main Goal	Architecture	SK	PK	LE	RN	PD	PR	FT	MB
						Techniques				
Single proxy [9]	Sender anonymity	Centralized	✓	–	–	✓	–	–	–	–
Mixes [27]	Unlinkability	Centralized	–	✓	✓	–	✓	–	–	–
Onion routing [116]	Unlinkability	Centralized	✓	✓	✓	–	–	–	✓	–
Tor [46]	Unlinkability	Centralized	✓	✓	✓	–	–	–	–	–
Crowds [117]	Sender anonymity	Decentralized	✓	–	–	✓	–	–	–	–
Hordes [76]	Sender anonymity	Decentralized	✓	✓	–	✓	–	–	–	✓
GAP [14]	Sender anonymity	Decentralized	✓	✓	–	✓	✓	✓	✓	–
DC-nets [28]	Unobservability	Decentralized	✓	–	–	–	–	–	–	✓
Herbivore [53]	Unobservability	Decentralized	✓	✓	–	–	–	–	–	✓

Notations: SK, Symmetric-key encryption/decryption; PK, public-key encryption/decryption; LE, layered encryption; RN, source identity renaming; PD, temporal packet delay; PR, packet replay; FT, fake traffic injection; MB, multicast or broadcast communications.

Finally, note that the various techniques employed by these solutions could be used to further break down the classification into new categories. For example, the schemes could be classified as high-latency or low-latency solutions depending on whether the systems introduce large delays before relaying the packets received or not. To avoid complicating the presentation of solutions with many categories, the exposition and analysis of solutions will be focused on the architectural (i.e., centralized or decentralized) perspective, which is more natural and consistent with the evolution of research in the field of anonymous communications systems. Nonetheless, the various techniques used by these systems (e.g., temporal packet delay) as well as the corresponding notation for these techniques (e.g., PD) will be used during the overhead analysis of the solutions.

2.2 Centralized Schemes

Centralized anonymous communications systems rely on a set of partially trusted devices* that are responsible for conveying data from senders to receivers in a privacy-preserving manner. Whenever a user wants to communicate anonymously with another party, it does so by means of any of the devices comprising the anonymity network. The anonymity relay(s) will eventually deliver the received data to the final destination on behalf of the user, thereby obscuring the actual data source. In short, the communication ends (i.e., sender and recipient) are not members but clients of centralized anonymity systems.

As a result, an attacker capable of observing all the nodes involved in the system can easily spot the communication ends. This is the case of global adversaries, who can observe all the transmissions in the network. Consequently, centralized anonymous communications systems are unable to protect themselves from such a powerful adversarial model. Thus, only local observers and internal attackers will be considered in the analysis of solutions throughout this section.

2.2.1 Single-Proxy

Single-proxy solutions (e.g., Anonymizer [9]) have been proposed to allow Internet users to access online services, like surfing the web, without disclosing their identity to service providers.[†] In other words, single-proxy solutions aim to provide source anonymity against potentially dishonest service providers mostly interested in tracking and profiling.

---

* Devices are usually not considered fully trusted because even honest relays may be forced to reveal information under legal compulsion.

† In most cases, when we talk about identity, we are actually referring to any information that is linked to or can be used to identify an individual, usually an IP address in the case of Internet communications.

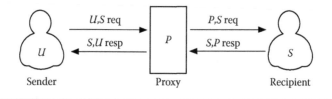

Figure 2.2 Single-proxy operation.

These solutions are based on a trusted third party that acts as an intermediary between the user and the real destination. The operation is very simple as depicted in Figure 2.2. Whenever a user U wants to communicate with a server S, it issues a message to the proxy P informing them about the intended recipient and the original request. Then, the proxy forwards the user request to the server but first removes the true source of the request. In this way, as far as the recipient is concerned, the proxy appears to be the original data sender, thus hiding the true identity of the true sender to the destination. Finally, the recipient responds to the message as if it came from the proxy, which needs to keep track of connections to send the reply back to the user. Additionally, some single-proxy solutions create an encrypted tunnel from the user to the proxy in order to prevent eavesdropping on that link. The communication from the proxy to the server can also be encrypted if the server provides that functionality, for example, using HTTPS.

From a computational point of view, single-proxy solutions introduce relatively low overhead, which is an interesting feature for hardware-constrained devices like sensor nodes. Source sensor nodes are only required to transmit their data to a proxy node and, in the worst case, encrypt it. A proxy node, on the other hand, must decrypt the data from different sources (if encrypted) and change the source ID of incoming packets with their own identifier. This process is referred to as renaming and must be done for every single message. Note that given that the communication is assumed to be unidirectional from sensor nodes to the base station only, a proxy node does not need to keep track of messages in order to send a reply back to the data source. Additionally, the data source could opt to apply end-to-end encryption in order to protect the data on its way from the proxy to the base station. This would imply an extra encryption operation on both ends of the communication but could also relief the proxy from decrypting in the first place. Table 2.2 summarizes the total number of operations that different network nodes will need to perform depending on the (best- or worst-case) scenario. Note that the values in the table refer to a single message transmission. The terminology used in this and subsequent tables is consistent to that described in Table 2.1.

Despite the low overhead introduced, given the threat model under consideration, a single-proxy approach alone cannot prevent the location privacy problem in WSNs. In the case of a local observer, this solution is unsuitable because the adversary uses strategies that lead him or her to the target regardless of the packet contents or

Table 2.2 Single-Proxy Overhead

Node	Case	
	Best	Worst
Sources	—	$2SK$
Proxies	RN	$RN + SK$
Sink	—	SK

headers. When looking for a source node, the attacker uses a traceback strategy based on the angle of arrival of signals, whereas an adversary willing to find the sink can simply turn to rate-monitoring or time-correlation attacks. To prevent these attacks, it is necessary to prevent the use of persistent paths by randomizing the routes to the proxy, using different proxies for each new message, and so on. In fact, Phantom Routing [66] and other solutions use random intermediate nodes (similar to proxies) from where the source data are finally routed to the base station. However, the protection mechanism does not reside in renaming or data encryption but on the selection of random intermediate nodes, which lead to ephemeral routes that confuse the adversary.

On the other hand, the use of renaming and end-to-end encryption provides some protection against internal adversaries. However, the level of protection is insufficient considering that only the nodes located after the proxy node would not have access to the true source identifier. Also, note that the attacker may be able to identify a proxy node and compromise it, thus easily gathering the identifiers of all the source nodes using the proxy. A potential countermeasure for this is to have proxies at various distances from the base station forming a multitier proxy architecture, but this is something that will be discussed in the next section.

2.2.2 Mixes

A mix is a store-and-forward device that receives public-key encrypted messages, and after a sufficiently long period of time has passed, it outputs a reordered batch of all messages. In this way, mixes hide the correspondence between input and output messages because of temporal storage and decryption. This type of high-latency anonymity solutions were originally devised by Chaum [27] for noninteractive online communications, such as anonymous e-mail transmissions. Usually, mixes are arranged and selected in series (i.e., mix cascade) or deployed as a fully connected network and picked in a random order (i.e., mix network). In such arrangements, a single honest mix preserves the unlinkability between inputs and outputs along the whole path.

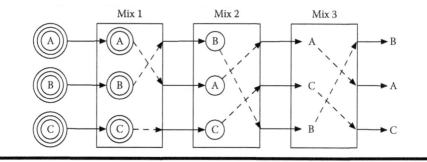

Figure 2.3   Communications in a mix cascade.

A mix cascade is depicted in Figure 2.3, where messages *A*, *B*, and *C* are encrypted with the public keys of the mixes they will traverse in reverse order. Each mix removes its corresponding encryption layer and outputs a lexicographically ordered batch of messages after a sufficiently large amount of time to prevent the correlation of inputs and outputs. After decryption, each mix adds a block of random bits at the end of each message to maintain their size constant. Additionally, both users and the mixes themselves can introduce dummy messages to hide the number of messages sent and received at each point.

The implementation of a mix-based solution over WSNs presents several limitations in terms of the computational overhead introduced. Source nodes are required to perform *N* public-key operations per transmitted packet.* Additionally, source nodes must have a global knowledge of the network topology in order to be able to determine the transmission paths and perform the public-key encryptions in the right order. Moreover, this implies that source nodes must store the public keys (P_K) of all potential mix nodes. Clearly, the size of the mix network has a tremendous impact on the number of operations and the amount of memory needed to store all the information required to satisfy the mix-based model. However, the recipient of messages, which is the most powerful device of the network, is freed from performing any operation.

Moreover, each intermediate node has to perform 1 public-key decryption per received packet as well as temporarily store a number of messages (T) that depends on the number of events in the field. Also, the closer the nodes are to the base station, the higher the traffic rate is. But the amount of memory fitted inside a typical sensor node is insufficient to accommodate a large number of messages. Besides, to preserve message indistinguishability and prevent leaking the direction of message flows, packets are padded (PAD) after decryption. This requires not only more computation but also more wirelessly transmitted bits. Finally, many WSN applications require real-time monitoring capabilities but mixes introduce significant delays at each node, thus precluding their use in these scenarios.

---

* An extra operation, be it symmetric or asymmetric, satisfies the end-to-end encryption principle.

Table 2.3   Mixes Overhead

Node	Requirements	
	CPU	RAM
Sources	$N \cdot PK$	$M \cdot P_K + topo$
Mixes	$PK + PAD + PERM$	$S_K + T \cdot mess$

A summary of results is provided in Table 2.3, where, for the sake of simplicity, only the best-case scenario is represented. Note that the worst-case scenario (i.e., source nodes performing end-to-end encryption) implies that for every message transmitted, a source node performs an extra cryptographic operation and, moreover, the base station must share keys with all potential source nodes. Furthermore, we do not consider scenarios where the destination responds to the source. In such cases, the base station would perform the same number of operations as a source node and mix nodes would have to perform roughly the same number of operations as in the forward path. Additional terminology appears in this table: S_K is the node's own private key, N is the number of nodes in a path, and M is the number of mixes. Additionally, "topo" refers to the topology of the network and $T \cdot mess$ indicates the temporal storage of messages. We acknowledge that some of these values may vary over time depending on the workload of the network. However, our goal is not to make an exhaustive and accurate to the milliwatt overhead study as this would require having real implementations running on the motes. Rather we are more interested in gaining an overall idea on the potential cost of deploying these solutions.

In addition to the high computational and memory overhead imposed by mix-based schemes, there are other limitations that hinder the successful deployment of the mixes, taking into account the types of adversaries considered in WSNs. The main aspect is that the adversary wins if he or she is able to obtain the location of either the source node or the base station, contrarily to the goal of the adversary in the traditional scenario, where he or she wants to determine whether a particular sender is communicating with a particular recipient. In such scenarios the temporal mix of messages provides the desired property but, in sensor networks, it makes no difference whether the adversary reaches one source node or another. The adversary is interested in no particular source node; any of them can lead him or her to an event in the field. Therefore, if the adversary is able to reach the entry point of the mix network (i.e., the mix closest to the source), he or she will start to receive packets from the source node, thus revealing its location. The same applies to the exit point of the mix network and the protection of the base station. Finally, it is worth mentioning that the mix model provides attractive countermeasures against internal adversaries. They are successfully prevented from determining the source node and the base station unless they are precisely the entry or exit nodes of the mix network, respectively. The use of layered encryption prevents any compromised mix node or intermediate observer from obtaining information about the true data source since all these data are contained in the innermost layer. Also, the use of padding helps to hide the number of layers that were peeled by intermediated mixes. After traversing several mixes, the messages are closer to the base station, thus padding prevents adversaries from learning the distance to the base station.

2.2.3 Onion Routing and Tor

Onion routing [116] is a low-latency anonymous communications systems based on a network core composed of onion routers (ORs), whose functionality is similar to Chaum's mixes. Indeed, onion routing is like mix networks except that the security of onion routing does not come from introducing significant delays to messages but from obscuring the route they traverse. ORs are connection-oriented devices, which means that once an anonymous connection (i.e., circuit) has been established through the network, the route remains unchanged for a given period of time. Circuits provide near real-time communications by multiplexing several connections in a single data stream using fixed-size cells. Moreover, circuits are established by means of a public-key layered data structure, called the onion. Each layer of the onion contains the cryptographic material needed to derive the symmetric keys used later during the data transmission phase by each of the ORs of the circuit. The onion also tells each element of the circuit that is the next member. Once the circuit has been established and ORs have their session keys, application data are optionally sanitized to remove any sensitive information and then they are passed to the onion proxy that adds one layer of symmetric-key encryption for each of the ORs in the path. Then, the entry OR peels the outermost layer of encryption and sends the resulting message onto the next router. The process is repeated until the exit node removes the last layer and sends the data to the intended recipient. A simplified illustration of the onion routing architecture and its transmission process is provided in Figure 2.4. Tor [46], the second-generation onion routing, added several changes to the original design, its new circuit setup process being the most relevant one. Instead of using an onion, the circuits are established incrementally, that is, node by node, based on authenticated Diffie–Hellman key exchange. Moreover, the number of ORs in a circuit is reduced from 5, in the original design, to only 3 as it was shown to provide reduced latency and similar security.

Onion routing reduces the overhead compared with mixes, principally for two reasons: data encryption and decryption are not based on public-key cryptography, and the core nodes are not required to temporarily store messages. Nonetheless, the computational and memory requirements are still costly for sensor nodes. Specifically, source nodes are required to be aware of the network topology as well as the public keys of each OR to enable them to establish the anonymous path. Moreover, if the path is set by means of an onion, the source must perform several layers of public-key encryption containing the key seed material for each of the ORs in

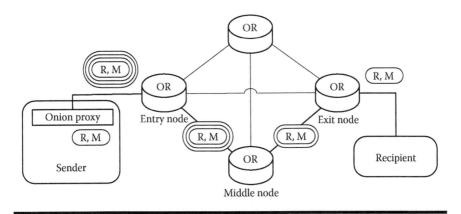

Figure 2.4 Onion routing communications.

the path. In the case of incremental path establishment, it implies that the source must contact the onion nodes one by one to make authenticated handshakes. This implies even more energy consumption because it requires the exchange of many messages, which is known to be much more power consuming than computations. Once the circuit has been established, the source node must apply as many layers of symmetric-key encryption to the data messages as ORs in the path. Later, each of the path members must decrypt the messages and multiplex several messages within a single link-encrypted transmission. In an attempt to further complicate traffic analysis, packet padding and reordering is introduced by onion routing, but Tor dismisses the idea because they introduce a significant cost and are still unable to yield effective resistance against various attacks. The base station might receive the data in clear text or encrypted with a shared key.

In Table 2.4, we summarize the computational and memory demands of onion routing schemes. The table considers both the path setup process, which only occurs occasionally, and the data transmission period. We place some operations in parenthesis those that are only performed by the original onion routing design and not

Table 2.4 Onion Routing Overhead

Node	CPU		RAM
	Path Setup	Transmission	
Sources	$N \cdot PK$	$N \cdot SK$	$M \cdot P_K + N \cdot S_K + topo$
Onion nodes	PK	$SK + LE$	$P_K + R \cdot L_K + S \cdot S_K$
		$(+PAD + PERM)$	

by Tor. Extra terminology is defined: S_K is the session key, LE and L_K are the link encryption and link key, R is the number of neighbors an onion node shares links with, and S is the number of sessions an OR handles at each given moment. During path setup, the sources need to perform an N public-key operation, and during data transmission, these become symmetric-key operations. Note that the cost associated (these values) is for a single transmitted message. Moreover, the source nodes need to know the public keys of all M nodes in the onion network, and somehow the topology, in order to be able to apply encryptions in the right order. Additionally, they need to store N session keys for each circuit, one for each of its nodes. We can assume that there is only one circuit per data transmission to the base station. The onion nodes only perform one decryption operation for each transmitted message. These decryptions are either based on public-key or symmetric-key cryptography depending on whether it is during the path setup or the data transmission. Moreover, onion nodes keep long-standing link-encrypted connections with every other onion node. This is represented in the table as LE during data transmission. These together with padding and reordering are present during the whole communication; thus, they could have also been included in the path setup, but it was done in this way for the sake of clarity. In terms of memory, onion nodes must keep their own public-key pair and as many link keys and session keys as there are neighboring onion nodes and active circuits. Note that we used R instead of M to represent the number of link-key encrypted connection an onion node has, but as an OR should be able to connect to any other OR in the network, this value may be equal to M. As a result, source nodes could be released from having to know the network topology. Again, we have considered the simplest case, where the source node does not use end-to-end encryption and the sink does not send responses back to the sources.

These schemes can be regarded as an evolution of the mix-net approach in the sense that they reduce some of the tight requirements imposed by the original mix design. Despite the overhead reduction, onion routing solutions still present the same limitations with respect to the capabilities of the adversarial model considered in WSNs. The main drawback is that a local adversary will eventually identify the edges of the onion network. This issue allows him or her to identify the source nodes and the base station if messages follow similar or fixed routes to reach and leave the onion network. Therefore, the best strategy for an adversary is to reach entry or exit nodes and wait for messages to arrive. Overall, it can be stated that the edges of the onion network are the most critical points. This is also true if the adversary is capable of compromising nodes.

2.3 Decentralized Schemes

Contrary to centralized solutions, where the communicating parties are not involved in the anonymity network, in the solutions considered in this section, all members collaborate to conceal the identities of other participants. In this way, there is more cohesion in the network, which positively affects the level of protection of the members since it is not trivial to identify the communicating parties from mere intermediaries. However, the elimination of a semitrusted network core introduces new challenges. Note that some of these solutions are only partially decentralized because they rely on a central server, which is in charge of providing all the information necessary to communicate with other participants.

2.3.1 Crowds and Hordes

Crowds [117] is a partially decentralized solution where a set of geographically diverse users are grouped and cooperate to issue requests on behalf of its members. Whenever a crowd member (i.e., a jondo*) wants to send a message, it chooses a random jondo, possibly itself, to act as an intermediary. The receiving jondo decides, based on some biased probability, whether to forward the data to another jondo or to finally submit it to the destination. Subsequent requests from the same jondo and same destination follow the same path. Finally, the reply is sent back using the same path in the reverse order. Both requests and replies are encrypted using pairwise keys provided by a trusted authority, namely, the blender, at the time jondos join the Crowd. This process is exemplified in Figure 2.5, where *jondo*1 communicates with *Server*2 using three intermediaries, while *jondo*5 issues requests to *Server*1 using only two relays. The first path, initiated by *jondo*1, is represented with ordinary arrows, while the other path is represented with dashed arrows. Interestingly, *jondo*5 is both the data source of one path and the last node in the other path. Hordes [76] is based

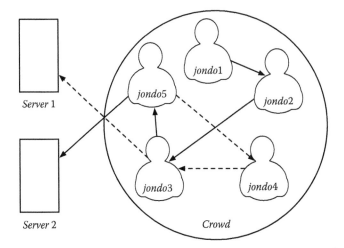

Figure 2.5   Crowds communications.

---

* Pronounced as John Doe.

on the Crowds model but its main contribution is the incorporation of multicast messages to reduce the latency and overhead on the return paths, that is, from recipients to initiators. Additionally, it uses public-key cryptography to obtain the session keys from a trusted authority to be later used for message forwarding.

The Crowds model presents a low overhead when compared to other solutions. Instead of requiring computationally heavy mechanisms such as public-key operations, dummy traffic or padding, the Crowds is based on symmetric-key packet reencryption, sender ID renaming, and random node selections.* Consequently, any intermediate jondo is only aware of the previous and next hop in the path, and from the receiver's perspective, the message is equally likely to have originated from any crowd member. Each member must perform one decryption and one encryption for every packet it forwards within the Crowd, but if it decides to submit the packet to the destination, it only needs to decrypt and forward it. In order to perform these operations, crowd members must share keys with any other member. Therefore, the number of keys each node must store is dependent on the size of the network. Also, for every received message, the node changes the sender ID for its own and assigns an identifier to keep track of all messages belonging to that path. They must keep a translation table with as many records as the number of paths the node handles, because any subsequent packets from this connection will follow the same path.

Table 2.5 represents the number of operations and the amount of memory consumption introduced by the Crowds model to nodes with different roles in the network. Note that even when these roles are separated in the table, a node might have several roles at the same time. A similar table could have been constructed for Hordes but since we are not considering the communications on the return path in WSNs, this is not really useful. Additionally, in Hordes all participants hold the public key of the server, which is used to obtain a signed list of all other members and their public keys. Later, each participant chooses a subset of jondos to use as message forwarders. The selected nodes receive a symmetric key encrypted with the

Table 2.5 Crowds Overhead

	Requirements	
Node	CPU	RAM
Initial	SK	$N \cdot S_K$
Intermediate	$SK + RN$	$N \cdot S_K + R \cdot paths$
Final	$SK + RN$	$N \cdot S_K$

---

* Additionally, the user might establish end-to-end encrypted channels to prevent en route eavesdropping by other crowd members.

node's private key. In this way, Hordes not only requires the storage of all participants' public keys but also the exchange and storage of session keys, which implies more computational operations and more memory consumption. For simplicity, we provide a single table corresponding to the Crowds solution. In this table, R represents the number of records in the translation table of an intermediate node. The remaining notation has already been introduced.

In general, the Crowds scheme imposes relatively low computational and memory requirements precisely due to the adversarial model under consideration. This solution provides a sufficient protection level against local adversaries that are able to observe the inputs and outputs of a single node, but the attackers are considered to be static because of the geographic dispersion of the crowd members. This feature makes a big difference with respect to the WSN domain. The Crowds model considers a random but fixed path for all communications with a given server; however, this involves a serious risk when the adversary can move toward the immediate sender of a packet. Likewise, by performing time-correlation attacks, the adversary could determine the next hop in the path, and after several hops, he or she finally reaches the sink. Internal adversaries are partially countered by means of source renaming at every hop but the main drawback is that renaming also prevents the base station from learning the actual data source unless specified in the packet payload. Finally, this model provides no protection mechanisms against global adversaries, who can easily spot the data sources because crowd members start a transmission as soon as they have a request to issue. In other words, the transmission of real messages is not hidden by any means. Similarly, the base station can be easily detected by a global adversary because it is not part of the anonymity network.

2.3.2 GNUnet Anonymity Protocol

The GNUnet Anonymity Protocol (GAP) [14] was originally devised to provide anonymous file sharing in peer-to-peer networks. GAP is based on the idea of making initiators look like mere intermediaries in order to hide their own actions. To achieve this, each node takes advantage of the traffic generated by other nodes but they also inject some baseline fake traffic in order to cover their own messages. Basically, GAP nodes perform the following actions: forwarding, renaming the identity of packets (i.e., indirection), injecting fake traffic, replaying messages several times, introducing short packet delays, and using message padding. Most of these actions are represented by different sorts of arrows in Figure 2.6. An ordinary arrow means message forwarding, but these arrows may have forks that represent the replay of packets to arbitrary nodes. Indirection is depicted by means of dotted arrows, while the short arrow starting from inside the node symbolizes the fake packet injection.

The security of the GAP model is based on the idea that the more traffic a node transmits, the more unlikely it is, to the eyes of an adversary, that a particular message was created by that node. In other words, a source node must route

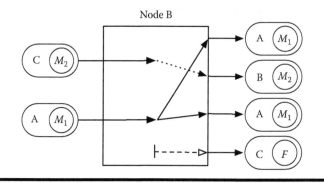

Figure 2.6 GAP node operation.

a sufficient number of packets from other participants so as to maintain an adequate protection level. Received messages can be either forwarded, indirected, or dropped. Message forwarding implies no modifications to the message, while indirection involves the modification of the sender address and thus the handling of subsequent packets belonging to that connection. However, in this analysis as we are considering traditional sensor networks where messages only flow from sensors to the base station, there is no need to handle replies, thus alleviating the problem of storing large translation tables. Only the forward path will be considered for the rest of this section.

Additionally, each node holds a public key that is used to establish encrypted links between nodes. Public keys are periodically propagated throughout the network. Also, both queries and data traversing the network are encoded using a particular scheme [15], which is similar to a symmetric-key encryption, but it allows intermediaries to verify whether the encoded data match a specific query or content. In this way, packets change their appearance at each hop but this also provides intermediaries with plausible deniability as they cannot decrypt what they are transmitting. This can also be considered a means of protection against internal adversaries. Finally, to further prevent the correlation between incoming and outgoing messages, short random delays are introduced, and packets can be either forwarded or indirected to a random number of nodes.

The GAP model imposes extremely expensive requirements for hardware-constrained nodes, especially in terms of energy consumption since the network must maintain a baseline noise in the form of fake traffic and sensor nodes are battery-powered devices. The overhead introduced by this solution is summarized in Table 2.6. Each node must contribute a given amount F of fake traffic to the network.* Moreover, for each received message, a GAP node can decide to simply

---

* This value F may vary on time depending on the network load.

Table 2.6   GAP Overhead

Node	Requirements
CPU	$F \cdot FT + R \cdot PR \, (+RN) + SK \, [+SK]$
RAM	$N \cdot P_K + N \cdot S_K + T \cdot mess$

replay this message to a random number $R \geq 0$ of nodes* or alternatively perform an indirection, which is represented within parenthesis. Also, after receiving a packet, the node must decrypt it and then encrypt it with the key from the output link. Furthermore, source nodes perform an additional encryption operation, which is represented within brackets. From the point of view of memory, the node stores a number N of public keys, which are used to establish pairwise secrets for enabling link encryption with neighboring nodes. Moreover, each node introduces a short random delay to messages, that is translated into the need of a buffer of a particular size T for allocating the messages. Recall that the variables represented on the table are node dependent and may vary over time.

Both local and global observers can be countered by the GAP model since they cannot easily determine the source of messages due to the use of a baseline fake traffic that hides the occurrence of events. On the one hand, a local adversary does not gain any information by following all the messages since these might be fake traffic, leading him or her nowhere. On the other hand, the global adversary is more difficult to deceive because in the presence of continuous events, there is an increase in the amount of traffic in that particular area compared to other more distant areas. Besides, internal adversaries are somehow, but not completely, countered due to the use of the encoding mechanism used for providing plausible deniability and the indirection mechanism. Finally, the base station can mimic the behavior of ordinary nodes, replaying and sending traffic in order to remain hidden, but it is likely that the area surrounding the base station still concentrates a larger amount of remote regions. In short, the presented mechanism might be useful for the protection of location privacy in WSNs but the overhead introduced will exhaust the battery of the nodes in a short period of time.

2.3.3 DC-nets and Herbivore

The Dining Cryptographers (DC) scheme [28] allows a group of users to share information while hiding the actual sender of messages even to other protocol participants.† To this end, each member needs to share a secret bit with any other

---

* The range includes zero because the node may drop the message.
† This scheme was proposed as a solution to the problem of determining whether someone on the table of a restaurant had paid for the dinner without revealing the identity of the payer.

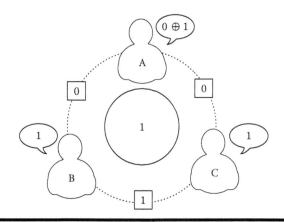

Figure 2.7   DC-nets operation.

participant. For example, in Figure 2.7, node C shares 1 bit with node B and 0 bit with node A. Also, the participants perform the sum modulo 2 (i.e., logic *XOR*) of their shared secrets. Subsequently, the obtained result is broadcasted to the rest of participants unless the participant is willing to communicate data to the rest of members, in which case it shares the inverse of the result. The inverse of any bit value can be obtained by simply *XOR*-ing that same bit value with 1 (see node *A* in Figure 2.7). The final result is obtained by performing the *XOR* of all contributions. Each protocol execution is called a round.

The idea behind this scheme is that the final result must be zero if nobody (actually, any even number of simultaneous senders) has transmitted because each secret is used twice and one if someone inverts the result. Provided that the initial shared bits are secret, there is no way to determine the actual sender. Although the original protocol considers the transmission of a single data bit, the DC scheme can be easily extended to transmit string messages by sharing random numbers instead of random bits. This modification enables the transmission of encrypted messages so that the actual recipient is the only entity capable of determining whether that protocol round conveyed a real message. Thus, it provides unobservability of both senders and recipients. The following analysis focuses on the bit-based version but it could be directly extrapolated to the extended version.

The application of the DC-nets model in WSNs has several impediments. One of these limitations is that sensor networks communicate wirelessly, which is a highly unreliable medium. The DC protocol is extremely vulnerable to noise and a single erroneous bit leads to undesirable results. Additionally, provided that participants' contributions must be broadcast* simultaneously in order to allow the *XOR* of their

---

* There are other potential communication techniques besides broadcasting but they imply an increase in the number of exchanged messages.

signals, the sensor nodes running the protocol are required to be tightly synchronized and within the transmission range of the other members. This suggests that the data recipient must be either one of the DC participants or an external observer within the communication range. Consequently, only neighboring sensor nodes can run the protocol or they must carefully adjust their transmission power; however, this would deplete their limited batteries in a short period of time. As proposed by Herbivore [53], the participants could be hierarchically arranged in order to reduce the complexity of the system. This arrangement would allow sensor nodes to reduce their transmission power but it also introduces more synchronization problems and increased delivery delays to data packets.

Additionally, there are high memory requirements in the DC model associated with the key sharing process because of the continuous protocol rounds. Two potential solutions exist for the provision of keys: either sensor nodes are preloaded with sufficiently large one-time keys or they share short keys that are periodically updated by means of a pseudo-random function. Given the memory limitation in sensor nodes, the first solution is quite impractical since the shared keys will rapidly expire. In the second solution, memory is traded by computational operations and thus present other impediments. In any case, the overhead introduced is directly dependent on the topology of the network. A ring topology, such as the one presented in Figure 2.7, requires each node to share 2 random bits, with the right and left participants. On the other hand, in a fully connected graph each participant shares one bit with every other participant, which adds up $N - 1$ random bits, where N is the total number nodes. Note that these values are for a single protocol round (i.e., for the transmission of a single bit). Moreover, a protocol round occurs even if no participant is willing to transmit; otherwise, an adversary would identify which nodes are interested in transmitting. Clearly, this implies a high waste of bandwidth and energy because of the continuous flow of messages.

Another substantial problem has to do with simultaneous communications. The DC model does not allow various data senders at a time because their messages would collide. This issue highly constrains the usability and nature of sensor networks, which were conceived to provide a highly distributed sensory system. This problem might be reduced by using a slot reservation protocol as proposed by Herbivore; however, this introduces more messages and thereby more energy waste. Moreover, this countermeasure cannot solve the increased delivery time in the communications, especially when the sensor networks under consideration are extremely large with a substantial amount of potential data senders. A summary of these and other features constraining the application of this model to WSNs is presented in Table 2.7, where *INV* refers to the inversion of the contribution. For every protocol round, each node is required to perform only two simple *XOR* operations and, optionally, an additional one if they want to transmit data. In terms of memory requirements, depending on the connectivity of the network, a single protocol round requires from 2 to $N - 1$ secret bits.

Table 2.7   DC-nets Overhead

Node	Requirements
CPU	$2 \cdot XORs$ (+INV)
RAM	[2 *to* $N - 1$] bits
Other	Topology restrictions, tight synch, proneness to error, simultaneity

Although the computational overhead introduced by the DC-net scheme is rather inexpensive even for sensor nodes, the memory requirements, topological restrictions, and the disruption of simultaneous event notifications preclude their application to WSNs. Nonetheless, the model is effective in the protection of location privacy because it hides the original data source to all participants and also external (local or global) observers. This could result in a problem for the base station that is unable to identify the data source unless the extended protocol is used. To this end, the source node would send both the event data and its identifier in an encrypted form so that only the base station knows the original sender. Therefore, the location of the data source is protected from disclosure to any other participant including internal passive adversaries, which are unable to determine the original data sender unless they collude. As a matter of fact, a collusion is successful only if all nodes sharing keys with the potential source node collude, which is highly unlikely.

2.4 Evaluation

Previous sections have delved into several features from centralized and decentralized anonymous communications systems that need to be further analyzed. This section is intended to provide this final discussion while outlining the most important aspects of this chapter.

As for the case of centralized solutions, these can be regarded as black box devices where the data sources stand on one side and the data recipients on the other. The communications originating from various sources change their appearance and are delayed or mixed within the network, but still the presence of incoming and outgoing messages is evident. In these settings, both source nodes and the base station are clearly exposed to a global observer, simply because they are not part of the network core and thus their actions can be easily detected, which implies the disclosure of their location. Contrarily, local and internal adversaries are placed somewhere within the network core and, in consequence, they cannot identify the communicating nodes so easily. These adversaries rely on a partial view of the communications but depending on their location they might be more likely to uncover the senders and recipients. The entry and exit points of centralized systems are especially sensitive since at these areas the adversary is capable of distinguishing the source nodes and the base station unless packets use different routes to reach that point.

In particular, single-proxy schemes are very lightweight because they are primarily based on source renaming at a single intermediate point. However, this together with the potential use of payload encryption for eavesdropping prevention can protect neither from the trace-back attack performed by local adversaries nor from compromised proxy nodes because they can retrieve the data source from the packet.

Mix-based designs depict a rather different situation. The overhead imposed by mix nodes is significant, not only because it demands the use of public-key cryptography but also because the source node must perform as many of these operations as nodes in the communication path each packet traverses. Additionally, the layered encryption implies the knowledge of the public keys of every mix node and the topology of the network to perform the encryptions in the right order. Moreover, mixes introduce large message delays, which are not suitable for time-critical applications, like critical infrastructures monitoring. Regarding the privacy protection, mix cascades present the same problem concerning local adversaries, which are able to follow the paths of messages since they are fixed and they follow any received packets regardless of the appearance or timing. Yet, the free-route selection proposed by mix nets provides some protection means against local adversaries but it might still be insufficient since they can eventually reach either edge of the mix network. From these positions, local attackers are much more likely to succeed. Similarly, internal adversaries who are at the edge of the network are capable of uncovering the communication endpoints. However, the use of layered encryption prevents intermediate nodes in the path from uncovering the data source. More precisely, intermediate nodes are only aware of the previous and next hop in the path.

Finally, onion routing solutions reduce some of the computational restrictions imposed by mixes by introducing the path setup process, which allows the establishment of session keys that are later used during the data transmission process. Also, these schemes reduce the delay introduced at every hop by multiplexing the communications of various data sources on a single stream. Although the overhead is reduced, it still demands layered cryptography and great memory requirements. Anyway, onion routing schemes present the same problems when countering the typical adversaries considered in sensor networks.

As for the case of decentralized approaches, their aim is to prevent the aforementioned problems at the edges by making all participants part of the system. In other words, any member of the system is potentially a data source as well as a data forwarder. This implies that it is not trivial for global observers to determine the communication endpoints and it also introduces the opportunity to more sophisticated internal attacks.

The Crowds schemes do not sufficiently protect against global adversaries because the data recipients are not part of the network and the data senders start new paths for new data connections, thus altering their behavior and becoming an easy target.

Moreover, in order to keep a low overhead, these solutions do not introduce protection mechanisms such as dummy packet injection, which might be helpful against both global and local adversaries. Local adversaries can also trace back sources and the base station because the paths are static once created to reduce the chances of internal adversaries. Internal adversaries are countered only slightly because, even if some protection means are placed (i.e., renaming), data sources can be easily detected by its neighbors for the same reason global adversaries can identify them.

On the contrary, GAP and DC-nets offer attractive safeguards, which improve the level of protection against the various types of adversaries considered in the WSN domain. However, these safeguards imply a significant increase in the number of messages being transmitted, replayed, or forwarded, which results in an unaffordable energy waste for battery-powered devices. Additionally, the DC-nets model presents extra limitations in terms of memory requirements, network topology restrictions, and also the inability to handle simultaneous data sources, which further precludes its application to the location privacy problem in WSNs.

A visual summary of this discussion is presented in Table 2.8, where the up and down arrows roughly indicate the overhead introduced and the impediments presented by these systems with respect to their applicability to WSNs. The tick, cross, and approx symbols ($\checkmark$, $\times$, and $\approx$) represent whether these solutions can provide, are not able to provide, or could provide some protection against the three adversarial models considered in WSNs.

In general, we can state that centralized approaches are less suitable for the protection of location privacy in WSNs than decentralized approaches given the highly

Table 2.8 Suitability of Traditional Systems

		Adversary		
	Overhead	*Global*	*Local*	*Internal*
Single proxy [9]	↓↓	×	×	×
Mix nets [27]	↑↑↑	×	×	$\checkmark$
Onion routing [116]	↑↑	×	×	$\checkmark$
Tor [46]	↑↑	×	×	$\checkmark$
Crowds [117]	↓	×	×	$\approx$
Hordes [76]	↓	×	×	$\approx$
GAP [14]	↑↑↑	$\checkmark$	$\checkmark$	$\checkmark$
DC-nets [28]	↑↑↑	$\checkmark$	$\checkmark$	$\checkmark$
Herbivore [53]	↑↑↑	$\checkmark$	$\checkmark$	$\checkmark$

distributed nature of these networks and their particular communication pattern. The typical many-to-one communication model makes it difficult to hide the location of the base station and the source nodes when they are located outside the limits of the centralized network core. A local adversary can eventually determine the entry points of the network core, while a global adversary can directly identify the source and destination of messages. Therefore, decentralized approaches are more appropriate as they integrate all the nodes within the anonymizing solution, thereby hindering the identification of the current participants to adversaries with either local or global eavesdropping capabilities. However, not all decentralized solutions are capable of providing suitable protection.

Although some solutions are sufficiently lightweight to run in a sensor node, we have shown that the real weak point is that they do not fit the requirements and the adversarial models considered in the sensors, domain. Similarly, another group of solutions are suitable for the protection of location privacy in WSNs, but they are rather expensive in terms of computational, memory, and battery requirements or they present additional limitations. However, the analysis of these solutions has provided us insight into a variety of mechanisms and techniques that can be applied to the sensors' domain to preserve location privacy.

Chapter 3

Analysis of Location Privacy Solutions in WSNs

After the analysis of computer-based anonymous communications systems, it has been concluded that these solutions present several impediments that limit their application to the location privacy issues in wireless sensor networks (WSNs) despite the apparent similarity of both problems. Nonetheless, some of the mechanisms and techniques used by computer-based systems have been successfully applied to sensor networks with some adaptations in order to fit the particular requirements of the new domain.

As a result, this chapter delves into the numerous solutions devised to protect both source- and receiver-location privacy in sensor networks to give insight into which techniques are useful in this new scenario and how they need to be applied. Based on the analysis of the advantages and disadvantages of existing solutions, it will be possible to detect open research problems as well as to formulate new and improved schemes capable of dealing with the limitations of the established state of the art.

Since the identifiers of the nodes can be directly mapped to physical locations in the field, the first step to location privacy protection is node identity concealment. Therefore, this chapter starts by describing and analyzing several solutions based on the use of pseudonyms to hide the true identity of sensor nodes. Once identities are sufficiently protected, it is necessary to deal with traffic pattern, as it can be exploited to identify the area where events of interest are detected by the network or the location of the data sink. Therefore, the rest of the chapter concentrates on traffic pattern obfuscation in the presence of different adversarial models.

The chapter concludes with the presentation of a comprehensive taxonomy of existing solutions. This taxonomy is organized in several tiers. The first level of the taxonomy considers the resource that demands protection while the second level groups solutions depending on the capabilities of the attacker model. This allows to identify at a glance what are the types of mechanisms that can effectively counter each type of adversary. Moreover, the taxonomy also reveals the presence of some research gaps that will be addressed in the following chapters.

3.1 Node Identity Protection

Despite the use of cryptographic mechanisms to protect the payload of data packets, there is much relevant information contained in the packet headers that is available to anyone eavesdropping on the wireless channel.

Packet headers consist of various data fields containing, among other elements, the identifiers of the data sender and the destination (see Figure 3.1 for the structure of a typical WSN frame). These data are sent in clear text because any intermediate sensor node must be capable of using packet header information to perform routing tasks. Therefore, an attacker can, after a sufficient amount of time capturing network traffic, elaborate a map of the network relating node identifiers to locations in the field. Being in possession of such a network map, a local attacker may simply wait next to the base station for incoming messages because all packets are addressed to this single location. Upon the reception of a packet, the adversary can retrieve the identifier of the data source and, by using the map, he can translate the identifier into a physical location, where the event occurred.

Several techniques have been proposed in the literature to provide node anonymity. Most of these solutions are based on the creation, distribution, update, and use of pseudonyms, which are intended to hide the true identifiers of the nodes.

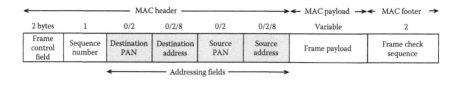

Figure 3.1 General IEEE 802.15.4 MAC frame format. (From The Institute of Electrical and Electronics Engineers (IEEE), IEEE Standard for Information technology—Telecommunications and information exchange between systems— Local and metropolitan area networks—Specic requirements, Part 15.4: Wireless Medium Access Control (MAC) and Physical Layer (PHY) Specifications for Low-Rate Wireless Personal Area Networks (LR-WPANs), 2003.)

Persistent pseudonyms provide no means of protection in the long term as they become the new identifiers of the nodes and thereby the attacker is able to easily correlate a node to a pseudonym. Therefore, pseudonyms are only effective if they are periodically updated, that is, pseudonyms must be dynamic if they are to provide node anonymity.

Some authors have approached the management of pseudonyms by means of pools of pseudonyms while others have turn to cryptographic mechanisms for the same purpose. Note that most of the solutions fall into the second category since the use of cryptographic techniques for the creation of pseudonyms have several benefits over the use of network pools. Next, we review these solutions in detail.

3.1.1 Pool of Pseudonyms

The first authors to provide a set of solutions for node identity protection based on the use dynamic pseudonyms were Misra and Xue [100]. The first of their solutions, called the simple anonymity scheme (SAS), is based on a network-wide pool of pseudonyms that are distributed among the sensor nodes. The base station divides the pool into subranges of l bits and provides each node with a random set of these subranges (see Figure 3.2a). Moreover, the base station stores correspondence between the identity of each sensor node and its subranges in order to figure out the correct decryption key for received messages. After deployment, each node builds a pseudonyms table where it stores the pseudonym ranges and secret keys used for communicating with its near neighbors. In each row of the table, the node keeps two ranges of pseudonyms for traffic coming from and directed to a particular neighbor. When the node wants to send data to a neighbor, it selects a random value from the range of pseudonyms belonging to that node and concatenates the index of the row from where it picked the pseudonym. The recipient node checks whether the received pseudonym belongs to the incoming range corresponding to the given index

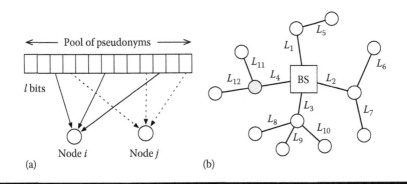

Figure 3.2 Pool-based approaches. (a) Distribution of pseudonyms in SAS. (b) Label assignment in DCARPS.

and, that being the case, it uses the shared key to decrypt the message. The principal limitation to SAS is the large memory space necessary to store a sufficiently large pseudonym space. Note that each sensor node is assigned several ranges of l bits from a preestablished pool of pseudonyms, and uses two ranges for each of its neighbors. This imposes a high memory overhead for hardware-constrained devices, especially in densely populated networks.

Instead of providing pseudonyms to sensor nodes, Nezhad et al. [101,102] suggest to assign dynamic pseudonyms to communication links. The proposed solution is part of their Destination Controlled Anonymous Routing Protocol for Sensornets (DCARPS) and operates as follows. After each topology discovery phase, the base station is aware of the location of the sensor nodes and is able to build an updated map of the network. This information is used to assign labels (i.e., identifiers) to each and every network link, as depicted in Figure 3.2b. These labels serve as pseudonyms and whenever a node has to send a packet to the base station, it uses the label assigned to the link connecting it to a neighbor that is closer to the base station.* Upon the reception of the packet, the neighbor node checks whether the label corresponds to one of its input labels. If the label is known to the node, it replaces the input label with its own output label. For example, the gray node in Figure 3.2b checks whether an incoming message has either label L_{11} or L_{12} and, in the case it does, it forwards the packet after changing the original label with L_4. The main drawback to this labeling solution is that it is not sufficiently dynamic. Labels are only modified sporadically, after a topology change has been discovered in the network, which gives the attacker the opportunity to observe the same labels for large periods of time. This allows the attacker to correlate labels with specific nodes, thus completely compromising anonymity.

3.1.2 Cryptographic Pseudonyms

The second solution by Misra and Xue [100] was the first one to use a cryptographic scheme to preserve the identity of the nodes. This solution is intended to reduce the amount of memory needed to handle the ranges of pseudonyms in SAS at the expense of increased computational overhead. The Cryptographic Anonymity Scheme (CAS) uses a keyed hash function to generate the pseudonyms. Before the deployment of the network, each node x is assigned a pseudo-random function f^x and a secret key K_{sx} as well as a random seed a_{sx} for communicating with the base station. After that, each pair of neighbors agree upon a random seed and a hash key generated using the pseudo-random function f^x. This information together with a sequence number *seq* is stored in a table, which is used to generate the

---

* Each node is considered to use only one path to send data to the base station for simplicity reasons. There is probabilistic version of DCARPS where nodes select, for each packet, a random node from all possible communication paths.

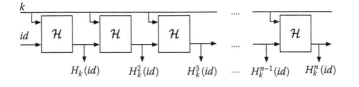

Figure 3.3 Keyed hash chain generation.

pseudonyms during the data transmission period. Whenever a node x wants to communicate with the base station, using node y as intermediary, it creates a message $M = \{sID, rID, EncryptedPayload, seq\}$, where sID consists of the concatenation of the index of node y in the table and the hash function of the bitwise *XOR* operation of the random seed shared with the base station and the sequence number keyed with the secret shared with the base station (i.e., $sID = I_y || H_{K_{sx}}(a_{sx} \oplus seq_{xy})$). The contents of rID are very similar except that instead of using the key and seed shared with the base station it uses the ones shared with the neighbor y. Clearly, the first field is used for identification with the base station and the second is used for identification with the next hop in the communication. This scheme is more memory efficient but it introduces a relevant computational cost, not only to intended recipients but also to the remaining neighbors that need to compute a keyed hash value before discovering that the packet is not addressed to them.

The CAS ensures that an external observer cannot learn the real sender (or recipient) of a message by simply observing the identifiers contained in the packet headers. The authors assume that an attacker cannot compromise the secrets shared between the nodes. For example, if an attacker captures a node, he learns all past, present, and future pseudonyms. To reduce the impact of secrets being compromised, Ouyang et al. [107] propose two methods based on keyed hash chains. The Hashing-based ID Randomization (HIR) scheme uses the result of applying a keyed hash function to the true identifier of the node as pseudonym. More precisely, after the topology discovery process, sensor nodes determine which neighbors are closer to (uplink) and which are farther from (downlink) the base station, and share pairwise keys with them. Then, sensor nodes create a table that includes, for each link, the keyed hash identifier of the uplink node of that neighbor.* After the transmission or reception of a message on a particular link, the node rehashes the value contained in the table to generate a fresh pseudonym. The process is depicted in Figure 3.3, where the identifier of the node id and the secret key k is the first input to the first hash function box $\mathcal{H}$, while subsequent hash functions use the same key k but the identifier hashed $i \geq 1$ times. Additionally, packets convey another identifier used for the base station to be able to identify the original data source. This value is also an

---

* If the node itself is the uplink of its neighbors, it stores the hash value of its own identifier keyed with the secret shared with the corresponding neighbor.

element of a hash chain keyed with a secret shared with the base station. Since hash values are assumed to be non-invertible, this solution provides backwards secrecy, that is, an attacker compromising the node or the secrets cannot retrieve previous identifiers.

However, if the adversary compromises the key used for the hash functions, he can easily generate future pseudonyms since he only needs to rehash the last values used by the node. The second solution by Ouyang et al. [107] attempts to further reduce the risk of secrets being compromised. Instead of creating the identifiers on the fly as they are needed, in reverse HIR (RHIR), the nodes first create the hash chain, store it locally, and then use the elements of the chain in reverse order. Once a pseudonym has been used, it is no longer needed and it can be deleted from the memory. Also, even if the attacker obtains the secret key used to create the hash chain, he cannot generate any fresh pseudonyms since he cannot invert a hash. The main drawback to this solution with respect to the previous one lies in the need for increased memory space to accommodate a lengthy hash chain.

Later, Jiang et al. [65,128] introduced the anonymous one-hop communication scheme as part of the Anonymous Path Routing (APR) protocol. The proposed anonymity scheme introduces an enhancement that improves the resilience against secret compromise attacks compared to previous solutions. Similar to the solutions by Ouyang et al., in this scheme each node creates a table to keep the uplink and downlink identifiers of each neighbor. These hidden identities are calculated by hashing the values of the secret keys plus the identities, a sequence number and a nonce shared by the nodes. The novelty of this approach is that both the shared keys and the hidden identities are updated (i.e., rehashed) after each successful transmission between neighboring nodes.

The same idea has been developed by Chen et al. [31,32] in the Efficient Anonymous Communication (EAC) protocol. Before the deployment of the network each sensor node is preloaded with two hash functions, a secret key and a random nonce shared with the base station. These data are used to generate a pseudonym that is included in packets addressed to the base station in order to allow the identification of the data source. The pseudonym is updated for every new packet by applying one of the preloaded hash functions to the current identifier xor-ed with the random nonce. The problem with this scheme is that, after deployment, each node exchanges their preloaded information with its neighbors in order to generate and update pseudonyms for one-hop communications. This information includes the keys and nonces shared with the base station, which allows any node to determine whether the true source of the packet is a neighboring node. Indeed, a node could even impersonate any of its neighbors.

None of these schemes can successfully protect the system from attackers who are able to capture a node and access its internal memory. When a node is compromised, its secrets are exposed and the adversary retrieves all current pseudonyms and is able to generate all future pseudonyms. Notwithstanding, we acknowledge that coming up with a solution capable of dealing with this type of threat is rather challenging.

Some kind of node revocation mechanism would be necessary to diminish this sort of problem.

Finally, it is worth highlighting that node anonymity is only a first line of defense to preserve location privacy. This problem is a huge challenge due to the resource limitations of the scenario and the peculiar communication model of these networks, which together allow a skilled adversary to perform more sophisticated traffic analysis attacks to determine the location of the nodes of interest to him. In the following sections, we present and analyze the most important solutions that have been developed to diminish the threat of different types of adversaries. The exposition will be based on the capabilities of the adversaries, more precisely on their eavesdropping power and their ability to capture nodes.

3.2 Source Protection

Source-location privacy refers to the ability to protect the location of the sensor nodes reporting event data to the base station. The physical sensor node itself is not particularly attractive to the attacker. The attacker is interested in finding the data source because its location is directly related to the location of the events in the sensing area and these events may, in turn, be associated with individuals or valuable resources.

This problem has drawn the attention of the research community due to the challenging nature of the scenario. Many solutions have been devised for countering passive adversaries with a local or a global view of the communications but only a few authors have concentrated on the threat of internal attackers. The following analysis is precisely guided by the capabilities of the adversary.

3.2.1 Local Adversaries

A local adversary can only monitor a small portion of the network, typically the equivalent of the hearing range of an ordinary sensor node, that is why they are usually referred to as mote-class attackers. Therefore, they must turn to moving in the field following packets until they find their target. This strategy is called a *traceback attack* since the adversary attempts to reach the target by moving along the path of messages in reverse order, from the base station to the data source.

A traceback attack is successful in typical WSNs because the packets transmitted by a particular node tend to follow the same path over and over again. Consequently, most of the solutions to this problem are based on the randomization of routes (i.e., using different paths for different packets) to hinder traceback attacks. The goal is to mislead the adversary in order to increase the *safety period*, that is, the number of packets sent by the source node before the attacker reaches it. The application of route randomization protocols come at the cost of increased latency, higher packet loss probability, and most importantly, increased energy waste. The research community has struggled to find the right balance between network performance and privacy protection.

In the following, we analyze a number of solutions falling into some of the categories, namely, undirected random paths, directed random paths, network loops, and bogus traffic. In the first category, we include solutions where the communication paths are not clearly guided by a mechanism to improve the safety period while the solutions in the second category introduce a technique to direct the random walks. The solutions in the third category use a strategy based on the creation of loops of fake messages in order to deceive the adversary into believing he is following a real path. Bogus traffic has also been used in another ways to protect the data sources. Finally, note that some solutions may belong to more than one category but are only presented in the most representative category.

3.2.1.1 Undirected Random Paths

The first solution to provide source-location privacy was devised by Ozturk et al. and is called Phantom Routing [108]. This scheme results from the analysis of two widely used families of routing protocols in WSNs, flooding-based and single-path routing protocols. Surprisingly, both provide the same privacy protection level although it may seem that an attacker could be confused in a flooding by the number of messages coming from all directions. However, the attacker only needs to pay attention to the first message it observes since this is following the shortest path. Besides that, a baseline flooding wastes a significantly greater amount of energy compared to single-path routing but the latter is less robust to packet loss. Probabilistic flooding tries to find a balance between reliability and energy efficiency by making sensor nodes flood messages with a given probability. As a side effect, this approach reduces the likelihood of the attacker reaching the data source.

Based on the previous analysis, Phantom Routing proposes making each packet undergo two phases, a walking phase and a flooding phase. In the walking phase, the packet is sent on a random walk for h hops until it reaches a node, which is called the phantom source. Then, in the next phase, the phantom source initiates a baseline or probabilistic flooding, which eventually delivers the packet to the base station. This two-phase process is repeated for each new message thereby selecting random phantom sources. Having different phantom sources implies that messages traverse different paths, which reduces the location privacy risk for the actual data source. Later, a new version of protocol, called Phantom Single-Path Routing, was proposed in [66]. This variant replaces the flooding in the second phase by a single-path routing, which results in even longer safety periods due to the fact that the adversary misses some of the single paths coming from different phantom sources. Figure 3.4 depicts the transmission of two messages using the Phantom Single-Path Routing protocol, where dashed arrows represent the walking phase and the ordinary arrows represent the single-path phase. The gray node in both subfigures represents the phantom source for each transmission.

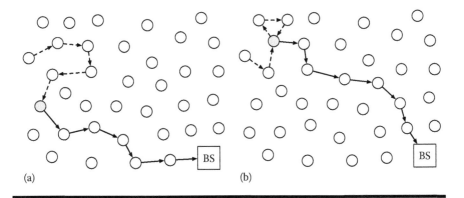

Figure 3.4 Phantom single-path routing. (a) First transmission and (b) next transmission.

The main limitation to Phantom Routing protocols is in the walking phase. Pure random walks tend to stay close to the source node and the definition of a large value for *h* does not solve the problem. Indeed, a larger value of *h* does not provide a direct improvement in the safety period, it only increases the energy waste. This problem is represented in Figure 3.4, where phantom sources are within a distance of two or three hops regardless of the definition of a five-step random walk.

To reduce the concerns about pure random walks staying close to the source node, Xi et al. [147] propose GROW, a two-way greedy random walk. The idea behind GROW is that using random walks is desirable for protecting source-location privacy because routing decisions are made locally and independently from the source location. However, using pure random walks as the only routing mechanism is impractical because the average delivery time of messages goes to infinity. GROW exploits the fact that the probability that two random walks will not intersect decreases exponentially in time [122]. First, it creates a permanent path of receptors by transmitting a special packet on a random walk from the base station. Then, the source node sends all subsequent data packets on a greedy random walk that will eventually hit a node from the path of receptors. From there, the packet is forwarded to the base station following the established path in reverse order. This process is illustrated in Figure 3.5. The protocol is said to be greedy because it uses a Bloom filter* to store previously visited nodes in order to extend as far and as quickly as possible. Despite being designed as a greedy algorithm, one of the main limitations of GROW is the substantial delivery time of the packets.

Shao et al. [125] design a cross-layer routing protocol to further mitigate the problem of random walks staying close to the data source. This approach is basically

---

* A Bloom filter [18] is a simple data structure used for representing in a memory-efficient way (as a bit string) a set of elements and for supporting queries about whether an element belongs to the set or not.

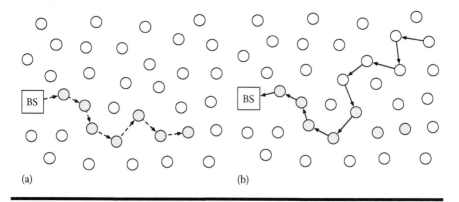

Figure 3.5 Operation of the GROW scheme. (a) Path of receptors and (b) data transmission.

a phantom routing that hides the walking phase by routing data using the data link layer. Beacon frames are periodically broadcast to inform about the node presence and other network-related parameters. Additionally, frame payload can be cryptographically obscured, which allows sensor nodes to convey event data insecurely. Since beacons are transmitted regardless of the occurrence of events, the attacker is unable to distinguish legitimate beacons from those containing event data. At the end of the walking phase, event data reach a pivot node where the information is extracted and sent to the base station using the implemented routing protocol. The pivot node is chosen by the data source at random from all its neighbors at h hops of distance. The operation of the protocol is depicted in Figure 3.6a, where the dotted arrows represent the routing phase at the data link layer, solid arrows represent the

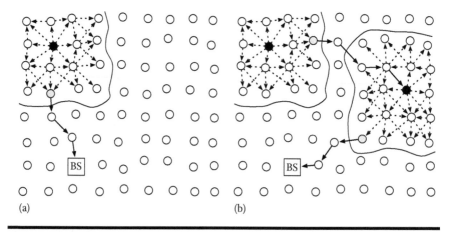

Figure 3.6 Cross-layer routing schemes. (a) Single cross-layer approach and (b) dual cross-layer approach.

transmission of messages at the routing layer, and the black and gray circles represent the data source and the pivot node, respectively. This solution provides perfect privacy for all attackers within the beaconing area as long as they are not close to the pivot node. Also, since the routing layer mechanism considered by the authors is a single-path protocol the attacker only gains some information if he is on the path from the pivot node to the base station. The main limitation to this approach lies in the trade-off between the level of protection it can provide and the delay introduced by large beaconing areas. Beacon frames are periodically sent out at intervals ranging from milliseconds to several hundreds of seconds. Therefore, the larger the beaconing area, the better the protection but also the longer the delay.

As the data travel from pivot nodes to the sink using a single-path strategy, choosing nearby pivot nodes very often allows an attacker to determine and reach the edge of the beaconing area. Also, due to the important trade-off involving the size of the beaconing area, the network administrator may turn to small values for *h* in order to boost the delivery time. This may result in pivot nodes close to the original data source (i.e., same problem as with the original Phantom Routing) and even if there is no evidence of messages leading to the target, the uncertainty region is considerably reduced. Therefore, an attacker can turn to a systematic field inspection to find the source node with no great effort. A double cross-layer solution is proposed by Shao et al. to further enhance location privacy in these circumstances. In this version of the protocol, instead of sending the data directly to the base station, the pivot node sends the data to another randomly chosen node using the routing layer. Then, this random node chooses a new pivot node and starts a second beaconing phase. Thus, the attacker cannot easily reach the edge of the beacon area to which the original data source belongs. The dual cross-layer approach is represented in Figure 3.6b.

The idea of hiding the walking phase is also leveraged by Mahmoud and Shen, who propose creating a cloud of fake traffic around the data source to hinder traceback attacks [91,92]. During the network setup, the base station floods the network with a discovery message in order to allow sensor nodes to learn the shortest path to the base station as well as the nodes in that route. Then, sensor nodes choose a group of nodes at different distances to become fake source nodes, similar to phantom sources or pivot nodes. Finally, each node groups its immediate neighbors in such a way that the members of each group are not contiguous so as to allow each group to send packet in different directions. During the data transmission phase, for each message the source node chooses one node *Fs* from its list of fake sources and sends the message to the group where there is a member that knows how to reach *Fs*. As the packet travels to the fake source, it generates fake traffic to cover the route. A node from the addressed group generates fake traffic if it is not in the direction of the fake source. In that case, the node chooses one of its groups at random and sends a fake message that lasts for *h* hops. Consequently, if groups are carefully chosen, traffic flows in any possible direction, generating clouds with dynamic shapes.

Compared to the cross-layer scheme, the main limitation to the cloud-based approach is that the clouds of fake messages consume substantially more energy than beacon frames since they are present even if there are no event data to transmit. On the other hand, routing data in the link layer is very slow and introduces significant delays but it is an interesting countermeasure when there are high privacy demands.

3.2.1.2 Directed Random Paths

Sending packets at random has shown to be moderately effective and somewhat energy inefficient. Therefore, some authors have proposed using mechanisms to guide the walking phase. By having a walking phase governed by certain parameters, either the packet delivery time is reduced or the privacy protection level is increased, or both.

The first solution to include a mechanism to guide the walking phase is Phantom Routing itself [108]. The authors suggest changing the pure random walk in favor of a directed random walk (DROW). By doing this, they prevent packets from staying close to the source node and at the same time they reduce the energy waste and achieve a similar safety period. The proposed mechanism is very simple and consists of separating each node neighbors into two groups depending on whether they are in the same direction or in the opposite direction to the base station. Thus, during the walking phase, the next hop in the path is still selected uniformly at random but only from the set of nodes in the direction of the base station.

Later, Yao and Wen [151] devised the DROW. The idea behind this solution also is quite simple. Any sensor node having a data packet to transmit must send it to any of its parent nodes (i.e., a node closer to the sink) with equal probability. This applies to both data sources and intermediaries. The level of protection provided by DROW is therefore highly dependent on the connectivity of the network. A path with a limited number of neighbors implies a short safety period since most of the packets follow very similar routes to the base station. In 2010, Yao alone published another paper describing the directed greedy random walk [150]. This solution is a mere copy of DROW with a different name. Also, the forward random walk scheme by Chen and Lou [30] does exactly the same thing. However, the authors argue that this solution cannot obtain a high level of protection and it would be necessary to inject dummy messages in the network to reduce the chances of the adversary.

The phantom routing with locational angle (PRLA) [143] prioritizes the selection of phantom sources leading to larger inclination angles. This solution results from the observation that one of the most critical factors during the walking phase period is not the length of the walk but its inclination. Long random walks do not necessarily increase the safety period unless the phantom sources are placed in a safe location to initiate the routing phase. A location is considered to be safe if it is not close to the straight line between the data source and the sink. The reason is that if phantom sources are close to this line too often, the single paths originated by them will be very similar to each other and thus the attacker has more opportunity to overhear packets. This problem is depicted in Figure 3.7a, where the curly lines

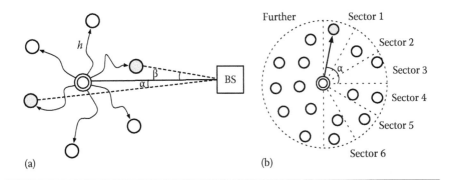

Figure 3.7   Angle-based privacy solutions. (a) Problematic phantom sources and (b) sector-based selection in WRS.

represent directed random walks from the source node to the phantom sources and the dashed lines represent the single-path routing phase. To prevent this situation, in PRLA a sensor node assigns its neighbors forwarding probabilities based on their inclination angles in such a way that neighbors with larger angles will be more likely to receive messages. After h hops, the node receiving the message becomes a phantom source and finally sends the packet to the base station using the shortest path. By using this strategy, the authors manage to reduce the number of hops necessary in the walking phase while keeping an adequate safety period. A major downside to this work is that it is not fully clear how the nodes obtain the inclination angles* of their neighbors without built-in geolocation devices or directional antennas.

Wang et al. [139] propose the Random Parallel routing scheme, which assigns each sensor node n parallel routing paths to the base station. Messages are evenly distributed to different paths in such a way that the adversary traceback time is the same at any path. Also, the paths must be sufficiently geographically separated in order to prevent the attacker from overhearing packets from various paths. The underlying idea is that if the adversary chooses one of the paths he is forced to stay on that single path. This improves the safety period, which is now equivalent to the sum of all the parallel paths. More formally, let L_i be the length of each of the paths and let p_i be the probability of choosing the path i as the transmission path. Then, the traceback time for an attacker (i.e., the safety period) is equal to $\sum_{i=1}^{n} \frac{L_i}{p_i} p_i \approx nL$, where L is the mean length of all paths. However, this approach is only theoretically feasible. In practice, the generation of n truly parallel paths is a complex task, especially in large-scale sensor network deployments. It is also impractical for sensor nodes to store a large number of routing paths locally. Moreover, some of these paths may

---

* The authors claim that the inclination angle of neighbors is calculated in terms of the number of hops. Nonetheless, two nodes at the same distance are likely to have different inclination angles.

become useless over time due to the death of nodes or due to simple disruptions performed by an attacker in order to force the source node to use some particular paths. Finally, since the paths are parallel to each other, retrieving several packets from any of the paths provides a good idea of the direction to the source. A savvy adversary can use this information to significantly reduce the traceback time to the data source.

Besides developing the Random Parallel routing scheme, Wang et al. [139] proposed the weighted random stride (WRS). This algorithm is similar to PRLA in the sense that both of them decide the next hop of the data path based on the inclination angle of its neighbors. Whenever a sensor node transmits a message to the base station, it uses two parameters to guide the path, a forwarding angle and a stride. First, the data source randomly picks a forwarding angle and chooses a neighbor that matches that angle. After receiving the message, the node uses the same forwarding angle to select a new neighbor. This process continues until the stride, which defines the number of hops for a particular forwarding angle, reaches zero. Once the stride expires, the recipient node selects a new forwarding angle and starts a new stride.* In practice, instead of sensor nodes having to store the forwarding probabilities of all their neighbors, they are divided into closer and further nodes. Closer nodes are additionally divided into sectors and only nodes from these sectors are selected to forward the packet. In order to produce larger routing paths and thus deter the traceback attacks, sectors with larger inclination angles are prioritized. Within a particular sector, the node selects the neighbor that has the largest forwarding step. For example, in Figure 3.7b, sectors 1 and 6 are more likely to be chosen than sectors 2 and 5, and sectors 3 and 4 are the least likely. The main difference between this approach and PRLA is that in WRS there are no phantom sources from where the packets are finally routed to the base station using a single-path approach.

Li et al. [78,118] proposed routing through a random selected intermediate node (RRIN) as another solution to the problem of selecting phantom sources close to the data source.† The authors assume that the network is divided into a grid and that each node knows its relative location (i.e., cell position) in the grid as well as the grid dimensions. In this way, instead of making each node in the walking phase take routing decisions independently, the source node can pick a random point in the field and send the packet to that location. The source node does not know whether there is a node in that particular location but in that case, the node closest to that location becomes the point from where the packet is finally transmitted to the base station using the shortest communication path. Li et al. propose two versions of

---

* The stride is set to a value of 5 for a large-scale sensor network with an average of 20 neighbors per node during the simulations.
† They also argue that directed random walks leak information about the data source since the forwarding direction must be contained in the packet headers in order to allow nodes to route packets correctly. However, this is not strictly necessary as this information may be encrypted or encoded in the payload thereby alleviating the problem.

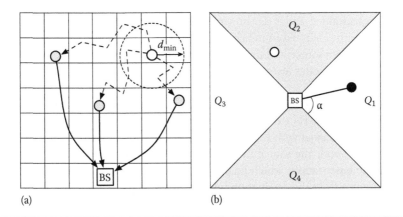

Figure 3.8   Routing through random selected intermediate node(s). (a) Distance-based RRIN and (b) quadrant-based multi-RRIN.

RRIN. In the first version, the intermediate point is chosen uniformly at random but it is forced to be placed at least at a distance d_{min} from the source as shown in Figure 3.8. The main drawback to this scheme is that the probability of being selected as an intermediate node is proportional to the distance to the data source. As a result, the intermediate nodes concentrate around the location of the source node and no mechanism prevents them from being picked from the proximities of the source-destination shortest path, which was one of the problems addressed by PRLA and WRS. In the second version of RRIN, any location in the network has the same probability of being selected as the random intermediate point. The consequence is that some intermediate nodes will be very close to the data source thus exposing its location while some others will be extremely far, not only resulting in energy-intensive paths but also in more chances for the adversary to trace packets.

The RRIN scheme has been used by Li et al. as a building block to location privacy solutions. As such, the idea has been extended and used in several other research papers. In [80], they propose two schemes that use multiple random intermediate nodes instead of only one. In the angle-based multi-intermediate node selection, the source node selects a maximum angle β to limit the location of the last intermediate node within the range $(-\beta, \beta)$. Once the maximum angle has been determined, the source node uniformly chooses a random angle θ between itself and the node with respect to the base station, such that $\theta \in (-\beta, \beta)$. Then, the data source selects the rest of the n intermediate nodes to be evenly separated between itself and the final intermediate node. In the quadrant-based multi-intermediate node selection, each sensor node divides the network into four quadrants in such a way that it is placed in the first quadrant and the base station is in the middle. The source node location is determined within the first quadrant based on a random angle α. The last intermediate node is selected to be somewhere within its adjacent quadrants, namely, quadrant 2 and 4 as shown in Figure 3.8b. Both extensions ensure that nodes are neither selected from behind the base station nor close to the shortest path between the data source and the destination. However, the reasons for using multiple intermediate nodes instead of a single intermediary are not clearly motivated in the paper.

The Sink Toroidal Routing (STaR) protocol [83,84] is also designed to improve upon the initial RRIN designs. In particular, it has been designed to reduce the energy cost associated with the selection of pure random intermediate nodes in the field. To that end, the source node picks random points within a toroidal region around the base station, which guarantees that intermediate nodes are, at most, a given distance from the destination but also not too close in order to prevent traceback attacks. The toroid is defined by three parameters: the center of the toroid (x_0, y_0), where the base station is placed; r, the inner edge of the toroid; and R, the outer edge of the toroid. Therefore, for each message a source node picks a distance value d uniformly from the interval $[r, R]$ and an angle θ from $[0, 2\pi]$. The intermediate node will be the one closest to the point $(x, y) = (x_0 + d \cos \theta, y_0 + d \sin \theta)$. The main drawback to this solution is again with the selection of random intermediate nodes. No mechanism ensures that these nodes are not often chosen close to the shortest path between the data source and the base station or behind it.

3.2.1.3 Network Loop Methods

A network loop is basically a sequence of sensor nodes that transmit messages in a cycle. These loops are primarily used to keep the adversary away from his target for as long as possible. They are either used to cover the presence of real traffic or as a mechanism to deviate the adversary from the path of real messages that would otherwise lead him to the data source.

The cyclic entrapment method (CEM) [106] sends decoy messages in a loop to attract the adversary and distract him from the true path to the data source thus increasing the safety period. After the deployment of the network, each sensor node decides whether it will generate a network loop with a given probability. Then, the node selects two neighboring nodes and sends a loop-creation message that travels h hops from one of the neighbors to the other. All the nodes receiving the loop-creation message become members of a loop. During the normal operation of the network, a loop is activated whenever a loop member (i.e., activation node) receives a real packet being routed from a source node to the base station. Interestingly, CEM is not a routing protocol itself but rather an add-on that can be used with different routing protocols to enhance source-location privacy. This implies that, when used in conjunction with single-path routing, real traffic reaches the base station in the shortest time possible without incurring extra delays but inducing some energy waste to the network. Figure 3.9a depicts such a scenario where two loop members (in gray) become activation nodes after receiving real traffic. During a traceback attack, when the adversary reaches an activation node he must decide which packet to follow.

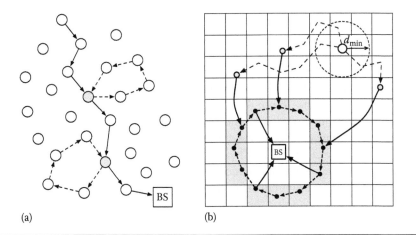

(a)   (b)

Figure 3.9   Network loop methods. (a) Cyclic entrapment method and (b) Network mixing ring.

If he chooses the fake message, he is trapped in the loop for h hops until he realizes. However, a skilled adversary might avoid loops by observing the angle of arrival of packets since those with a larger inclination angle are more likely to lead to a loop.

The information Hiding in Distributed Environments (iHIDE) scheme by Kazatzopoulos et al. [69,70] is another solution that uses network loops. In this scheme, the sensor network consists of a set of ring nodes that are interconnected with each other and with the base station by means of a wireless network bus. The main difference between this arrangement and the one depicted in Figure 3.9a is that in iHIDE, all sensor nodes belong either to a ring or to the network bus. During the data transmission period, a source node that wishes to communicate data to the base station first sends the data to the next ring member in a (counter-)clockwise direction. If the node belongs to multiple rings simultaneously it randomly selects one of them to forward the message. When the bus node receives the packet, it forwards it to the next bus node closer to the sink but the packet continues to loop in the ring for a random number of hops. As the packet travels through the bus, each bus node decides, based on a given probability, to forward the packet into its own ring or to directly submit it to the next bus node. The main limitation to iHIDE is that because it has such a well-defined architecture and roles for the nodes, it is easy to learn the topology of the network and thereby identify the bus and the rings. Once a bus node has been reached, the adversary can wait until he observes that the bus node receives a message from another bus node that it forwards to the next one. This implies that somewhere in a previous ring there is a data source. In this way, the adversary can slowly reduce his uncertainty.

The network mixing ring (NMR) scheme [79,81] creates a ring of nodes surrounding the base station, which is not intended to trap the adversary but to mix up real messages with fake traffic in order to make them indistinguishable to the adversary. This scheme consists of two phases. In the first phase, the source nodes pick a random intermediate node that is in charge of initiating the next phase. The selection process is based on the distance-based RRIN approach described earlier. In the second phase, the intermediate node sends the packet to the closest node in the network mixing ring. Once there, the packet is placed in a vehicle message and relayed clockwise for a random number of hops before it is finally send to the base station. These vehicle messages are created by a few nodes within the mixing ring and consist of several data slots, which are initially filled with random bits. To further complicate traffic analysis, vehicle messages are re-encrypted at every hop. In this way, the attacker cannot distinguish real packets from random data, and even if he reaches the ring node that forwarded the data, to the base station, he is unable to figure out the entry point of that packet to the ring. Moreover, reaching an entry point does not lead to the data source as they change over time due to the use of the distance-based RRIN approach in the first phase. The whole process is depicted in Figure 3.9b, where the gray cells represent the area defining the network mixing ring. This scheme not only presents the limitations as the STaR approach described earlier but there is another major limitation to it, which is energy consumption at the ring nodes. These nodes are more likely to deplete their batteries than other nodes as they are constantly relaying traffic. This event not only ruins the source protection mechanism but also isolates the sink from the rest of the network, rendering the whole system useless.

The authors acknowledge the energy imbalance problem between ring nodes and ordinary nodes and discuss on some potential solutions. They suggest predefining several rings and activating only one at a time according to the residual energy of their members. Additionally, they briefly discuss the possibility of having several active rings simultaneously to improve the level of protection of the data sources. More recently, Yao et al. [152] have continued with the idea of organizing the network using a multiring approach to protect source-location privacy. This scheme consists of three phases: initialization, path diversification, and fake packet injection. During initialization, the base station floods the network with a discovery message that includes a hop count. This process allows sensor nodes to obtain their distance to the base station as well as to determine which of their neighbors are at the same distance, which means that they belong to the same ring. In the following phase, the data source picks, uniformly at random, two rings (one closer and one farther) and an angle α between 0 and π. Then, the data packet is sent out to the farther ring and once there it is relayed counterclockwise until the angle is reached. From this point, the packet is sent to the closer ring and once more travels counterclockwise for an angle $\beta = \pi - \alpha$. Finally, the packet is routed directly to the base station. During transmission of real traffic on the rings, fake packets are injected by the nodes on contiguous rings to further complicate traffic analysis. Clearly, these ring-based solutions require the network to be densely populated in order to enable the creation of full rings.

3.2.1.4 Fake Data Sources

The use of fake data sources was first accomplished by Ozturk et al. [108]. Two strategies were proposed to simulate the presence of real events in the field by making some sensor nodes to behave as true data sources. In the first strategy, called the Short-lived Fake Source, whenever a sensor node receives a real message it decides, based on a particular probability distribution, whether to generate a fake message and flood the network with it. This scheme provides a poor privacy protection since fake data sources are ephemeral. The second strategy, called the Persistent Fake Source, aims to increase the level of protection by creating sources of fake messages that are continuously injecting traffic. During the network setup, each sensor node decides with a probability to become a persistent fake data source. The efficiency of this strategy is very much dependent on the positioning of the fake data source. If fake data sources are far from a real data source, it helps to improve the safety period significantly, otherwise it may lead the adversary to the real data source. Moreover, this strategy can only increase the safety period, but after the attacker reaches a data source, he can discard it and eventually he will be able to discard all of them.

Jhumka et al. [62] devised two solutions based on the creation of fake data sources in order to study the effectiveness of this approach to protect source-location privacy. These solutions, which are built on top of a baseline flooding protocol, are called the Fake Source (FS) 1 and 2, respectively. In the former, when a node has something to transmit, it first floods the network with a data message containing the event data and a hop count. When this message reaches the base station, it floods the network with a new message to inform about the distance d_s between the data source and itself. Once this message reaches nodes at the same distance than the data source, they transmit a choose message. This new message is forwarded to nodes further away, which decide to forward it based on a given probability. When the hop count of the choose message reaches 0, the recipient node generates a random number, and, if above a given threshold, the node becomes a fake data source. The result is that a number of nodes at distance larger than d_s from the base station become fake sources. The second protocol, FS2, is very similar but now all the nodes that receive a message forward it, while in FS1 the forwarding of messages is determined by a given probability. Consequently, more nodes are likely to become fake data sources in FS2, and thereby the level of protection achieved by this scheme is better. A major limitation of both schemes is the complexity and the amount of messages that need to be exchanged before fake data sources are finally chosen. In fact, these protocols can be simplified since each node knows which of its neighbors are at the same distance than itself from the base station.

Finally, Chen and Lou [30] designed a set of solutions that make use of fake data sources to create branches of fake messages along the communication path to mislead the adversary. In the bidirectional tree (BT) scheme, real messages travel along the shortest path from the source to the base station and several branches of fake messages flow into and out of the path. The branches that flow into the path are intended to

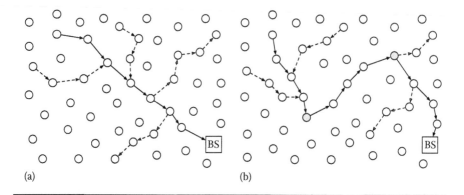

Figure 3.10 **(a) Bidirectional tree schemes and (b) zigzag bidirectional tree scheme.**

make it difficult for the adversary to find out which of the flows of messages lead to the real data source. On the other hand, the branches that flow out of path aim to protect the base station.* To achieve this, the source node sends a packet along the communication path prior to the transmission of event data. This packet contains its own distance to the base station H_s, which is used to determine the area that may receive fake branches and the area that may generate them. Nodes in the path whose distance to the sink is greater than $(1 - p)H_s$, being p a network parameter, will generate an input branch with a given probability.† Similarly, the nodes satisfying pH_s will choose whether to generate an output branch. This solution is depicted in Figure 3.10a, where dashed arrows represent (input or output) fake branches and solid arrows represent the real communication path.

Although the idea behind the creation of fake branches is to misdirect the adversary from the real path while event data reach the base station in the shortest time possible, it is not difficult for a skilled adversary to realize that nodes deviating from the already traveled path are fake branches. To prevent this, the authors propose a new solution called the dynamic bidirectional tree (DBT) scheme. Instead of using a shortest-path routing to transmit real data to the base station, the DBT scheme suggests to make real messages travel with a DROW. When a node receives a real message, it decides the next hop uniformly at random from its list of those neighbors closest to the base station. Similar to the BT scheme, fake branches are created

---

* These solutions are originally devised to protect both source- and receiver-location privacy simultaneously but will be covered here in full detail to prevent the replication of contents across multiple sections.
† Input messages cannot originate from a node belonging to the shortest path but from a remote node. The authors do not specify how remote sources of fake data are selected. A possible solution is to send a message on a directed random walk from the node in the shortest path.

in order to complicate packet tracing attacks further. In this case, input branches are generated with a probability when the hop count is smaller than $H_s/2$, and output branches otherwise.

Chen and Lou also propose the zigzag bidirectional tree (ZBT) scheme to further prevent leaking direction information. In this scheme, real packets zigzag along three segments: from the source node to a source proxy, from there to a sink proxy, and finally to the real sink. First, two candidate sink proxies are selected, one on each side of the sink and at a distance of h hops. Then the sink and the two proxies initiate a flooding so that each node learns its distance from each of them. In this way, the source node can select the sink proxy that is furthest away from itself. Having a single sink proxy may imply that a source node is very close to that proxy, which would negatively impact source-location privacy. Before the transmission of data to the sink, the source node picks a source proxy h hops away from itself. The source proxy should be selected in such a way that it is not close to the sink. However, this is not a trivial task unless the nodes are aware of the physical location of all other nodes. Finally, during the data transmission phase, each node in the path generates fake branches with a given probability. In the segment from the source node to the source proxy, the fake packets flow into the path, and in the segment from the sink proxy to the sink, the packets flow out. No branches are generated in the segment connecting the source and sink proxies. The operation of the ZBT scheme is depicted in Figure 3.10b, where gray nodes represent the source and sink proxy nodes. This scheme presents the same limitation as the original BT scheme, that is, fake branches can be eventually discarded. Either the attacker discards a fake branch after tracing it or due to an unusual inclination angle. Moreover, the segment between the source and sink proxies does not generate any branches, which implies that an attacker can easily determine their locations and from there reach its target.

3.2.2 Global Adversaries

The aforementioned techniques are only effective against adversaries performing traceback attacks with a limited hearing range. A more powerful adversary is capable of monitoring the behavior of a larger number of nodes simultaneously, which allows him to better correlate messages and guess routing paths. In particular, global adversaries are capable of monitoring all the traffic generated and forwarded in the network. Such adversaries can easily detect the data sources among mere intermediaries because sensor nodes are programmed to report event data to the base station as soon as it is detected.

Dealing with global adversaries is very challenging especially in scenarios where there exist topological, functional, or hardware constraints, as we learnt in Chapter 2. There are two main approaches to hide the location of data sources, either using fake traffic to cover the presence of event messages or introducing significant delays in the transmission of messages. Both solutions present some disadvantages in the sensor domain. The former implies a massive energy waste while the latter has a negative impact on the ability of the network to provide the base station with timely reports about events, which is essential for time critical applications.

Most solutions in this area have concentrated on the injection of fake traffic to provide event source unobservability but these solutions are extremely energy consuming. Therefore, much of the research effort has been devoted to reducing the amount of fake traffic while maintaining a suitable level of privacy.

3.2.2.1 Dummy Traffic Injection

The threat of global adversaries was first considered by Mehta et al. They proposed the periodic collection scheme in this paper [97]. This scheme makes every node transmit fake messages at regular intervals to hide the presence of events in the field. However, it is necessary to prevent real messages from changing the message transmission pattern to prevent the adversary from easily distinguishing real from fake transmissions. In Figure 3.11a, a flawed fake transmission scheme is shown. This figure depicts a timeline where the transmission of fake messages F_i are represented as white-headed dashed arrows, while the real transmissions E are represented with ordinary arrows. The scheme is flawed since the transmission of the real message changes the transmission pattern. In the periodic collection scheme, each sensor node transmits messages at a given rate $\mathcal{R}$ regardless of the presence of events. Instead of transmitting a message immediately after the detection of an event, the message is temporarily stored until the next scheduled transmission time, as shown in Figure 3.11b. This method provides perfect event source unobservability because the transmission rate is not altered by the presence of events and the adversary cannot distinguish an encrypted (real) message from a random-looking (fake) message.

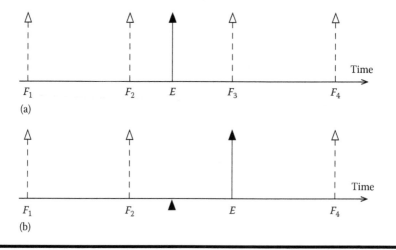

Figure 3.11 Periodic fake packet injection. (a) Detectable event and (b) perfect event source unobservability.

This scheme presents two conflicting parameters. First, real messages need to be delayed in order to conform to the established transmission pattern. This poses an important limitation in time-critical applications. To reduce this problem, the network administrator can change the transmission pattern in order to have shorter inter-transmission times and thereby reduce the delivery delay. However, this has a serious impact on the lifetime of the network as more fake traffic needs to be injected. Therefore, the transmission rate must be carefully adjusted in order to ensure the durability of the network without incurring an excessive delay in the delivery of messages to the base station.

3.2.2.2 Energy-Aware Approaches

An extensive body of research has focused on reducing the overhead imposed by the injection of fake messages at regular intervals by all sensor nodes. These proposed solutions have approached the problem in different ways: simulating the presence of events in the field, filtering out fake traffic, using already existing traffic to convey event data, and sending messages according to a given probability distribution.

A first attempt to reduce the overhead produced by the periodic collection scheme was devised by Mehta et al. [97]. This scheme, called source simulation, is based on the idea of saving energy by reducing the number of nodes transmitting fake messages. Instead of making all nodes send out messages at regular intervals, the network simulates the presence of real events in the field. The main problem with this approach lies in the difficulty of accurately modeling the movement of an object so it appears as real to the adversary. In such a case, having a static subset of sensor nodes transmitting fake messages is not enough to deceive an attacker. Therefore, sensor nodes must be carefully programmed to transmit fake messages following a coherent pattern that resembles a real object. Moreover, this process should be carefully tailored to any type of asset being monitored, which turns it into a challenging and laborious protection mechanism. Mehta et al. propose a source simulation protocol as follows. During network deployment, a set of L nodes are preloaded, each with a different token. These nodes generate fake traffic during the data transmission phase, and after a predefined period of time, the token is passed to one of its neighbors (possibly itself) depending on the behavior of real objects. The size of L determines the level of protection as well as the energy consumed by the network.

Although the cross-layer scheme proposed by Shao et al. [125] (see Section 3.2.1.1) was originally devised to counter local adversaries, it can be used to protect from global adversaries in a similar way to the periodic collection scheme described earlier. Event data are conveyed within beacon frames, which are periodically transmitted, until it eventually reaches the base station. Basically, this version of the cross-layer solution removes the single-path transmission path on the routing layer. Therefore, the main difference with the periodic collection scheme is that instead of using ordinary network traffic it takes advantage of the beaconing phase.

This scheme also provides perfect event source unobservability at no additional cost since event data are hidden within beacon frames, which are broadcast regardless of the occurrence or not, of events in the field. However, since the time between consecutive beacons is relatively large, the solution is only practical for some applications where no tight time restrictions exist. Moreover, this solution is inadequate for large-scale sensor networks since the delivery time is highly dependent on the distance from the data source to the base station.

Ortolani et al. [105] suggest to simulate the movements of objects in the field to hide the presence of real moving objects in the presence of global adversaries. In particular, they concentrate on events originating at the perimeter of the network and eventually expiring at some point inside it (see Figure 3.12a). A clear example is the transportation of goods to an industrial area. Their scheme, namely, Unobservable Handoff Trajectory (UHT), generates fake mobile events with the same probability distribution as real events. Real events follow a Poisson distribution of rate l while fake events are generated with rate $k - l$. In consequence, the overall distribution of messages in the network follows a Poisson distribution of ratio k thus covering real events. The generation of dummy events starts at the perimeter of the network and propagates for a number of hops according to the length of real events. Each perimeter node decides to generate a new dummy event independently based on a Poisson with parameter $k - l/P$, where P is the number of perimeter nodes and l, although unknown, can be estimated by choosing a statistical estimator. To do this, perimeter nodes record the number of real events they observe over a time window. The propagation of fake event messages works as follows. All nodes within the radius of a fake node receive the fake packets sent toward the base station. This packet contains who will be the next fake source in the path and also the length of

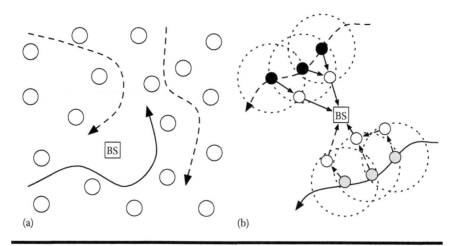

(a)   (b)

Figure 3.12 Unobservable handoff trajectory. (a) Real and fake mobile events and (b) modeling of event propagation.

the current event. This process is represented in Figure 3.12b, where fake sources are shaded in gray and real sources in black while fake and real messages are represented with dashed and ordinary arrows, respectively.

In order to reduce network traffic while maintaining source unobservability, Yang et al. [148] proposed a bogus traffic filtering scheme. In this approach, the network is divided into cells and some sensor nodes operate as filtering proxies. Cells send real or fake messages at a given rate and on their way to the base station they reach some of these proxy nodes. Upon the reception of traffic, a proxy node discards bogus traffic and real traffic is temporarily buffered and re-encrypted before being forwarded.* In the case where there are no event messages available, a proxy node sends encrypted dummy messages to prevent the attacker from learning which proxies are receiving real traffic from some of its associated cells. Two filtering schemes are proposed, the Proxy-based Filtering Scheme (PFS) and the Tree-based Filtering Scheme (TFS). The PFS is the baseline approach where a number of nodes are selected as proxies but the traffic generated by each cell is only filtered once by its default proxy node. In TFS, a multilayered proxy architecture is proposed to further reduce dummy traffic. As packets move toward the base station they can be processed by several proxy nodes, which reduces fake traffic at the expense of increased network delay due to the buffering at each proxy node. Thus, the number and location of proxy nodes is very important to the performance of the solution. It should be noted that a drawback to this solution is that an attacker can still use rate-monitoring techniques to identify the proxy nodes, which are important for the operation of the network.

Several other authors have concentrated on the concept of *statistically strong source unobservability*, which was first introduced by Shao et al. [126]. The idea is to relax the tight requirements of perfect event source unobservability while maintaining a statistical assurance on the protection of data source. Before network deployment, sensor nodes are configured to transmit according to a particular message distribution F_i, as shown in Figure 3.13. During the data transmission phase, when an event E occurs, the real message can be transmitted before the next scheduled transmission, F_4, without altering the parameters of the distribution (e.g., the mean and variance). The process is depicted in Figure 3.13b. Sensor nodes keep a sliding window of previous intermessage delays $\{\delta_1, \delta_2, ..., \delta_{n-1}\}$, and, upon the occurrence of an event, δ_n is set to a value very close to 0 and gradually incremented by a small random number until the whole sliding window passes an Anderson–Darling goodness-of-fit test. Thus, the real event transmission can be sent ahead of the scheduled time without alerting the adversary even if he performs statistical tests on intermessage delays. However, in the presence of burst of real messages the mean of the distribution might be skewed. To prevent this, the scheme also include a mean recovery mechanism that delays subsequent transmissions.

---

* Cells are assumed to share pairwise keys with proxy nodes to allow them distinguish real from fake messages.

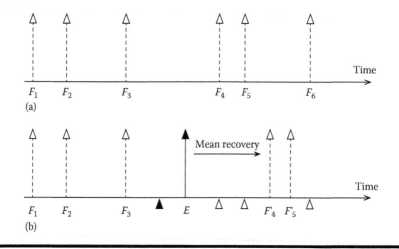

Figure 3.13 Statistically strong source unobservability. (a) Predefined message distribution and (b) message distribution adjustment.

Despite the efforts of Shao et al., a few years later Alomair et al. [6,7] showed that a global adversary can detect the presence of real messages thus breaking statistically strong unobservability. To that end, the adversary needs to spot differences between two consecutive sliding windows. To distinguish between an interval (i.e., a sliding window) containing real events from another one with no real events is to identify short intermessage delays followed by long intermessage delays. These patterns are common in intervals containing real events because the delay of real messages is usually shorter than the mean in order to reduce the latency, and subsequent messages are delayed in order to adjust the mean of the distribution as proposed by Shao et al. [126]. On the contrary, intermessage delays are independent identically distributed random variables in fake intervals. Consequently, an attacker might be able to identify intervals containing real messages by counting the number of short–long intermessage delays. Alomair et al. propose to introduce some statistical interdependence between fake intermessage delays in order to make fake intervals resemble intervals with real messages and thus reduce the success probability of an adversary performing this type of attack.

More recently, Proaño and Lazos [113] pointed out that the adversary cannot exactly determine the transmission rate of each and every sensor node. This is due to the fact that a global vision of the network is usually achieved by means of an adversarial sensor network. Each adversarial node only knows the number of packets sent within its hearing range but it is unaware of which node is sending each of the packets unless these data are present in the packet headers. As a result, not all sensor nodes need to be active sources of fake traffic to deceive the adversary. The problem of reducing the number of fake data sources is solved by partitioning the network into a minimum connected dominating set (MCDS) rooted at the

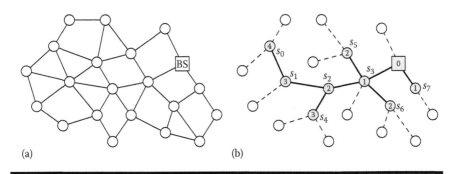

Figure 3.14 **Minimum connected dominating set. (a) A graph representation of the WSN and (b) a potential MCDS.**

base station. The MCDS covers the whole network by using the minimum number of nodes in such a way that each node in the network either belongs to the MCDS or is one hop away from it, as depicted in Figure 3.14. In this way, the nodes in the MCDS transmit (real or fake) traffic at a given rate $\mathcal{Z}$ and the rest of the nodes regulate their transmissions in order to conform to the statistical traffic properties observed by an eavesdropper. Since the location of the eavesdropper is unknown, each sensor node divides its hearing range into several regions so as to consider all potential locations and computes a rate that satisfies the original rate $\mathcal{Z}$ for all of them. Later, in [114], the same authors added a deterministic assignment scheme for coordinating sensor transmissions and thus reduce end-to-end delay for real packets. Time is divided into intervals of duration T and each interval is in turn divided into subintervals of duration T/l, where l is the height of the MCDS. Nodes deeper in the MCDS are scheduled to transmit sooner, so that any real packet reaches the sink at the end of each interval. For example, in Figure 3.14b, each time interval I_k is divided into four subintervals since the maximum depth of the MCDS is four. Sensor node s_0 transmits at subinterval I_k^1, node s_1 at subinterval I_k^2, and so on.

The solutions considered so far deal with a passive global adversary that observes the network traffic and based on his observations tries to determine whether an event has been detected by the network and, if so, where it occurred. Yang et al. [149] go a step further by considering a global attacker who, upon detecting suspicious areas, devises an optimal route to efficiently visit these spots. The attacker performs traffic analysis as usual and after an observation period he obtains a suspicion level for each cell. The suspicion level is used to determine which cells (areas) to visit and in what order. Since this problem has a factorial time complexity on the number of suspicion cells (i.e., $\mathcal{O}(s \cdot s!)$), Yang et al. propose two potential strategies to find a (pseudo-) optimal route to visit all suspicious cells. The first strategy is based on a greedy algorithm, which ends in polynomial time but is not globally optimal, and the second one is a dynamic programming algorithm, which finds the optimal solution but requires an exponential time to finish. Subsequently, the authors evaluate the impact of the proposed attacker model to two existing solutions: statistically strong source unobservability and source simulation. They conclude that the former behaves well when the rate of real messages to be delivered is low while the latter approach is suitable when the rate is high. As a result, Yang et al. propose a dynamic approach that combines the merits of both solutions by switching from the one to the other based on the load of the network.

3.2.3 Internal Adversaries

In addition to performing traffic analysis attacks some adversaries might turn to tampering with the hardware in order to compromise and take control of some legitimate sensor nodes. These nodes become internal adversaries since they can participate in the same tasks performed by any other network nodes but they work on behalf of the attacker. Thus, compromised nodes can provide the attacker with any information contained in the packets they overhear since they share cryptographic material with their neighbors.

The solutions devised to deal with these types of attackers are very limited and their approaches rather diverse. To the best of our knowledge, very few (only three) solutions have been devised, and they have concentrated on the implementation of a trust-based routing scheme, the modification of packets in transit, and the decoupling of the location where the data are sensed, from the location where it is temporarily stored before it is collected by the base station. Next we review them in more detail.

Shaikh et al. [121] describe their identity, route, and location (IRL) privacy algorithm as a network-level privacy solution. The primary goal of this solution is to provide source anonymity and location privacy as well as provide assurance that packets reach their destination. Although the authors do not consider the threat of internal adversaries, one of its features is suitable for just this purpose. The authors introduce the notion of trust and reputation to prevent routing through misbehaving adversaries. First, each node classifies its neighbors into four groups depending on their position with respect to the base station: forward (F), right backward (B_r), left backward (B_l), and middle backward (B_m), as shown in Figure 3.15. Furthermore, each node classifies its neighbors as either trustworthy or untrustworthy based on the number of successfully forwarded packets. Nonetheless, the calculation of the trust values could be extended to incorporate new parameters, such as the presence of communications with external entities or with other nonneighboring nodes in order to identify internal adversaries. When a node needs to send a message to the base station, it checks whether there are any trustworthy nodes it can select in the direction of the base station. From among all the trustworthy nodes it picks one uniformly at random. If there are no trustworthy nodes, the same process is repeated for B_r and B_l. As a last resort, the node tries to send the packet in the opposite direction to the base station. In the case no trustworthy nodes are found, the node simply drops

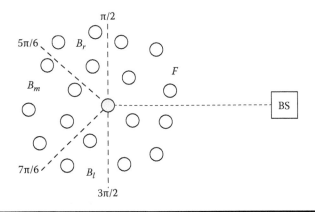

Figure 3.15 Neighbors partition in the identity, route, and location.

the packet. Therefore, each message follows a different (random) path composed of trustworthy nodes only.

Additionally, IRL includes a renaming mechanism to protect the identity of the data source. Whenever a node receives a packet it replaces the identifier contained in its header with its own before forwarding it. In this way, dishonest en-route nodes are unable to determine whether the sender is the real data source or a mere intermediary. This implies that the identity of the real data source is conveyed in the packet payload, encrypted with a pairwise secret shared with the base station. The use of end-to-end encryption is efficient against internal adversaries, but it impedes the use of data-aggregation mechanisms, which is a useful feature for reducing network traffic and thus preserving energy.

A more sophisticated packet transformation approach is proposed in [111,112]. The Source Privacy under Eavesdropping and Node compromise Attacks (SPENA) is based on the application of some cryptographic operations on the packets at dynamically selected nodes in the route to the base station. Packets have the following structure: {*DstID, SrcID Hash, Obfuscating Partial Hash, Rehash Seed, Payload Length, Payload | SrcID, Filler*}, and nodes are pre-loaded with two unique hash functions, a mapping function f_p that returns 1 with probability p and 0 with probability $1 - p$, a rehash function, and a symmetric key shared with the base station. One of the hash functions H_i is used to generate a hash chain $(h_i^1, h_i^2, \ldots, h_i^n)$ used in reverse order as the identities of the nodes and the other hash function F_i is used in conjunction with the mapping function to determine whether a node should modify the packet or not. In particular, a node j transforms a received packet if $f_p(F_j(Rehash\ Seed)) = 1$. Nodes that transform packets in transit are called rehashing nodes. At the data source, the *SrcID Hash* field is loaded with an element of its hash chain (i.e., h_i^m) and later replaced by a rehashing node j by a value of its own hash chain (i.e., h_j^k). The *Obfuscating Partial Hash* (OPH) is initially set to the next element of the hash chain concatenated with the payload and encrypted with its symmetric key (i.e., $E_{K_i}(h_i^{m+1}|Payload)$). A rehashing node j generates a new OPH_j by first applying the rehashing function to the received OPH and then encrypts it with its own key. Additionally, the rehashing node concatenates the *SrcIDHash* obtained from the received packet to the payload, which is then encrypted with its own symmetric key. It also uploads the new payload length and subtracts that amount of bits from the filler to keep the packet size unchanged. At the base station, the payload is recursively decrypted until the *SrcID Hash* of the true data source is found. Finally, the base station checks the validity of the OPH. The verification process requires the base station to keep track of the hash chains of all the nodes in order to find the key corresponding to each of the concatenated hash values. Another limitation to this approach is that the attacker can trivially learn the real size of the payload by inspecting its corresponding header field and thereby guess the number of modifications the packet has suffered based on the probability p of the mapping function. By having access to this information the attacker can estimate its distance to the data source.

In data-centric sensor (DCS) networks, there are two types of nodes: sensing nodes, which collect and forward information about events of interest, and storage nodes, which temporarily store the data from a subset of sensing nodes and respond to the queries of the itinerant base station. The relationship between sensing and storage nodes is defined by a publicly known mapping function that determines where the data are stored. In this way, the data can be accessed more efficiently when the base station collects the data, but it also allows an attacker to easily determine which nodes to compromise if he is interested in a particular type of data. After compromising such nodes, he can also identify the location where the data were originally collected. Shao et al. [127] present a solution called pDCS that is intended for this type of network with an itinerant base station. In particular, pDCS concentrates on preventing node compromise and mapping attacks, that is, impeding the retrieval of any event data stored in storage nodes as well as preventing the attacker from identifying the relationship between sensing and storage nodes. The proposed scheme is based on the use of a secure mapping function, which is basically a keyed hash function that uses as input the type of event and other secret information shared by a group of nodes, and the storage of encrypted data in a remote location. In the case where the adversary compromises a storage node, he is not able to decrypt the data contained in it because these data are encrypted with the key of the sensing nodes which collected them. If a sensing node is compromised, the attacker cannot determine where previous data were stored because the secure mapping function prevents this from happening. Moreover, when a node is found to be compromised there is a node revocation mechanism in order to prevent the attacker from obtaining the location of future event data. Finally, the authors suggest to use any existing location privacy solution in order to prevent the adversary from learning the data source using some sort of traffic analysis attack.

3.3 Receiver Protection

Receiver-location privacy refers to the protection of the destination of messages but it primarily concentrates on hiding the location of the base station. This device demands exceptional protection measures given its importance for both the physical protection of the network and strategic reasons. An attacker aware of the location of the base station may compromise it for his own benefit. For example, the attacker may be interested in gaining access to the data collected by the network, change configuration and operation parameters, or even destroy the base station and thereby render the whole system useless. Additionally, the base station provides strategic information because it is usually housed in a relevant facility (recall the scenario depicted in Section 1.4.1).

The location of the base station is exposed due to the peculiar communication pattern of WSNs. Each sensor node transmits data messages to a single base station using a multihop routing protocol, which results in a high volume of traffic in the proximities of the sink. Intuitively, the solution is to normalize the traffic load by making each sensor node transmit, on average, the same number of messages. Thus, a baseline flooding protocol provides the maximum protection but it also incurs a prohibitive network overhead. Solutions in this area have concentrated on providing a sufficient protection level at a reasonable cost.

In the following, we review the existing solutions according to the capabilities of the adversary. We analyze proposals dealing with local adversaries followed by solutions considering the threat of global adversaries. There are no solutions in the literature that study the threat of internal adversaries or node compromise attacks. To the best of our knowledge, the first receiver-location privacy solution to consider this type of threat is presented in Chapter 5.

3.3.1 Local Adversaries

In a local adversarial model, the attacker usually starts at a random position in the network* and waits or moves around until he overhears some transmissions in the area surrounding him. The typical types of attacks performed by an adversary who wishes to find the sink are: content analysis, rate monitoring, and time correlation. In content analysis, the adversary looks for any valuable information that might lead him to the base station in either the packet's headers or the payload. This attack may be taken a step further by adding undetectable marks to data packets as proposed by Shakshuki et al. [123] in order to allow the adversary to track them on their way to the sink. Nonetheless, content analysis is usually a poor source of information.

Additionally, an attacker can observe the packet sending times of neighboring nodes in order to determine the direction of the communication flow. Assuming that the network is using a single-path routing protocol, the attacker can learn that

---

* Placing the adversary at the edge of the network is possibly more realistic.

a sensor node is closer to the base station than one of its neighbors if it is used as a relay. In other words, if a node transmits immediately after one of its neighbors, the former node is closer to the sink. Finally, in a rate-monitoring attack, the strategy of the adversary is to move in the direction of those nodes with higher transmission rates since nodes in the vicinity of the base station receive more packets than remote nodes.

Next we analyze some basic countermeasures against the aforementioned attacks followed by a set of more advanced solutions that provide enhanced security to the base station. Most of these solutions aim to balance the amount of traffic between all network nodes by selecting the next hop based on some probability while other solutions attempt to disguise or emulate the presence of the base station at different locations. Again, some solutions may fall into several categories depending on the features analyzed.

3.3.1.1 Basic Countermeasures

In order to prevent the aforementioned traffic analysis attacks, some basic counter-measures have been proposed. First, content analysis can be hindered by applying secure data encryption on a hop-by-hop basis. Deng et al. [41] suggest this process should be applied throughout the whole lifetime of the network, but it is not easy to satisfy this requirement until each node shares pairwise keys with all its neighbors. Thus, they propose an ID confusion technique to conceal the source and destination during the route discovery phase. This technique is based on reversible hash functions so that when a node x sends a message to node y, it randomly selects an element from $C_x = \{h_x : x = H(x)\}$ as the source address, and an element from $C_y = \{h_y : y = H(y)\}$ as the destination address. Finally, it encrypts the whole packet with a network-wide shared key pre-loaded on all sensor nodes. A receiving node decrypts the message and obtains the true sender and intended recipient by reverting the hash function.

As data packets move toward the base station, each node in the communication path must decrypt any received packet and then re-encrypt it with the key shared with the next node in the route. This ensures that packet change their appearance at every hop and complicates the correlation of inputs and outputs. However, even if the packets change and the attacker has no access to the contents of the packets, he can learn some information from packet sending times and eventually infer the relationship between parent and child (i.e., closer and further) nodes. To prevent this, Deng et al. [40,42] propose applying random delays to the transmission of packets. Additionally, the authors suggest creating a uniform sending rate to prevent rate-monitoring attacks. This can be achieved by making a parent node accept packets from a child node only if its own packet has been forwarded. In the case the parent node has nothing new to send, it can simply inject fake traffic or continue to send the same packet.

These basic countermeasures present some limitations that require the development of further solutions. These limitations are related to the delay introduced at each forwarding node and the energy wasted due to the application of uniform data transmission rates. The following solutions aim to reduce these limitations.

3.3.1.2 Biased Random Walks

The use of random walks has also been extensively used to protect the location of data sources from local adversaries (see Section 3.2.1). This category includes schemes where the routing process is random but packets are more likely to be sent to neighbors closer to the base station, that is, random walks are directed or biased.

The first solution in this category is also presented by Deng et al. [40,42] and is called multiparent routing (MPR). The MPR consists of making each sensor node pick the next element in the path uniformly at random from its set of parent nodes. See in Figure 3.16a comparison between a single-path routing and an MPR scheme. In single-path routing, all transmissions use the same transmission path, which is represented by a straight arrow, while in MPR, two different packets are likely to two different communication paths, as shown in Figure 3.16b. The MPR scheme obtains a better load balance as data packets spread within a band of nodes next to the shortest path from the data source to the base station. However, the traffic flow still points to the base station as the next communication hop is always selected from parent nodes, which are closer to the base station.

To further diversify routing paths and introduce packets in different directions, the authors suggest combining MPR with a random walk (RW) routing scheme. In this version of the protocol, nodes forward packets to a parent node with probability p_r and to a randomly chosen neighbor with probability $1 - p_r$. Consequently, packets may travel not only toward the base station but also in any other direction. Figure 3.16c shows two routing paths that at some points even move in the opposite

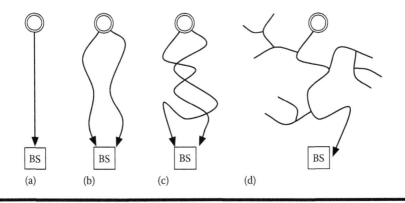

Figure 3.16 Schematic of multiparent routing techniques. (a) Single-path, (b) MPR, (c) MPR + RW, and (d) MPR + RW + FP.

direction to the base station. This scheme provides better security at the cost of increased message delivery delay.

Similarly, the location privacy routing by Jian et al. [63,64] proposes to make every sensor node divide its neighbors into two groups. The first group contains nodes that are closer to the base station and the second group contains the rest of their neighbors. So, nodes forward packets to further nodes with probability P_f and to closer nodes with probability $1 - P_f$. To ensure that packets reach the base station, the value of P_f must be below $1/2$. This implies that after a sufficient number of observations, the attacker is able to determine which of the neighbors of a node belong to each group. By following this strategy at different nodes, the attacker is able to infer the direction toward the data sink. To prevent this, the authors propose injecting fake packets in the opposite direction to the base station. When a node forwards a real packet, it generates with probability P_{fake} a fake packet to a random node in the group of further nodes. This packet travels for $M_f \geq 2$ hops away from the base station.* In general, the adversary cannot distinguish real from fake traffic, which makes this solution secure since packets flow in any direction with an even probability. However, if the adversary observes a node that does not forward a packet he knows that it is a fake packet. As fake packets are sent to further neighbors exclusively, the adversary learns that the base station is in the opposite direction.

3.3.1.3 Fake Traffic Injection

The aforementioned MPR solutions are still vulnerable to traffic analysis attacks since p_r is typically set to values more than 0.5 for reasons of efficiency. Therefore, after a sufficient number of observations, an attacker can learn which of the neighbors of a node are its parents. To mitigate this problem, Deng et al. [40,42] propose an additional technique called fractal propagation (FP) to be used in conjunction with MPR and RW. The main idea behind this mechanism is to generate and propagate fake packets in random directions in order to introduce more randomness into the communication pattern. When a sensor node observes that a neighboring node is forwarding a data packet to the base station, it generates a fake packet with probability p_c and forwards it to one of its neighbors. The durability of fake packets is controlled by means of a global time-to-live parameter K. Also, if a node observes a fake packet with parameter k $(0 < k < K)$ it propagates another fake packet with time-to-live parameter $k - 1$. Figure 3.16c shows the trace resulting from the transmission of a single packet using the three mechanisms together.

The main limitation of the FP scheme is that since nodes in the vicinity of the base station observe a greater amount of traffic, they generate much more fake traffic than remote nodes. This implies that the traffic rate in the area surrounding the

---

* A value $M_f = 1$ implies that the node receiving the fake packet does not retransmit the packet, which can be detected by the attacker.

base station is significantly higher than in other areas, which is not only detrimental to the operation of the network as it increases the number of collisions but also helps the adversary to track down the base station. To address this problem, the authors propose a new solution called the differential fractal propagation (DFP). In this scheme, sensor nodes adjust their probability of generating fake traffic p_c according to the number of packets they forward. Below a given threshold, sensor nodes behave as in FP, but if their forwarding rates are higher (i.e., they are close to the base station), they reduce the probability p_c by a specific factor. Besides reducing the energy waste and packet loss rate, this scheme provides better privacy protection to the base station because it balances the network traffic load more evenly.

Most of the solutions that are to be presented in the following rely on the use of fake traffic to keep the adversary away from the true base station. However, they are analyzed in a separate section since fake traffic is injected with some particular goal, such as mimicking the presence of the base station in far away locations. These are precisely the solutions covered next.

3.3.1.4 Sink Simulation

Some solutions try to reproduce the behavior of the base station at different locations in the field in order to provide some form of k-anonymity [120], which refers to the ability to remain anonymous (i.e., unidentified) within a set of at least k entities with similar attributes. Simulation techniques are based on the generation of fake traffic but, instead of being transmitted in random directions, it is addressed to particular network locations. This results in a concentration of high volumes of fake traffic, called hotspots, that attract local adversaries and keep them away from the true base station. The main challenge is to create hotspots that are evenly distributed throughout the network with a minimum overhead.

Yao et al. [153] devised another fake packet injection scheme to protect sink location privacy. In this scheme, real packets are sent along the shortest path from the data source to the base station. When two paths of real messages intersect at some point, the node receiving these packets sends two fake packets to two fake data sinks after a timer expires or a packet counter reaches a certain threshold. In this way, real and fake data sinks receive a similar number of packets. Moreover, when a packet reaches subsequent intersection points, the intersection node sends N_f packets to some random destinations. This process is depicted in Figure 3.17, where dark-gray nodes represent intersection nodes, light-gray nodes are fake sinks or some random data destinations. Ordinary arrows symbolize real data packets while dashed arrows represent fake packets. In Figure 3.17a, the first intersection node transmits fake traffic to both fake data sinks. Meanwhile, the second intersection node introduces fake traffic to other random destinations as well.

The main problem of Yao et al.'s approach is its privacy protection level. An attacker starting from a data source and tracing packets can trivially reach the first intermediate node. From that point, the attacker has to decide on his next move.

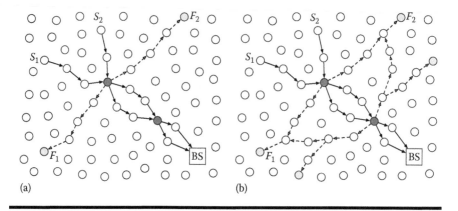

Figure 3.17 Yao et al.'s fake packet injection scheme. (a) Injection at first intersection node and (b) injection at second intersection node.

Since fake traffic is sent after certain conditions have been satisfied, the attacker can distinguish real from fake traffic. Additionally, since real data packets are sent using the shortest path, the transmission of fake traffic may imply an abrupt change in the angle of transmission and thus reveal the flow of real messages. This problem is also present in the BT scheme, which was devised by Chen and Lou [30] as a solution for protecting source- and receiver-location privacy simultaneously in the presence of a local adversary. As such, the BTS scheme was covered under Section 3.2.1.4.

Chang et al. [26] present a solution called maelstrom that generates a number of points in the network with a high traffic density that are intended to drag the attacker to them. After network deployment, the base station sends N special configuration packets, each of which is configured to travel H_s hops away from the base station. After that, each of these packets travel H_r random hops to any node on the same level or further away. The final recipients of these packets become the center of a maelstrom area and announce this by sending a discovery packet to nearby nodes. During data transmission, when a node receives a real packet it generates with probability p_f a fake message and forwards it to its closest maelstrom. Additionally, any packet addressed to the sink or a maelstrom is sent to a node closer to its destination with probability p and to a node at the same distance as itself (if any) with probability $1 - p$. By carefully adjusting the values of p_f, N, and p, the authors claim that it is possible to evenly distribute the number of packets being received at the base station and the various maelstroms. However, once an intelligent attacker reaches a maelstrom area he can discard it as the true data sink. Moreover, the base station is more or less in the center of all maelstroms.

Similarly, Biswas et al. [17] describe an approach to simulate several data sinks in the network. These fake data sinks are intended to be evenly distributed such that each of them receive the fake traffic within its neighborhood. The selection criteria

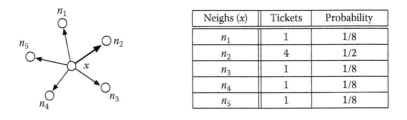

Neighs (x)	Tickets	Probability
n_1	1	1/8
n_2	4	1/2
n_3	1	1/8
n_4	1	1/8
n_5	1	1/8

Figure 3.18 Decentralized hotspot generation in differential enforced fractal propagation.

is that fake data sinks should not be close to the base station, be neighbors with each other, or have neighbors in common. The goal is to maximize the number of neighbors that each of the fake base stations have, since this implies more incoming traffic. During data transmission, each node is configured to transmit a fixed number of messages either real or fake so that after a given time period all nodes have sent the same amount of traffic. Fake traffic is directed to fake base stations by its neighbors except for nodes that are not neighbors. The selection of a fake destination is done in a round-robin fashion. The result should be that fake base stations receive at least the same amount of traffic as the actual base station. This approach may deal with naive rate-monitoring adversaries but it can be easily defeated by informed global observers.

The FP solutions by Deng et al. [40,42] were refined into a new scheme called differential enforced fractal propagation (DEFP). This scheme creates hotspots in a decentralized and dynamic way. To generate hotspots, sensor nodes are pushed to send fake traffic to an already used neighbor with higher probability as opposed to FP and DFP where dummy packets are sent in any direction. This is achieved by keeping track of the number of fake packets forwarded to each neighbor. New fake traffic is more likely to be sent to neighbors who have previously received more fake traffic, as shown in Figure 3.18. In this way, there is no need for a central authority or a complex coordination system to establish where the hotspots should be placed. The most interesting feature of this solution is that the hotspots can be deactivated by simply resetting the forwarding probabilities of each node. This prevents smart adversaries from easily discarding fake data sinks as after resetting the forwarding probabilities new hotspots are likely to appear.

3.3.2 Global Adversaries

Routing-based countermeasures are known to be effective only against local adversaries but some of the aforementioned techniques, particularly those based on the injection of bogus traffic, may provide some means of protection against global adversaries. As a matter of fact, they can be useful if the global adversary has no real-time analyzing capabilities, that is, he is only able to retrieve a snapshot of the amount of traffic transmitted over a period of time. Also, this is made possible by the fact that the adversary is usually unaware of the forwarding rate of each particular node rather he only knows the overall rate in its vicinity, as noted by Proaño and Lazos [113]. However, there is still a chance that there can appear global adversaries with real-time monitoring capabilities, which needs to be tackled.

The injection of fake traffic is one of the main approaches for protecting from global adversaries also in the case of protecting the base station. Notwithstanding, making the base station mimic the behavior of sensor nodes, simulating the presence of several data sinks, and moving the base station to a different location might also be useful solutions. These schemes are usually more energy efficient but also imply more management and configuration issues.

3.3.2.1 Traffic Homogenization

At the beginning of Section 3.3, we mentioned that flooding the network with messages is a simple yet efficient mechanism to homogenize network traffic and thus protect the location of the base station. The main drawback to flooding is the cost associated with the retransmission of the same message to every corner of the network.

The idea of Backbone Flooding [98] is to reduce the scope of the baseline flooding approach to a limited area of the network, the backbone, and thus reduce the communication cost associated with this process. Any data packet generated in the network is addressed to a backbone. Once a data packet reaches a backbone member, it forwards the packet to all its neighbors. Backbone members will repeat the process while ordinary sensor nodes will remain silent. Thereby, the backbone must satisfy two conditions. First, any data sinks must be located within the range of at least one backbone member in order to overhear all messages. Second, the backbone is created in such a way that it contains a sufficient number of nodes to achieve the desired level of privacy. A major limitation to this approach is that the backbone is static and thus backbone members will deplete their batteries sooner than the rest of the nodes. The authors suggest that this problem can be alleviated by (1) periodically rebuilding the backbone based on the energy remaining on the nodes or (2) defining several backbones from the beginning so that each packet is addressed to different backbones. Figure 3.19 illustrates the transmission of a data packet to the backbone as well as its eventual propagation and delivery to the base station.

Ying et al. [154,155] also try to homogenize the traffic in the network by making each sensor node transmit at the same rate regardless of its distance to the base station. After network topology discovery, each sensor node knows its distance from the base station and can adjust its transmission rate accordingly. The Concealing Sink Location (CSL) [154] calculates the traffic that has to be transmitted by each single node located at distance h from the sink. This value is calculated as the number of nodes with distance $d \geq h$ divided by the number of nodes at distance h.

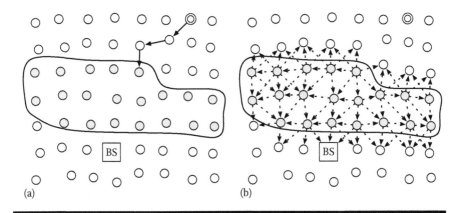

Figure 3.19 Backbone flooding. (a) Data packet reaches the backbone and (b) packet flooding reaches data sink.

This ratio represents the number of messages to be transmitted by each individual node at distance *h*, considering that each node must send its own traffic and forward the traffic from nodes further away from the sink. The number of nodes at a given distance *h* is estimated via geometric analysis considering the size of the deployment area and a uniform distribution of the nodes in the field. However, these estimations may differ significantly from the reality. Also, it is important to note that the authors assume that sensor nodes have a similar transmission rate for real messages but this might not be the case in the presence of bursts of messages at different network locations.

The transmission rate of sensor nodes is calculated in [155] similarly. The rate is based on the number of child nodes an immediate neighbor of the sink has. The reason is that this provides an estimation of the total amount of traffic that each node should generate to transmit a similar number of messages. The rationale is to make all sensor nodes in the network transmit as many messages as a sink neighbor has to since they are the most loaded nodes. This fixed number of messages is split into real and fake messages. When a sensor node receives a message, it first checks whether it is fake or real. In the former case, the packet is simply dropped, while in the latter, the packet is temporarily buffered before being transmitted. In the meantime, the sensor node generates fake traffic to satisfy the overall transmission rate. Ying et al. claim that by instructing sensor nodes to forward the same number of messages as the neighbors of the base station, the lifetime of the network is not reduced. The argument is that the neighbors of the sink are always the first nodes to deplete their batteries. However, the authors have not considered several important issues that may call into question their claims. First, they should have considered that a transceiver in listening mode consumes almost as much battery as the micro-controller in a typical sensor node [129]. Second, sensor nodes must decrypt received packets in order to be able to discern which of them are real. Finally, it is necessary to consider that increasing the traffic rate of every single sensor node also has a negative impact on the reliability of the communications, which results in packet collisions and retransmissions.

3.3.2.2 Sink Simulation

Sink simulation is based on the notion of k-anonymity because its goal is to make the base station indistinguishable from several other fake base stations. This approach is also suitable to protect from adversaries with a global view of the communications in the network.

This idea is exploited by Mehta et al. [98] who devise a scheme that simulates the presence of several data sinks in the field. During the deployment of the network, a number of sensor nodes are picked as fake data sinks and the true data base stations are manually placed within the communication range of some of these nodes. Clearly, the number of fake sinks must outnumber the number of true sinks. Later, during data transmission a data source sends data to all the fake data sinks, which on reception broadcast the message locally. Since the true base stations are within the range of fake data sinks, they receive the message. This process is illustrated in Figure 3.20a, where the data source sends four messages, one for each of the fake data sinks $(F_1, \ldots, F_2)$, and each of them broadcast the message locally. The attacker cannot determine where is the base station because all fake data sinks receive the same amount of traffic, they are all equally likely to be next to a true data sink. The main limitation of this approach is that fake data sinks are static and thus the attacker can visit them and check for himself. Therefore, the number of fake sinks, has a clear impact on both the level of protection of the network and the communication

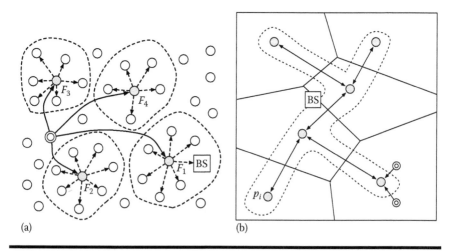

(a)   (b)

Figure 3.20 **Examples of sink simulation approaches. (a) Mehta et al.'s approach and (b) Chai et al.'s approach.**

overhead. The larger the number of fake data sinks, the better the protection but the higher the volume of traffic in the network.

Chai et al. [25] present a solution also based on the concept of k-anonymity. The idea is to have at least k nodes with a communication pattern similar to the nodes around the base station. To that end, the network is partitioned into k nonoverlapping regions, each of which contains a node that collects all the information sensed in that region. These nodes p_i are organized as a Euclidean minimum-spanning tree (EMST), and the data they received from their own region are forwarded to all other tree members. The base station is manually placed after the formation of the EMST in order to ensure that it is within the communication range of the tree. The authors show in the paper that the Voronoi tessellation* of the network is the optimal partition that minimizes the total routing energy and provides a reasonable protection level. Figure 3.20a shows a Voronoi partition of the network for the designated nodes p_i, in gray. Note that all nodes connecting the designated nodes see all the network traffic and thus the base station simply needs to be placed close to one of them. As a result, the uncertainty of the attacker is much greater than in the previous scheme for the same value of k. However, there is a limitation to this approach in relation to the connectivity of the tree. The nodes forming the tree are highly likely to deplete their batteries much sooner than the rest of the nodes, thereby ending up with no alternative routes to the base station.

Wang and Hsiang [140] propose another solution based on the creation of artificial hotspots that is intended to counter a global adversary. The hotspots are generated by means of a decentralized protocol that starts by generating a shortest-path tree rooted at the base station. After that, neighboring leaf nodes from the tree can establish communication links in order to generate network cycles. During data transmission, the shortest-path tree is used to transmit data to the base station and, simultaneously, fake packets are injected into the cycles. Fake traffic continues moving along the cycle until it is completed. The center of a hotspot is, indeed, a node where several cycles intersect as it is the recipient of all the bogus traffic generated along the cycles. Moreover, during cycle generation, they include a mechanism that establishes that two leaf nodes only create a cycle if their least common ancestor is at least h hops away from both nodes. This mechanism is interesting because it reduces the number of hotspots and, in this way, each of the hotspots receives a greater amount of traffic. However, if h is too large, it may result in very few hotspots, which turn out to be placed very close to the base station. Another drawback is that leaf nodes may be physically distant from each other and if this is the case they are unable to communicate with each other in order to establish a link for the cycle. Finally, it is worth mentioning that even though the authors assume a global adversarial model, this solution does not seem suitable for that purpose. As a matter of fact, their simulations concentrate on the communication cost and efficiency

---

* A Voronoi diagram for a given set of locations is a partition of the plane into disjoint regions such that any given region contains all the points closest to each of the locations.

compared to DEFP but no security analysis nor simulation results are provided with respect to the level of privacy achieved by their solution. The main problem is that the true sink behaves differently from the rest of the artificial hotspots. While the transmission rate of the base station is negligible, fake hotspots must forward the real data packets coming from its child nodes. Consequently, the base station can be uncovered by calculating the node with the largest reception–transmission ratio.

3.3.2.3 Relocation and Disguise

Having itinerant or mobile base station is possible in WSNs [135]. Mobile sinks present several advantages since they can obtain sensor data from isolated sensor nodes, may help to reduce the number of hops on communication paths and achieve a uniform energy consumption across the network. In fact, mobility has also been considered a mechanism for enhancing security. As far back as 2003, Deng et al. [41] considered sink mobility as a mechanism to prevent packet dropping from compromised nodes.

Possibly motivated by previous works, Acharya and Younis present the Relocation for Increased Anonymity (RIA) scheme [1]. The base station moves to a new location by considering both the impact over network performance and its own level of protection. The network is divided into cells and the base station knows the transmission rate of each cell as well as the number of nodes in them. With this information, the base station calculates a score for each cell (i.e., $score_i = densitiy_i / threat_i$) and moves to the cell with the highest score. The idea behind this scoring mechanism is that by moving the base station to a cell with a low threat (i.e., low transmission rate), the cells with high activity need to send packets to remote areas, which increases the delivery time and consumes more energy. Likewise, if there is a low transmission rate due to a reduced node density, moving the base station to that cell would cause the few nodes in the cell to become overwhelmed with traffic and their batteries would soon be depleted. Once the base station knows which is the most suitable cell to reside in, instead of moving there using the shortest path, the base station follows the safest route to reach the final destination. In Figure 3.21a, we depict the path selected by the base station for relocation based on the scores of each of its cells, the cells with higher scores are depicted in a lighter color.

The authors also suggest using a completely different approach to hide the base station from global adversaries. The base station anonymity increase through selective packet re-transmission (BAR) [1] is based on the idea of making the base station mimic the behavior of ordinary sensor nodes. After receiving a packet, the base station decides whether to send the packet to a random neighbor. Packets will be retransmitted away from the base station for a given number of hops. The length of the walk is dynamically adjusted based on the level of threat perceived by the base station. If the base station needs to increase its level of protection it defines longer walks. The rationale is that by doing this, the number of transmissions in remote cells increases and thus the attacker cannot clearly identify the actual location of the

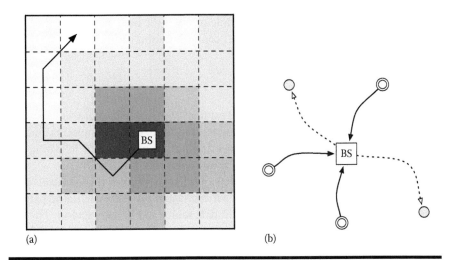

Figure 3.21   Relocation and disguise examples. (a) Safest route in the RIA scheme and (b) selective packet retransmission.

base station based on the transmission rate of a cell. An example of this approach is illustrated in Figure 3.21b, where source nodes and destination nodes are represented as gray and white circles, respectively. The main problem with this approach is that all traffic passes through the base station. By forwarding packets to random remote locations, the base station is also increasing the transmission rate of the cells in its vicinity. Consequently, the attacker may still spot the base station as the cell with the highest transmission rate. Another limitation is that a local adversary can easily find the base station if the network uses a shortest-path routing algorithm.

Finally, the Decoy Sink Protocol [36] tries to hide the base station by reducing the amount of traffic it receives. To that end, this scheme combines indirection and data aggregation. Instead of sending the event data to the base station directly, sensor nodes are programmed to transmit their packets to an intermediate node (i.e., the decoy sink) and on their way the data are aggregated. Finally, the decoy sink sends the result of the aggregation to the base station. Although this would reduce the amount of traffic addressed to the base station, a global observer can still detect the communications from the decoy sink to the true base station. Moreover, this protocol exposes the location of the decoy sink, which can be destroyed or compromised by the attack thus impacting the network in the same way as if he managed to reach the true data sink. To reduce this threat, the authors suggest picking several random nodes during the deployment of the network. During data transmission, sensor nodes will send their readings for a preestablished period of time to a particular decoy sink. This version of the protocol adds robustness to the network and balances the traffic load but a motivated adversary will end up destroying all decoy sinks until he achieves his goal. This protocol also present the limitation that if a local adversary finds a decoy sink he may be able to reach the base station as aggregated data travels to the base station using fixed communication paths.

3.4 Summary

This chapter has presented and analyzed a number of schemes for protecting location privacy in WSNs. Based on this analysis, we have come up with a complete taxonomy of solutions (see Figure 3.22). This categorization has been created following the same criteria as those used to guide the exposition of this chapter.

The first tier of the taxonomy considers the element or asset that demands protection, namely, node identity or traffic pattern. More precisely, the traffic pattern branch considers both the protection of the data source and the base station. The different categories of solutions are considered at a second level, where the capabilities of the adversary are also taken into account.

There are two main approaches for node identity protection, both of which are based on the generation, distribution, and use of dynamic pseudonyms. The first category of solutions consider the use of pools of pseudonyms that are either assigned to nodes or communication links in order to hide the true identity of the nodes. These solutions present several impediments due to the constrained memory budget of sensor nodes and this is where the second category of solutions come into play. Cryptographic-based solutions make use of cryptographic operations to update the pseudonyms thus reducing the memory demands of sensor nodes at the expense of increased computational power and complexity. In particular, these schemes rely on the repetitive application of keyed hash functions on the true identifier of the node.

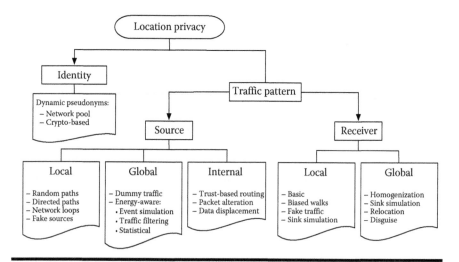

Figure 3.22   Taxonomy of location privacy solutions in wireless sensor networks.

Most of the research in this area has endeavored to prevent the attacker from being able to link past and future pseudonyms to a given pseudonym.

Once node identity is sufficiently protected, it is necessary to obfuscate the traffic pattern in order to prevent the adversary from inferring the location of the data sources and the base station. Solutions are classified according to the capabilities of the adversary. The adversarial model considered in the literature is mostly passive and external although some few papers have also looked into the threat of passive internal adversaries. External attackers can be further classified into local or global adversaries depending on whether they are capable to monitor a limited portion of the network or the hearing range can cover the entire network.

The most common approach to protect from local adversaries is to randomize the routing paths in order to prevent the adversary from trivially following the communication path until they reach a target. The primary reason for this is that random routing can increase the safety period without introducing a significant overhead to the network in terms of message delivery delay and energy consumption. However, the protection level offered by this type of solutions is usually insufficient when the application scenario is critical. As such, some solutions have turned to the injection of fake traffic in order to somehow hide differences between ordinary and sensitive sensor nodes. Several solutions exist that use fake data source to simulate the presence of real events in the field as well as solutions that simulate the presence of data sinks at various locations by delivering high volumes of traffic to areas distant from the true base station.

Although the injection of fake traffic, in general, and simulation techniques, in particular, exist in the context of local adversaries, they are primarily used against global adversaries since random routing schemes are essentially useless in the presence of such powerful attackers. Most of the solutions designed to protect data sources from global adversaries have strived for reducing the amount of fake traffic necessary to hide data sources without introducing an excessive delay in the transmission of sensor nodes while preserving their batteries. To that end, some solutions devised mechanisms to filter out fake traffic at some points of the network but the most successful area of research has been the study of statistically modifying the transmission pattern to introduce real messages without being detected by the adversary. On the side of receiver-location privacy, most solutions have exploited the injection of fake traffic to create hotspots (i.e., sink simulation) and to homogenize the number of transmissions of the nodes in the network. Notwithstanding some authors have turned to more innovative solutions like moving the base station to a safer location or making it to behave as an ordinary node.

Finally, little work has been done on the protection of location privacy against internal and active adversaries. In fact, this problem has only been considered in the presence of attackers willing to uncover the location of data sources and no papers have deal with this type of adversary when the goal is to hide the location of the base station. To that end, only three solutions have been devised. A routing protocol that prevents forwarding data to potentially compromised nodes, an in-transit packet alteration scheme that renames the headers of event messages, and a mechanism for DCS networks that unlinks the nodes that collect the data from those which store them until the base station queries for the data.

Besides the information that can be easily derived from the proposed taxonomy, there are some other interesting issues that will be exploited in the following chapters to enhance location privacy in WSNs. First, it is interesting to observe that protection mechanisms are mostly blind, in the sense that they are executed without having any feedback on whether they are actually being useful against adversaries. Moreover, the network is unaware of whether the protection mechanism is necessary because there are no adversaries trying to compromise privacy. Knowing the whereabouts of the attacker can be a very useful information that can be exploited in different ways to enhance location privacy and to reduce the costs associated with the protection mechanism. With this sort of information, the network can intelligently decide when to activate the protection mechanism instead of assuming a constant threat. If the network knows the exact or approximate location of the adversary, it can carefully adjust the protection mechanism to impose a minimal impact on the network both in terms of energy consumption and data delivery delay. This idea is exploited in Chapter 4 to protect source-location privacy in the presence of a mobile adversary.

Another interesting observation is that most of the solutions devised to protect the location of the base station are either too costly because they require large amounts of fake traffic to create hotspots or they leak location information in some specific circumstances. Additionally, none of the existing solutions deal with node compromise attacks and more precisely with the threat of routing table inspection. An adversary being able to retrieve the routing tables of a node trivially learns which of its neighbors are closer to the base station. After very few repetitions of this process, he gains a very good idea of the direction toward the base station. In Chapter 5, we elaborate on these research gaps and develop a solution that provides receiver-location privacy against adversaries capable of performing both types of attacks.

Chapter 4

Context-Aware Source-Location Privacy

This chapter presents a novel source-location privacy solution, called context-aware location privacy (CALP). The general trend toward source-location privacy protection has been to randomize routing paths in order to reduce the number of packets the adversary is capable of capturing, thus minimizing his chances of tracing back to the source of messages. However, it is well known that sending packets on randomly chosen paths does not necessarily reduce the likelihood of the attacker reaching the source of events. The primary reason is that the data routing process is blind, that is, there is no knowledge of the paths that are being traversed or the location of the attacker.

The CALP mechanism offers an original solution to the location privacy problem that takes advantage of the ability of sensor nodes to feel their environment. CALP exploits sensor nodes' context awareness to detect the presence of a mobile adversary in their surroundings so that packets are routed in a more efficient and privacy-preserving manner. The solution aims to anticipate the movements of the attacker in order to minimize the number of packets he is able to capture and analyze, hence reducing the likelihood of the attacker finding the source. Unlike state-of-the-art solutions, the devised protection mechanism is operative only when the adversary is present in the field. Since the network is expected to be free from threats most of the time, the use of the CALP mechanism translates into significant energy savings and increased efficiency compared to previous source-location privacy solutions.

Prior to describing the scheme, the general assumptions about the network and threat model are presented. Then, the chapter details the main building blocks of the CALP approach and continues by presenting the implementation of the shortest-path CALP routing algorithm, which combines the CALP approach with an energy-efficient routing algorithm. Finally, extensive simulations are performed in order to evaluate the robustness and efficiency of the shortest-path CALP routing scheme.

4.1 Problem Statement

This section describes the network and attacker models considered throughout this chapter. It also presents the main assumptions that are relevant for the development in the CALP mechanism.

4.1.1 Network Model

We consider WSNs used for monitoring purposes that follow an event-driven data reporting method, meaning that individual sensor nodes transmit data packets to the base station as soon as they observe a relevant phenomenon in their vicinity. Therefore, all data are received at the base station after several forwarding hops.

The network is assumed to be composed of n sensor nodes that are uniformly and randomly distributed in a field. Sensor nodes cover a large area so that the attacker can only control and monitor a small portion of the communications at any given moment. Also, we assume that each node is aware of its adjacent neighbors and the connectivity of the network is high. This allows sensor nodes to choose the next communication hop from various neighboring nodes.

The most important assumption for the correct operation of CALP is that each node in the network has the ability to detect the presence of moving objects in the field. This can be done by means of one or various types of sensors such as infrared, acoustic, thermal, pressure, and magnetic sensors. Additionally, as shown in [156] and [145], the location of transceiver-free moving objects can be estimated due to the interferences they cause in the radio signal strength of several network nodes.

In addition, we require sensor nodes to share keys with its immediate neighbors in order to be able to encrypt and decrypt messages at each hop. We assume these cryptographic algorithms are semantically secure, thus enabling message confidentiality and indistinguishability to an external observer, who is unable to retrieve packet contents nor link messages. Moreover, the headers of the packets contain no information about the identity of the data sources. This can be achieved by means of pseudonym schemes, as described in Section 3.1. Notwithstanding, these are not strict requirements since the protocol leverages on the concept of undetectability. In order words, the solution aims to prevent the adversary from being able to detect the presence of traffic in his proximities.

4.1.2 Threat Model

The adversarial model under consideration is an external, passive attacker with local eavesdropping capabilities. The adversary has the ability to move in the sensor field and follow messages based on the angle of arrival of the signals, which can be obtained by measuring the difference in received phase at each of the elements of an antenna array [94]. The attacker turns to traceback attacks (i.e., follow messages in reverse order) in order to reach data sources. Besides, we assume that the attacker is able to move at a reasonable speed but never exceeds the time it takes for a packet to reach a neighboring node. Thus, the speed of the attacker is not a critical factor, although it affects the response time of our scheme.

A passive adversary does not interfere with the communications or the normal operation of the network by injecting, modifying, or blocking packets. In general, passive adversaries limit their actions to performing traffic analysis attacks. This is not an important assumption to the CALP mechanism even though it relies on the use of some alert messages to inform their neighbors about the presence of the adversary in a particular location. An active adversary could block the communications to prevent these messages to arrive to their destination but by doing this the attacker is also unable to observe any communications originated by the network. Consequently, the adversary loses his ability to trace back packets to the data source.

The attacker might start to monitor the communications from either an internal position or the edge of the network. We follow the same approach as most authors, that is, letting the adversary start next to the base station. In this way, the adversary will eventually overhear data packets since all the traffic is addressed to this single node. We consider two different strategies for the adversary: a patient or inquisitive adversary. Formally,

Definition 4.1 ($\mathcal{ADV}_{PAT}$). *Let $X = \{x_1, x_2, \ldots, x_n\}$ be the set of sensor nodes comprising the network and let x_0 be the base station. $\mathcal{ADV}_{PAT}$ is an attacker that starts at x_0 and waits until he observes a packet from another node x_i. The adversary moves to node x_i and waits for a new transmission from a node x_j, where $i \neq j$. If no packets are received after a time t, the attacker returns to node x_i. This process is repeated until $x_i = x_0$.*

The patient adversary waits until he overhears a data packet or a predefined time period passes without any observations, in which case he returns to his previous position. Eventually, the attacker may return to the original position, the base station. The inquisitive adversary behaves similarly but he does not wait for packets.

Definition 4.2 ($\mathcal{ADV}_{INQ}$). *Let $X = \{x_1, x_2, \ldots, x_n\}$ be the set of sensor nodes comprising the network and let x_0 be the base station. $\mathcal{ADV}_{INQ}$ is an attacker that starts*

at x_0 and initiates a random walk until he observes a packet coming from node x_i. The adversary waits next to node x_i for new packets, but if no packets are received after a time t, he initiates a new random walk.

A combination of both strategies is also possible but the proposed solution will be only evaluated against the $\mathcal{ADV}_{PAT}$ and $\mathcal{ADV}_{INQ}$ adversaries.

4.2 Context-Aware Location Privacy

This section provides the details of the CALP scheme. First, it gives an overview of the rationale of the solution and continues presenting how it fits in with the software components of sensor nodes. Second, it describes the process of detecting and alerting about the presence of the adversary in the field. Next, it shows how sensor nodes use the location of the adversary to update their routing information. Finally, this section concentrates on the data transmission phase and presents two different data forwarding strategies to counter local adversaries.

4.2.1 Overview

The basic idea behind the CALP mechanism is to anticipate the movements of the attacker in order to decrease the number of packets he is able to capture. The reason is that by limiting the access to data packets, the ability of the adversary to perform traceback attacks is hindered thus increasing the location privacy of data sources.

In order to detect the adversary in the sensor filed and anticipate his movements, the CALP scheme takes advantage of the ability of sensor nodes to perceive the presence of moving objects in their vicinity. Upon the detection of such an event, nodes react by broadcasting a route update message to its neighboring nodes. This message is forwarded several hops away from the position of the attacker and is used to modify the routing tables of the nodes in such a way that packets are routed around the region under the control of the adversary.

4.2.2 Software Integration

The CALP scheme can be regarded as a software plug-in that integrates neatly with the rest of components of the sensor nodes* to enable privacy-aware routing protocols. The interaction between components is depicted in Figure 4.1, where an outgoing arrow means that the component uses some of the functionality provided by the component receiving the arrow. Therefore, a monitoring Application might

---

* A typical approach to software development in sensor platforms is to follow a component-based model, where systems are built by the composition of loosely coupled, reusable software containers. TinyOS [77] is indeed a component-based operating system for sensor networks.

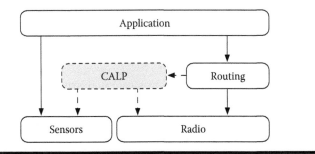

Figure 4.1 Integration of the context-aware location privacy component.

use the Sensors component to measure some phenomena and a Routing component to send the information to the base station. Additionally, the Routing component uses the Radio component to send the data through the wireless interface and might use the CALP component to make decisions on the next hop of the communication, thus allowing the sensor nodes to adapt their routing strategy depending on their privacy needs. Finally, the CALP component may use either the Sensors component or the Radio component, or both, to detect the presence of adversaries.

The main advantage of this approach is that by integrating the CALP component, any existing application can transparently benefit from privacy-enhanced routing. Moreover, the underlying routing protocol does not need to be modified or replaced by a specially tailored solution since the interaction between the routing and the CALP component is done seamlessly through an intermediate shared element, that is, the routing table of the node. More details will be given in the subsequent sections.

4.2.3 Adversary Detection

Prior to the route updating process, the network must identify whether there is an adversary in the field. This implies that the CALP mechanism is suitable for application scenarios where the tracking of moving objects is among the typical duties performed by the sensor nodes. The monitoring of endangered species, the surveillance of country borders, mineral deposits, or oil and gas fields are among the scenarios where sensor nodes already incorporate the object tracking functionality. Most of these scenarios are highly sensitive to the presence of intruders and the authorized-personnel-only policy must be enforced.

The use of traditional radio-based localization methods [94], where the target object carries a transmitter or transceiver whose radio signals are analyzed to determine its location, are not suitable for critical object tracking scenarios because an intruder might not have such a device or can simply drop it. Also, the use of physical barriers has been a means of protection but in some cases, such as a country's perimeter surveillance, this might be highly expensive or even infeasible. Given such circumstances, the use of WSNs capable of detecting and tracking objects crossing the area under observation is of great interest [75,85]. To that end, the nodes comprising the network can be equipped with motion sensors or they might measure the interferences in the signal strength of the radio signals [145] caused by the moving objects.

The aforementioned techniques allow sensor nodes to determine the existence of mobile targets in their vicinity. However, these techniques on their own provide no means of discriminating between adversaries and authorized users or other moving objects. As a matter of fact, being able to distinguish adversaries from other mobile entities is not a trivial task. The only difference is between entities authorized to move around the field (e.g., those being monitored or network administrators) and other moving objects, which may be adversaries or not. Therefore, the best strategy for the sensor network is to consider that any non-authorized moving object is an adversary although, ideally, the protection mechanism should be launched only in the presence of adversaries in order to reduce the extra overhead due to the performance of the privacy-aware routing mechanism. Anyway, this strategy is much more energy-preserving than already existing solutions, which are in continuous operation.

Consider a sensor network that monitors the behavior of an endangered animal species. This network needs to be able to distinguish between different species so that it collects only relevant information concerning the protected species. This can be done in several different ways, for example, by tagging the animals with some sort of wireless device (e.g., an under-skin transmitter) being able to broadcast authenticated information regarding each specific animal. Also, biologists might carry their own personal devices in order to be recognized as authorized users. On the other hand, other animal species or adversaries willing to capture the protected animals would trigger the protection mechanism as they are not in possession of a legitimate device.

A simple challenge-response protocol might allow the interaction of external authorized entities with the sensor network. After authentication, a temporal session key might be established between the sensor network and the external entity in such a way that this entity is able to securely transmit messages to the sensor network. Clearly, the session key must be occasionally updated. This process may require the use of public key operations. Several solutions have been devised for the user-authentication problem [29,136]. Also, similar solutions exist for unattended WSNs, where the sink sporadically visits the field to collect data from every single node [43]. Doubtlessly, the advances in Elliptic Curve Cryptography will not only simplify the process but also reduce the overhead introduced by the use of authentication mechanisms.

Also, in order to reduce the probability of erroneously identifying moving objects as adversaries, the sensor network might observe the behavior of moving objects in the field in the presence of messages. Therefore, if a nonauthorized moving object is detected by the network, the sensor nodes in the vicinity of the mobile object might mimic source nodes and send out fake messages. In the case the moving object traces back fake messages it is highly likely to be an adversary and thus the sensor nodes might alert their neighbors to this, by broadcasting route update messages.

4.2.4 Route Updating Process

Upon the detection of an adversary in the proximities of the network, the devised privacy-preserving mechanism is triggered. The sensor nodes, feeling the presence of an adversary, inform their neighbors of the situation in order to prevent packets from traversing the area where the adversary is located. As the adversary is capable of moving in any direction, it is also necessary to anticipate his movements in order to minimize the number of packets he might be able to capture. Thus, alert messages need to expand over several hops so that it is not only neighbors in a close range to the attacker that are aware of the distance to the adversary.

After the detection of an adversary in the field, the detecting node (at distance 0) informs their immediate neighbors about the presence of the adversary by broadcasting an alert message with distance value 1. Upon reception, the receiving nodes store the distance value and broadcast a new message with distance value 2. This process is repeated for a given number of hops to spread the alert. Clearly, the number of hops the alert spans depends on the ability of the attacker to monitor the communications. The more powerful the attacker, the larger the radius of the area covered by the routing update message. Figure 4.2 depicts the distance values obtained by each sensor node in a network of size 50×50, where two adversaries have been detected at positions $(20, 20)$ and $(0, 0)$.

The power of the attacker can be measured by two non-mutually exclusive means, namely, the communications area the attacker is able to monitor and the displacement speed. In the work presented here, we focus on mote-class attackers, which are

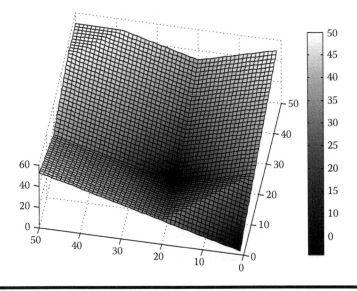

Figure 4.2 **Distance to detected adversaries.**

capable of eavesdropping and analyzing the traffic in a region r equivalent to that of any regular sensor node. This feature is also dependent on the size of the network since a large network is less vulnerable to an attacker with a hearing range of r than a network covering a small region. With regards to the speed of the attacker, it is important to note that an adversary moving at an infinite speed has the ability to capture every packet in the network. Obviously, this type of attacker is unrealistic and thus is beyond the scope of our solution. We assume that the network is agile enough to reconfigure the routing tables before the attacker reaches the next neighboring node. In fact, this is not such a strong assumption since the time of flight of packets between contiguous nodes and the processing time of packets can be considered negligible.

Whenever a detector node sends a route update message to its neighbors, this message contains information regarding the distance at which the attacker is placed. In general, the number of hops is a good indicator of the distance if the sensor network is uniformly deployed, though sophisticated devices might provide more precise information about the location of the attacker. Nevertheless, using a hop-based distance estimation simplifies the route updating process because upon the reception of an update message, the receiving node merely increments the hop count before forwarding the packet and the routing table is modified in consequence without having to perform any further calculations to determine the distance between the node and the adversary.

Finally, it is worth noting that route update messages do not provide the adversary with information regarding the location of the data sources because their transmission is independent of the presence of events in the network. Therefore, these messages may be either sent periodically or just in the presence of adversaries but the latter choice is recommended to extend the lifetime of the sensor nodes. An alternative is to benefit from beacon frames, which are configuration messages that are periodically broadcast regardless of the existence of events. Beacon frames have the ability to carry a few bytes of information in the payload, which is enough for alerting about the distance to the adversary. Beacon frames do not imply any extra energy consumption in the network and thus allow resources to be saved. However, this approach has some limitations in terms of the delay between two consecutive frames, which ranges from tens of milliseconds to hundreds of seconds, as described in [125]. Therefore, there is a trade-off between the energy consumption and the routing update speed, which impacts on the privacy preservation of the source nodes in the case of having to counter rapidly moving adversaries.

4.2.5 Data Forwarding Process

Whenever a sensor node has data to transmit to the base station it does so by using routing protocols. The routing protocol to use depends on the requirements of the application scenario and, as such, may differ from network to network. Nonetheless, almost any routing protocol relies on the routing information obtained from the network topology discovery protocol* and stored in the routing tables of each sensor node.

As aforementioned, the CALP mechanism can be regarded as a plug-in component that may be used with different routing protocols to enhance location privacy. The devised scheme is responsible for modifying the routing tables of sensor nodes in such a way that the selection of the forwarding nodes is conditioned not only by their distance from the base station but also by their distance from the adversary. Thus, upon receiving a data packet directed to the base station, the recipient node decides in which direction to forward the message based on the routing strategy and, additionally, the distance from its neighbors to the attacker. These data can be stored as an additional column in the routing table of each node.

There are at least two options when sending packets to nodes that are located at a close distance to the adversary. One might choose to impede sensor nodes from forwarding packets to those neighbors located at a distance of less than a *minimum safety distance* from the adversary, that is, data packets must circumvent the region where the adversary is. On the other hand, instead of simply blocking the arrival of data packets to sensor nodes in the proximities of the adversary, we might choose to penalize the selection of these nodes with respect to other neighbors outside the established minimum safety distance. We refer to these two strategies as strict and permissive data forwarding.

The use of a *strict* safety distance has the advantage of ensuring that the attacker will not capture any packets unless he moves fast enough to cover areas at a distance greater than the predefined minimum safety distance. We assume that adversaries are incapable of moving that fast (see Section 4.1.2). Nonetheless, the use of a strict security perimeter presents some drawbacks that might negatively affect the operation of the network. Specifically, the greater the minimum safety distance, the greater the number of hops a packet will traverse in the presence of an adversary in the proximities of the communication path. Consequently, the delivery delay and the overall energy consumption of the network will increase. This might also result in the non-delivery of data packets at the base station if the adversary is in its vicinity and the security perimeter is sufficiently large. In that case, data packets travel back and forth originating network loops until the adversary moves to another region. A possible countermeasure to this problem is to make sensor nodes temporarily store any received data packet, but if the adversary being countered is patient, that is, he does not move until the reception of a data packet, the delivery time significantly increases. Also, if the sensor nodes continue to receive data packets they might run out of memory and therefore, they should turn to dropping some packets.

On the other hand, a *permissive* security perimeter avoids the need of buffering data packets at intermediate sensor nodes in the vicinity of an adversary, thus

---

* This process is run during the network setup and can be periodically launched to prevent topology changes from disrupting the delivery of data to the base station.

saving memory and reducing the delays in the delivery process. Thus, a permissive minimum safety distance is more suitable for real-time applications while the strict version is convenient in delay-tolerant application. Notwithstanding, a permissive security perimeter provides a lower privacy protection level since data packets may be forwarded to nodes placed within the hearing range of the adversary. As a result, the adversary is more likely to reach the data source. Clearly, there is a trade-off between overhead and privacy protection associated with the data forwarding strategy. Further analysis and discussion is provided in Section 4.4.3.

4.3 Shortest-Path CALP Routing

The CALP mechanism can be used in conjunction with different routing protocols to enhance source-location privacy protection. Although this mechanism can virtually be applied to any routing protocol, here we focus on the application of CALP to a shortest-path routing algorithm since they provide interesting features such as minimal latency and reduced energy consumption.

4.3.1 Shortest-Path Routing

Several shortest- or single-path routing techniques can be found in the literature [68,103]. These energy-efficient routing protocols allow sensor nodes to deliver data packets to the base station using the minimum number of neighbors as data relays. Whenever a node has data to transmit, it picks the neighbor node that is closest to the base station and sends the packet to it. The recipient repeats the process until the packet is eventually received at the data sink. Since each sensor node always picks the neighbor that is closest to the destination, the path followed is the most energy-efficient and it also incurs the shortest delay.

Usually, these techniques require that either sensor nodes are equipped with additional hardware or that an initialization phase is performed. The simplest way to enable this sort of routing protocol is by means of a topology discovery protocol, where the base station floods the network with a distance value initially set to 0 that is incremented at each hop; similar to the route updating process described in Section 4.2.4.

The shortest-path routing technique considered in this section makes greedy forwarding decisions since it selects locally optimal neighbors. A neighbor is considered to be locally optimal when it minimally deviates from the straight line connecting the data sender and the destination. An example is given in Figure 4.3, where N represents the node sending data in the direction to the data sink (S) and A, B, C, D, E are the neighbors of N ($neighs(N)$). Also, $\alpha = \angle NAS$, $\beta = \angle NBS$, and $\gamma = \angle NCS$ are the angles formed between the line $\overline{NS}$, and $\overline{NA}$, $\overline{NB}$ and $\overline{NC}$, respectively. For the sake of simplicity, only some of the angles have been represented. Thus, X is the locally optimal neighbor of N if $\forall X, Y \in neighs(N) \land X \neq Y, \angle NXS \leq \angle NYS$.

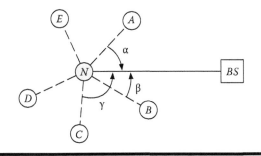

Figure 4.3   Locally optimal neighbor selection.

The main advantage of implementing a greedy shortest-path technique is that only a small amount of internal storage is required in the nodes to operate. In order to route data packets, a sensor node needs information about its own neighbors and the location of the base station, but it does not have to be in possession of information about other intermediate nodes. The main limitation of a greedy approach is that the path followed by the packets might not be globally optimal even though it is locally optimal, that is, there might exist more efficient paths. Nonetheless, this is not usually a problem as most shortest-path routing protocols rely on the distance to the base station rather than the deviation from the shortest path connecting the node and the base station.

4.3.2 Combination with CALP

When a greedy shortest-path routing technique is augmented with the location awareness provided by the CALP scheme, it acquires the ability to anticipate the movements of the adversary in such a way that the number of packets he might be able to capture is significantly reduced. Additionally, the packets will minimally deviate from the shortest path to the destination, thus the extra energy consumption incurred by the operation of our privacy preservation mechanism is notably reduced compared to other solutions. Moreover, note that the deviation from the most energy-efficient path only takes place when the adversary is located close to that area. Figure 4.4 depicts a scenario where the network adapts the routing path in order to circumvent an adversary moving in the vicinity of the shortest path. The area controlled by the adversary is represented as a dashed circle while dashed arrows represent a temporary suppression of messages.

Two versions of the shortest-path CALP routing have been devised. In the first version, a strict minimum safety distance is considered. Consequently, the route update messages are used to create an impassable security perimeter, which data packets never traverse. When the distance from the adversary to the shortest path is shorter than the minimum safety distance, that is the adversary is over the shortest path, data packets will deviate from the original path to avoid crossing the security perimeter. This behavior is described in Algorithm 4.1. Basically, whenever a sensor

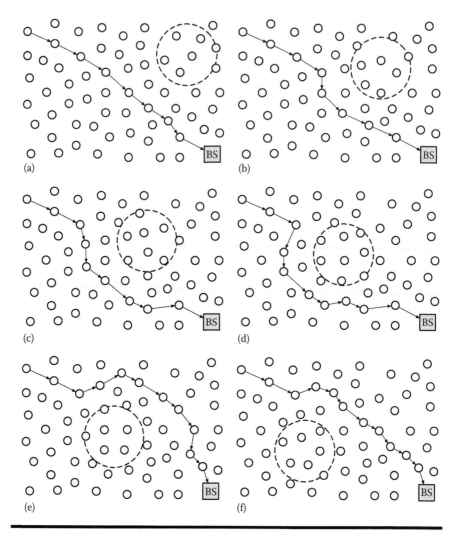

Figure 4.4 **Path adaptation based on the location of the adversary: (a) optimal path, (b) slight deviation, (c) deviation grows, (d) worst case, (e) adversary crosses, (f) going back to normal.**

node has data to transmit or forward, the node obtains a list of neighbors from its routing table and for each of them calculates a penalty based on their distance to the adversary. This penalty is maximum when the neighbor is in range of the adversary (lines 3–5), but it is a linear function of the distance and the deviation from the shortest path otherwise (lines 5–7). Finally, the data packet is sent to the neighbor with the lowest penalty.

In the permissive version of the protocol, data packets do not necessarily change their route in the case of an adversary placed in the shortest path. Packets are only

---

Algorithm 4.1 Sending Strategy: Strict CALP Routing

Input: *MIN_SAFETY_DIST*
Input: *data*
  1: *neighs* ← *get_neighbors*()
  2: **for all** n_i ∈ *neighs* **do**
  3:   **if** *distance*(n_i) ≤ *MIN_SAFETY_DIST* **then**
  4:     *penalty*[n_i] = ∞
  5:   **else**
  6:     *penalty*[n_i] = *angle*(n_i) + π/*distance*(n_i)
  7:   **end if**
  8: **end for**
  9: *next_hop* ← *minimum*(*penalty*, *neighs*)
10: *send*(*data*, *next_hop*)

Algorithm 4.2 Sending Strategy: Permissive CALP Routing

Input: *MIN_SAFETY_DIST*
Input: *data*
  1: *neighs* ← *get_neighbors*()
  2: **for all** n_i ∈ *neighs* **do**
  3:   *penalty*[n_i] = *angle*(n_i) + π/*distance*(n_i)
  4:   **if** *distance*(n_i) ≤ *MIN_SAFETY_DIST* **then**
  5:     *penalty*[n_i] = *penalty*[n_i] + 1/*distance*(n_i)
  6:   **end if**
  7: **end for**
  8: *next_hop* ← *minimum*(*penalty*, *neighs*)
  9: *send*(*data*, *next_hop*)

---

deviated if the cost associated with performing such a choice is greater than the cost of entering the adversary's hearing range. A detailed description of this behavior is provided in Algorithm 4.2. Similar to the strict version, the algorithm is activated when a node has data to transmit or forward. The node obtains the list of neighbors, and for each of them it calculates a base penalty (line 3), which is incremented by a factor that is inversely proportional to the distance of the neighbor to the adversary (lines 4–6) in the case the adversary is in its vicinity. The neighbor with the lowest penalty is finally chosen to receive the data.

As previously described, when the adversary is not present in the field, the proposed algorithms must behave as the original shortest-path routing protocol. Therefore, the locally optimal forwarding neighbor is chosen so that it minimally deviates from the straight line connecting the data sender and the base station. To that end, the distance to the adversary is used as a penalty value in such a way

Table 4.1   Routing Table of Node N

Neighs	Angle	Distance
A	$\pi/4$	2
B	$\pi/5$	4
C	$5\pi/9$	5
D	$8\pi/9$	3
E	$11\pi/18$	4

that the closer the adversary, the greater the penalty. In particular, we penalize the proximity of a neighbor to the adversary exactly $\pi/distance$ units. Depending on whether the version in use is strict or permissive, an additional penalty is introduced when the distance to the adversary is less or equal than the predefined minimum safety distance. The minimum safety distance is a parameter of the solution (*MIN_SAFETY_DIST*) that might be tuned by the administrator of the network to carefully balance between privacy protection and usability.

Finally, note that both algorithms are based on straightforward operations that can be performed even by extremely hardware-constrained devices. Additionally, the CALP requires some extra memory in order to store information about the distance from the adversary to each of the neighbors. Table 4.1 shows the routing table of a particular node, where the right-most column has been added to keep distance information. These values are updated upon the reception of the route update messages described in Section 4.2.4.

4.4 Protocol Evaluation

In this section, we evaluate the performance and privacy protection level of the proposed shortest-path CALP routing mechanism. First, we briefly describe the simulation scenario.

4.4.1 Simulation Scenario

We developed a discrete-event simulation environment in MATLAB® [134] and conducted extensive simulations on it. The simulator enables multiple simultaneous transmissions from various data sources as well as the presence of various local adversaries moving in the field. The simulator obviates the low-level communication problems (e.g., collisions) and focuses on the application and routing layers since our goal is to demonstrate the feasibility of the proposed solution.

The setup used for our simulations is similar to that commonly found in the literature [66,125]. We deployed a large WSN consisting of $n \times n$ uniformly distributed nodes, where $n = 100$. Each simulation instance is run 50 times and each of the instances consists of 500 simulation steps. A new data message is generated and forwarded by the data source at each simulation step. Also, a beaconing phase is scheduled so that the network is aware of the whereabouts of the adversary and thus packets are routed accordingly. Source nodes are placed at different distances from the base station but are static during each simulation.

In the first simulation step, the adversary is placed in the proximities of the base station, which is located at the center of the network by default. The adversary under consideration is either inquisitive or patient. The inquisitive adversary moves randomly until he overhears a transmission in his vicinity, in which case he moves in the direction of the received message. If he follows a trace of packets and after a period of time no message arrives at his current position he starts to move randomly in the search of new packets. On the other hand, the patient adversary only moves in the presence of packets in his vicinity. Moreover, adversaries might move at different paces with respect to the simulation steps, however the speed is fixed and constant within a single simulation instance.

By default, the network safety distance is set to five meaning that communication paths are modified when the adversary is closer or equal to that distance from the shortest path. Furthermore, the hearing range of the adversary has been set to a monitoring radius equivalent to that of a sensor node. Although the simulation environment allows for several simultaneous adversaries in the field, we study the effect of a single adversary. Note that the simulations were conducted such that the adversary is considered to be in the field at all times. However, in real scenarios this is not the case, the adversary enters and leaves the network at will.

The simulation ends under two circumstances, either when the adversary reaches the data source or when the last simulation step is reached without the adversary being able to find it.

4.4.2 Privacy Protection Level

This section evaluates the privacy protection level provided by both the permissive and strict versions of the shortest-path CALP routing scheme. The level of protection is measured as the number of source nodes the adversary is able to capture in each simulation instance. The two versions of the proposed mechanism are compared with each other and with respect to the traditional shortest-path routing scheme for various source–sink distances. Moreover, the simulations are conducted in the presence of both inquisitive and patient adversaries. The results are depicted in Figure 4.5 as a bar diagram where the x-axis represents the distance to the base station and the y-axis shows the total number of captures after 50 simulations of each instance.

From the simulations, we observe that the distance of the source node with respect to the base station has no clear impact on the privacy protection level. The adversary is able to reach the data source in roughly the same number of cases regardless of the distance. The patient adversary (see Figure 4.5b) always reaches the source

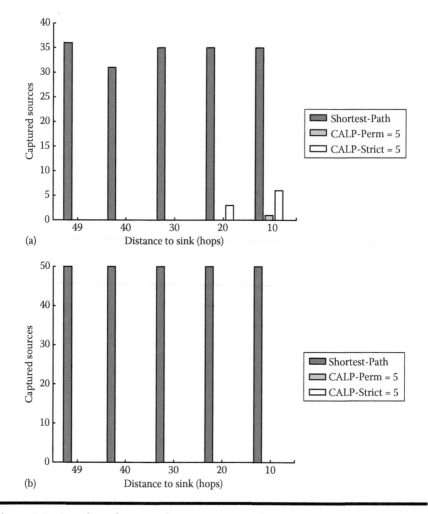

Figure 4.5 **Number of captured sources. (a) Inquisitive adversary and (b) Patient adversary.**

node because he waits next to the base station until he receives a packet addressed to it. After that, since all packets follow the same path, he reaches the data source in the minimum number of steps. On the other hand, the inquisitive adversary (Figure 4.5a) is less likely to find the data source even for a single-path routing algorithm. The main drawback for inquisitive adversaries is that at the beginning of the simulation they might move away from the original location thus missing some of the packets arriving at the base station several simulation steps later. These adversaries are only successful if at some point during the simulation they come across with the communication path.

When the shortest-path routing protocol is used in conjunction with the CALP mechanism, the situation improves enormously. When the adversary is inquisitive (see Figure 4.5a), he is only capable of compromising source-location privacy when the distance between the data source and the base station is relatively short. Surprisingly, the permissive version of the shortest-path CALP routing provides better protection level than the strict version. The reason is that, in the strict version, the movements of the adversary are never conditioned by the packets traversing the network since he is not able to overhear them given a sufficiently large safety distance, as the one being used. In the permissive version, an inquisitive adversary is able to overhear some of the packets because under certain circumstances the nodes might choose a node within the security perimeter as the next hop. This causes the adversary to move in the direction of the received packet but since the path changes dynamically based on his movements, he might overhear packets coming from different neighboring nodes that misleads him from the target.

When countering a patient adversary (see Figure 4.5b), neither version of our protocol ever leaks location information about the source node. Apparently the packets are able to circumvent the attacker without being detected. In the permissive version, the packets might reach the base station by traversing the safety distance thereby causing the patient adversary to move toward those packets. Being the adversary in a new location away from the base station, the new paths are re-adapted thus being able to circumvent the adversary and reach the base station. However, in the strict version, since the adversary is initially placed next to the base station and the packets are not allowed to traverse the safety region, the task of delivering the packets to the base station is not fulfilled. This issue is reviewed in more detail in the following sections.

4.4.3 Protocol Overhead

We evaluate the performance of the protocol by means of the length of the resulting routing paths. The length of the path not only determines the delivery time of the packets but also the overall energy consumption of the network. Larger paths result in more transmissions and consequently have a negative impact on the lifetime of the batteries. In general, single-path routing algorithms are considered energy-efficient algorithms since data packets are sent via the shortest path from the source node to the base station. However, these algorithms provide the lowest protection level as all the packets follow the same (shortest) path. Therefore, the inclusion of the CALP mechanisms to a shortest-path routing scheme effectively trades off between performance and privacy protection level.

The mean path length of the packets traveling from the source nodes to the base station is represented in Figure 4.6. In general, the mean path length is slightly higher than the minimum expected value, that is, the length of the path originated by the shortest-path routing algorithm. Clearly, in the presence of an inquisitive adversary (see Figure 4.6a), the permissive version of our scheme provides better results than

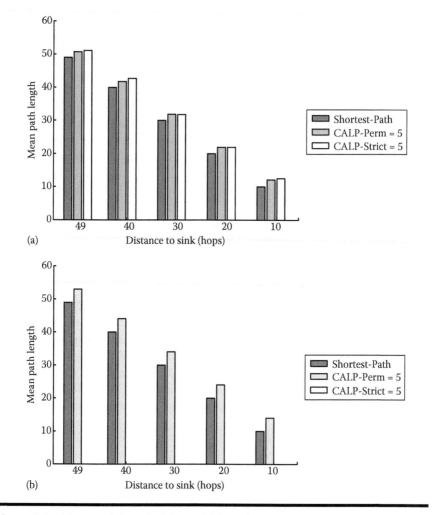

(a)

(b)

Figure 4.6   **Mean path length. (a) Inquisitive adversary and (b) Patient adversary.**

the strict version. On the other hand, for a patient adversary (see Figure 4.6b), the permissive approach originates paths that are on average slightly longer than those generated in the presence of an inquisitive adversary. The reason is that for a patient adversary the nodes need to deal with an adversary waiting in the vicinity of the base station. More importantly, the strict version is unable to generate data paths that circumvent the patient adversary and eventually deliver the packets to the data sink. Since the length of the packets is stored when they arrive at the base station, no data are shown for this scheme in Figure 4.6b. This problem is not due to the design of the CALP mechanism but is caused by the particular strategy followed by this type of adversary.

This problem can be lessened in several ways depending on the requirements of the network. In a sensor network with no real-time requirements (i.e., it tolerates moderate latencies), instead of sending messages back and forth at the border of the security perimeter, intermediate nodes could temporarily store the packets until the adversary decides to move away from the base station. However, if the adversary is patient enough, the highly constrained memory of the sensor nodes would require some of the packets to be dropped. Therefore, a more convenient approach to deal with this issue is to implement a mixed version of the CALP mechanism including the benefits of both the permissive and strict schemes. The idea is to switch from a strict to a permissive approach as packets approach to the base station. In this way, if a patient adversary is next to the base station using a permissive strategy attracts the adversary away from it and allows the delivery of packets. In addition, using a strict strategy is expedient when the adversary is close to the data source because at that point capturing a few packets might lead to the target. Also, it is possible to overcome the problem by dynamically re-adapting the safety distance depending on the whereabouts of the adversary or by switching from the CALP approach to one of the solutions based on the creation of random routes, such as the Phantom Routing.

Despite the mean path length being close to the minimum value, some isolated packets might traverse a large number of intermediate nodes before being delivered. Therefore, studying mean values is not enough and next we look into the path length distribution. In Figure 4.7 we present the path length distribution in the presence of an inquisitive adversary with box plots,* which is a useful way of describing the degree of dispersion and skewness in the data, and identifying outliers. On the left-hand side of the figure, we can observe that when using a permissive security perimeter, most of the packets travel a similar number of hops before reaching the destination. The mean value is very close or equal to the distance to the sink and there are only a few packets that travel long distances (outliers). However, the landscape changes dramatically when using the strict version of the scheme, as shown on the right-hand side of the figure. Some isolated packets may travel up to 134 hops before reaching the base station. The reason for such long paths is the creation of network loops due to the presence of the adversary in regions close to the sink. Packets are sent in the direction of the base station, but nodes on the border of the security perimeter cannot send them forward and choose to relay them to other nodes that are in the same situation. Finally, the packets are returned to any of the nodes which initially sent those packets. Keeping a list of already seen packets could help avoid network loops; however, since the adversary is able to move, the next time a node receives the packet the situation might be different, that is, the direction, which was previously occupied by the adversary, might currently be safe.

---

* In each box, the central mark is the median, the edges of the box are the first and third quartiles, and the whiskers extend to the minimum and maximum data points or to 1.5 times the interquartile range. Outliers ("+") are values behind the whiskers.

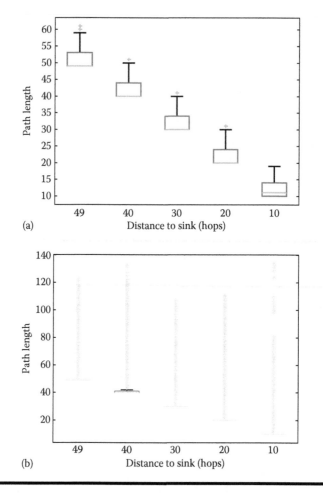

Figure 4.7 Path length distribution. (a) Permissive CALP and (b) Strict CALP.

In general, we can claim that the permissive version provides an adequate protection level without incurring an excessive overhead to the network. It is true that in a few special cases the protocol generates paths that are slightly longer than usual but this is not too problematic. However, we acknowledge that the overhead incurred by the strict version of the protocol might be overly high. Consequently, this strategy must be used only when the criticality of the scenario demands an extraordinary privacy protection level. Notwithstanding, a mixed strategy might be the best option to keep a reasonable path length.

4.4.4 Safety Distance Impact

In this section, we study the impact of the security perimeter on the privacy protection level and the mean path length. Security perimeters of size 2, 5, and 7 have

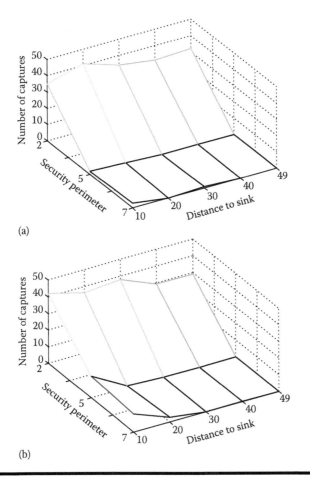

(a)

(b)

Figure 4.8   Impact on number of captures. (a) Permissive CALP and (b) Strict CALP.

been used for the evaluation. Again, we have considered an inquisitive adversary and source nodes at various distances from the base station. The results on how the security perimeter affects privacy protection and the length of data paths are given in Figures 4.8 and 4.9, respectively.

As expected, the size of the security perimeter has a clear impact on the number of captures. The larger the security perimeter, the better the privacy protection. In general, both the permissive and strict versions of the CALP mechanism behave well for a security perimeter size larger than 2. Also, the distance of the data source to the base station affects both versions but to a lesser extent. More precisely, the adversary is only able to capture a few packets in the permissive approach when the distance to the base station is not sufficiently large (see Figure 4.8a). This is also the case in the

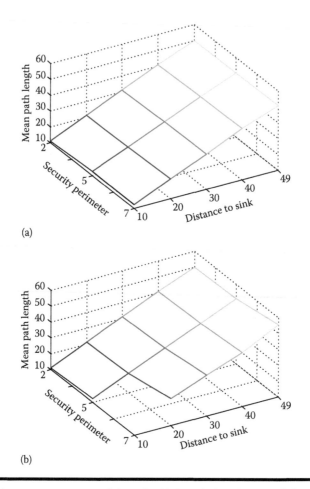

(a)

(b)

Figure 4.9   Impact on mean path length. (a) Permissive CALP and (b) Strict CALP.

strict approach but the problem is even more acute (see Figure 4.8b). In general, the problem is that by using a small security perimeter the network is incapable of readjusting the routing paths and thus the adversary is more likely to capture packets, which leads him to the data source.

Additionally, we observe that the security perimeter size has an almost negligible impact on the mean path length. However, there might be some packets traversing an undue number of nodes before reaching the base station destination, as already discussed in Section 4.4.3. The strict version is more sensitive to the size of the security perimeter. In particular, using a larger security perimeter when the source node is close to the base station might result in some executions with no packets reaching their destination. This particular case is depicted in Figure 4.9b for a security perimeter size of 7 and a source node located 10 hops away from the base station. Again, to counter the problem of having some packets not reach their target, a source–sink distance-dependent security perimeter might be used. In other words, the security perimeter might be larger for nodes that are located further away from the base station. Moreover, as the security perimeter size increases, the mean path length increase is more abrupt in the strict version than in the permissive version.

4.5 Summary and Improvements

This chapter has presented the CALP scheme, a novel approach to source-location privacy that, unlike previous solutions, is triggered upon the detection of the adversary only. This mechanism benefits from the ability of sensor nodes to detect the presence of objects in their vicinity to prevent the transmission of messages in the area controlled by the adversary. When a sensor node detects the adversary, it disseminates this information throughout the network thus enabling efficient privacy-preserving routing protocols.

The idea of feeding routing protocols with the location of the adversary has been successfully applied to a shortest-path routing technique. The combination of a shortest-path routing with the CALP scheme has a very clear advantage: data packets deviate from the most energy-efficient routing path only when the adversary is in the vicinity of that path. In particular, two versions of the protocol have been developed based on the way data packets are forwarded when an adversary is within a minimum safety distance from the sender. Moreover, two different strategies have been considered for the adversarial model. The extensive simulations performed have demonstrated that the devised protocol is capable of providing a solid privacy protection level with an average energy consumption very close to optimal. A combination of both strategies depending on the distance of the data source may result in an even more promising solution.

Although the idea of determining and using the location of the adversary has been exploited to enhance source-location privacy, since the devised solution is based on the notion of undetectability, it might also be exploited to preserve the location of the base station in the presence of an adversary with similar capabilities. Beyond the use of the CALP scheme as a mechanism to provide the property of undetectability, it might also be used to misdirect the adversary from potential targets by injecting controlled amounts of fake traffic in his vicinity. These decoy messages can successfully lead the adversary away from the data sources or the base station without introducing a significant overhead to the network.

Most interestingly, the context-aware capabilities of sensor nodes can be used to provide a holistic location privacy solution that is capable of preserving the location of both data sources and the base station. Achieving an effective and energy-efficient solution would be a significant breakthrough in the area since there is yet to be a single scheme capable of providing an integral solution to both problems simultaneously. The CALP scheme seems promising in this respect because it offers undetectability at a very low cost by modifying the data communication paths based on the location of the adversary. To that end, it is necessary to further investigate the way in which to provide sensor nodes with the ability to precisely identify and trace adversaries. By monitoring the movements of the adversary and not only the current position, the network may be able to infer the strategy of the attacker as well as its target.

Finally, to further enhance and complete this solution the threat of internal adversaries should be taken into consideration. The CALP approach in its current state assumes that route update messages are secure and legitimate. However, these messages might be generated by nodes that have been compromised by the adversary. To solve these problems, the notions of reputation and trust seem very suitable as it might allow legitimate sensor nodes to identify and revoke that misbehave during the route updating process or which behave differently as this may be an indication that they have been compromised.

Chapter 5

Probabilistic Receiver-Location Privacy

Wireless sensor networks are continually exposed to different types of attacks, but the most devastating ones are those that target the base station since this critical device is responsible for collecting and analyzing all the traffic generated in the network. Therefore, protecting the location of the base station is essential for the integrity and survivability of the network. Besides its importance for the physical protection of the network, the location of the base station is strategically critical because it is usually housed in a highly relevant facility.

As a result, a number of authors have struggled to provide receiver-location privacy, primarily, by randomizing and normalizing the traffic pattern of the network. However, this might be insufficient when the adversary is also capable of retrieving the routing tables of the sensor nodes. Normally, the routing tables contain information regarding the distance to or the location of the base station, which may be used by the attacker to effectively reach the base station thus rendering useless anti traffic analysis techniques. This serious threat to receiver-location privacy has never been taken into consideration in the literature.

This chapter presents the Homogeneous Injection for Sink Privacy with Node Compromise protection (HISP-NC) scheme, a receiver-location privacy solution that consists of two complementary schemes that protect the location of the base station in the presence of traffic analysis and routing table inspection attacks, which is a new type of node compromise attack that leverages on the analysis of the routing tables of the nodes in order to determine the direction toward the base station. This solution addresses, for the first time, both traffic analysis and node compromise attacks in a single solution. On the one hand, the HISP-NC data transmission protocol hide the flow of real messages by introducing controlled amounts of fake traffic to locally homogenize the number of packets being forwarded from a sensor node to its neighbors. On the other hand, the HISP-NC perturbation scheme modifies the routing tables of the nodes to reduce the risk of node capture attacks while ensuring that data packets eventually reach the base station.

This chapter first describes the network and threat models as well as the main assumptions applicable to the rest of the chapter. A detailed description of the HISP-NC data transmission and routing tables perturbation schemes is presented next. Then, this chapter provides a detailed analysis and evaluation of the potential limitations of the proposed solution with respect to the traffic overhead and delivery time of data packets. The evaluation includes extensive simulations.

Finally, extensive simulations are performed to evaluate the privacy protection level achieved by the HISP-NC scheme under different types of attacks.

5.1 Problem Statement

This section describes the network and threat models considered during the elaboration of this HISP-NC solution. The assumptions introduced here will be applicable to the rest of this chapter.

5.1.1 Network Model

The network model contemplated here is very similar to the one introduced in Chapter 4 and considered by most of the research papers in the location privacy literature. This is a network used for monitoring purposes that follows an event-driven approach and thus transmits event messages as soon as they are detected in the vicinity sensor nodes. As such, all the data flow from sensor nodes to a single base station. Having one or more base stations does not have a negative impact on the solution. In fact, having a single base station is the worst-case scenario as all the traffic is directed to the same area thus making the direction to the base station more evident. When several base stations are evenly distributed in the deployment area, the traffic is more homogeneous. Nonetheless, if the final goal of the adversary is to destroy the network, he has to reach each of the base stations and eventually the scenario will be exactly as the one considered here.

The network is deployed over a vast area and is composed of a large number of sensor nodes. This prevents the adversary from both controlling the communications in a large portion of the network and having all sensors within easy reach. Moreover, sensor nodes are aware of its adjacent neighbors and their distance to the base station. With this information, which is obtained after the deployment of the network by means of a network topology discovery protocol, they can make routing decisions. The routing table contained in each sensor node is responsible for keeping this information. Normally, there are no other requirements for routing tables than storing the identifiers of the neighbors and their distances to the base station, but for the operation of HISP-NC, it is also necessary that these data are sorted incrementally according to the distance to the base station. In this way, the neighbors closer to the base station than the original node ($L^{\mathcal{C}}$) are located at the top of the table, the neighbors at the same distance ($L^{\mathcal{E}}$) are placed in the middle of the table, and the neighbors that are one hop further away ($L^{\mathcal{F}}$) are placed next. Therefore, a routing table can be represented as $L^* = \{L^{\mathcal{C}}, L^{\mathcal{E}}, L^{\mathcal{F}}\}$, where each element in L^* is a tuple consisting of two elements, namely, the neighbor identifier and its distance to the base station.

Sensor nodes are not required to be equipped with additional hardware like energy scavengers or tamper-resistant modules. These components involve an extra monetary cost to the network but help to extend the lifetime of the network and improve its robustness and survivability in the presence of physical attacks. Sensor nodes must share keys with its immediate neighbors and packet header information must not be sent in clear text. Packet payloads must be encrypted, and data messages must be indistinguishable from fake messages. This feature can be achieved by adding some noise in the form of a secure random sequence [87] to the messages before they are encrypted.

5.1.2 Threat Model

The threat model defines the capabilities of the adversary that needs to be tackled by the HISP-NC scheme. This adversary is expected to be capable of performing not only traffic analysis attacks but also a particular type of node compromise attack, which is called the routing table inspection attack. Although an attacker with such capabilities is able to use both sources of information at any time, for the sake of clarity, it is assumed that the adversary either chooses to perform a passive or an active attack at a time. Next are given more details about each of these types of attacks.

5.1.2.1 Traffic Analysis Attacks

Traffic analysis attacks allow an adversary to obtain or infer information from the packets traversing the network. This type of passive adversary can monitor a portion of the network that is dependent on its hearing range and his ability to retrieve packet header information. Since the network is assumed to employ proper mechanisms to conceal the identities in packet headers [32], the focus here is on the hearing range.

With respect to the hearing range, adversaries might range from those capable of observing the transmissions of a single node to those powerful enough to monitor all the communications in the network. The attacker model considered here has a limited hearing range, similar to an ordinary sensor node, which in this chapter is referred to as $\mathcal{ADV}_1$. Next, we provide a formal definition of the adversarial model based on his hearing range:

Definition 5.1 (ADV_n) *Let $X = \{x_1, x_2, \ldots, x_m\}$ be the set of sensor nodes comprising the network and let x_i be an ordinary sensor node in the proximity of the adversary. ADV_n chooses first a node x_i and then observes the transmissions of node x_i and all its neighbors within distance n. In the next round, he may choose a different node $x_{i'}$. The choice of the next x_i depends on the movement strategy; see, for instance, time correlation and rate monitoring, in the following.*

An ADV_1 adversary is capable of monitoring any packets transmitted by nodes at distances no larger than 1. In Figure 5.1, two types of adversaries with different monitoring ranges are represented. The central node broadcasts a message that is received by all its immediate neighbors. Although the message is overheard by all the neighbors, it is usually addressed to only one of them, which is identified by the arrow head. This node forwards the message immediately after receiving it. In the case of an ADV_0, the attacker knows that the central node is transmitted, but he does not know which of the neighbors is the intended recipient of the message. On the other hand, the ADV_1 learns the recipient of the message after it forwards the message in its vicinity, but the attacker cannot learn the new hop of the communication.

Therefore, attackers with a hearing range n are capable of determining the next communication hop no further than n hops away from him. This is true unless the adversary owns an antenna array or a device alike that allows him to determine the angle of arrival of signals. Without this sort of device, the adversary observes that a node out of his hearing range transmits a message, but he cannot ascertain which one. On the contrary, if the adversary has access to the angle of arrival of signals, he can determine which node broadcasts the message and thus control an additional hop. Therefore, an ADV_0 carrying an antenna array is basically equivalent to an ADV_1 without it. For the sake of simplicity, the adversary is assumed to have the same capabilities as ordinary sensor nodes, which is referred to as ADV_1.

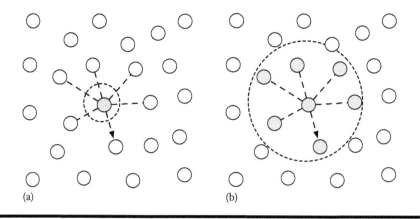

(a)   (b)

Figure 5.1 **Adversarial model examples. (a) ADV_0 and (b) ADV_1.**

Also, the attacker is assumed to be aware of the protection mechanism or he is able to deduce it after a period of time (i.e., Shannon's maxim [124]). As usual, the adversary is considered to be *mobile* and decides on which direction to move based on his observations of the messages traversing the network. The adversary may turn to two potential attack strategies to decide on his next move: the time-correlation and the rate-monitoring attack.

In a *time-correlation* attack, the adversary observes the transmission times of a node x_i and its neighbors. Based on the assumption that a node forwards a received packet shortly after receiving it, the adversary is able to reduce by one its distance to the base station. In a *rate-monitoring* attack, the adversary moves in the direction of the nodes transmitting a higher number of packets. The rationale behind this attack is that nodes closer to the base station have higher transmission rates as they not only send their own data but also forward the messages of remote nodes. The second strategy is more time-consuming than the first one because the adversary needs to wait for a sufficient number of transmissions before deciding where to move. Moreover, the rate-monitoring attack is not effective when the adversary is far away from the base station or when the number of data sources is rather limited.

5.1.2.2 Routing Tables Inspection

Physical attacks may range from node destruction to the modification or exfiltration of the software and data from the internal memories in the node. In this chapter, the adversary is assumed to be interested in capturing sensor nodes with the sole purpose of retrieving information that might be useful for reaching the base station. Routing tables inspection is a form of physical attack that consists of accessing the routing tables of the node and analyzing the data contained in it to determine which of the neighbors of the captured node are closer to the base station.

Despite the fact that physical attacks are very common in sensor networks, especially when they are deployed in unattended and hostile environments, physical attacks have received little attention from the research community working on location privacy issues in WSNs. An adversary with access to the routing table of a node trivially learns which of its neighbors are closer to the base station, as this information is necessary for the sensor node to choose the most suitable routing paths. Clearly, this is most valuable piece of information for an adversary willing to reach the base station. Moreover, after capturing several nodes, the adversary acquires a very good clue as to the distance and direction toward the base station.

Since this is, to the best of our knowledge, the first solution considering the threat of routing tables inspection in the area of receiver-location privacy, the strategy of the adversary is not clearly defined. Notwithstanding, the threat of node capture attacks has been considered by a number of authors. Several papers have dealt with the modeling and mitigation of node capture attacks in WSNs [33,137] particularly in the protection of secure communication channels for random key distribution systems. Some papers assume that the adversary capture nodes in the sensor filed at random, while others consider that the adversary is more likely to compromise nodes in a particular area. In this chapter, we consider that the adversary is more successful if he turns to the second strategy, that is, capturing nodes nearby rather than at random locations. The reason is that the information contained in the routing tables of several consecutive nodes allows the attacker to have a good idea of the direction toward the base station.

Some authors have also considered other features, such as the time it takes to compromise a single node. Although this is an important issue to take into account to understand the impact a node compromise attack can have on particular network, this aspect is not considered as such. Instead, this chapter assumes the adversary is not capable of capturing and inspecting the routing tables of more than a given number of nodes during a single data transmission phase. Indeed, this assumption is directly related to the time it takes for the adversary to compromise a single node. The exact percentage of inspected routing tables is provided in the following sections.

Once the adversary has captured a node and retrieved its routing table, he has to decide where to move next. Provided that the routing tables are correct, the adversary is certain that the first neighbor in the table is closer to the base station than the current node. Thus, the adversary is more likely to reach the base station if he moves toward the first neighbor in the routing table for each compromised node. This may not be the case after the routing tables perturbation scheme has been applied, but still the routing tables must allow packets to reach the base station. More details about the operation of the adversary are provided later on.

5.2 Homogeneous Injection for Sink Privacy

This section describes the data transmission protocol used by the HISP-NC scheme. First, the protocol is overviewed in order to highlight the core idea behind this solution. Then, some background information about the process of building the routing tables is provided since this is a critical element for the operation of the HISP-NC data transmission protocol. This background information is also relevant for understanding the next section of the chapter, where the routing table pertur- bation protocol is presented. This section also presents a set of properties that must hold so as to ensure the delivery of data messages to the base station while data flows are sufficiently protected from eavesdropping attacks. The data transmission protocol itself is described at the end of this section.

5.2.1 Overview

The basic idea behind the data transmission protocol used by HISP-NC is to hide the flow of real messages by injecting controlled amounts of fake traffic in its vicinity. Since fake packets are indistinguishable from real packets, an attacker observing the communications in his vicinity cannot identify which packets are real and which of them are fake. Moreover, real messages do not always follow the same path to reach the base station, instead a biased random walk protocol is used to guide messages to the data sink. The reason for using a random walk rather than a single-path routing protocol is to prevent the attacker from discarding paths of fake messages after following them without any success.

Essentially, the data transmission protocol used by HISP-NC is a biased random walk scheme that injects fake traffic. Whenever a node has something to transmit, it selects two random neighbors and sends one packet to each of them. This probabilistic process is repeated for each transmission, and it is devised to ensure that messages flow in any direction, evenly distributing the traffic among all neighbors. The protocol is devised in such a way that one of the two packets is more likely to be received by a neighbor in L^C and the other packet is sent with high probability to a neighbor in $L^{\mathcal{E}}$ or $L^{\mathcal{F}}$. Therefore, if the first packet contains encrypted event data and the second one contains garbage, this mechanism allows real traffic to advance (probabilistically) toward the base station while fake traffic is used as a cover, homogenizing the number of transmissions in the vicinity of the path of data messages and thus hiding it.

The process of selecting two neighbors is computationally inexpensive. In particular, a node generates all the combinations without repetitions of two elements from its routing table once and, for each transmission, selects one of these combinations uniformly at random. Since the neighbors closer to the base station (i.e., L^C) are placed in the routing table above neighbors at the same distance and neighbors farther away, there are more combinations whose first element is a neighbor from L^C. See Table 5.1 for an example. This table contains all the combinations resulting from the routing table of node x in Figure 5.2. There is a total of 15 combinations, of which there are 12 combinations whose first element (n_1) is a neighbor from L^C, 3 combinations where the first element belongs to $L^{\mathcal{E}}$ and no combination whose

Table 5.1 Combinations Resulting from the Routing Table of Node x

		n_1						
		L^C			$L^{\mathcal{E}}$		$L^{\mathcal{F}}$	
n_2	L^C	AB						3
		AC	BC					
	$L^{\mathcal{E}}$	AD	BD	CD				7
		AE	BE	CE	DE			
	$L^{\mathcal{F}}$	AF	BF	CF	DF	EF		5
		12			3		0	

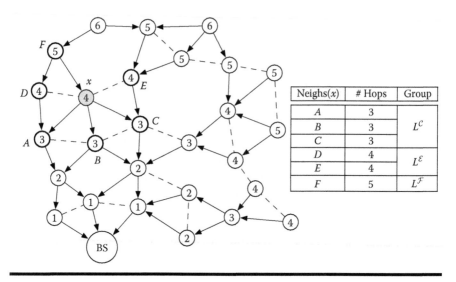

Neighs(x)	# Hops	Group
A	3	
B	3	L^C
C	3	
D	4	$L^{\mathcal{E}}$
E	4	
F	5	$L^{\mathcal{F}}$

Figure 5.2 Routing table of node x.

first element is from $L^{\mathcal{F}}$. Likewise, there are 3 combinations where the second element of the combination (n_2) belongs to L^C, 7 where it belongs to $L^{\mathcal{E}}$, and 5 where it belongs to $L^{\mathcal{F}}$.

Consequently, choosing combinations uniformly at random for each transmission has two implications. First, the first element of the combination is more likely to be a neighbor closer to the base station, and thus real traffic, which is sent to this neighbor, is more likely to reduce its distance to the base station. Second, each neighbor appears in the same number of combinations, exactly $N - 1$, where N is the total number of neighbors of the node. This means that all neighbors are to be selected, on average, the same number of times and thus traffic is evenly distributed.

Finally, nodes receiving fake traffic must also send two messages, both of which are fake, to prevent the protocol from leaking information. A time-to-live parameter is introduced to messages in order to control the durability of fake traffic in the network.

5.2.2 Routing Tables Creation

Routing tables are built shortly after the deployment of the network thanks to the topology discovery protocol. This process is initiated by the base station, which floods the network with a discovery message. This message contains a hop count value that indicates the distance (i.e., number of hops) to the base station and is initially set to zero. On reception of a discovery message, the node extracts the hop count value h and increments it by 1. If this is the first time the node receives a discovery message, it forwards the message with the new hop count to tell its neighbors that he know a route to the base station that is h hops long, that is, they are $h + 1$

hops away from the base station. Since all the nodes forward the first discovery message they receive, each node can build its routing tables with the hop count values broadcast by its neighbors.

Figure 5.2 shows the routing table of a particular node x. During the topology discovery phase, node x first receives discovery messages from nodes A, B, and C, which are 3 hops away from the base station. Since node x receives the first discovery message from one of these nodes, it knows that its distance to the base station is 4. Then, it forwards the discovery message after increasing the hop count value by 1. In this way, all its neighbors know that it is 4 hops away from the base station. Additionally, node x receives two separate discovery messages from nodes D and E, stating that they are 4 hops away from the base station, and another message from node F, which contains a hop count value equal to 5. The node thus complete its routing table.

To ensure the correct operation of the HISP-NC data transmission protocol, the routing table must be arranged incrementally, as shown in Figure 5.2. No other information apart from the ordering is necessary for the node to enable the convergence of real messages to the base station. Therefore, the distance or group columns can be removed. They are shown in this figure just for clarity.

5.2.3 Desired Properties

The HISP-NC data transmission protocol uses real and bogus messages. Any node in the communication path sends a real message and a fake message, while nodes receiving a fake message forwards two fake messages. To prevent the adversary from identifying real messages, these are encrypted at every hop and fake messages contain random data, so that they are indistinguishable from each other to the adversary. Besides providing messages indistinguishability, the transmission protocol must fulfill several properties to ensure the delivery of data and the concealment of the base station.

Real messages must be transmitted to nodes closer to the base station with a high probability. In other words, the expected distance to reach the base station should be reduced at every hop. This notion is formalized as the convergence property as follows:

Property 5.1: Convergence. *Let x be an arbitrary sensor node and BS be the base station. Also, let neigh(n) be the set of immediate neighbors of a particular node n. Then we say that a path is convergent if x chooses the next node $x' \in$ neigh(x) such that*

$$E(dist(x', BS)) < E(dist(x, BS))$$

where
  E is the mathematical expectation
  dist is the distance between two particular nodes

Additionally, a node must balance the number of packets delivered to each of its immediate neighbors in order to prevent the adversary from moving to the neighbor with the highest transmission rate. Formally, this property can be defined as follows:

Property 5.2: Homogeneity. *Let x be an arbitrary sensor node and neigh(n) be the set of immediate neighbors of a particular node n. We say that the transmissions of a node x hold the homogeneity property if*

$$\forall y, z \in neigh(x) \quad Frec_m(x, y) \simeq Frec_m(x, z)$$

where $Frec_m(x, y)$ represents the number of messages (real and fake) transmitted by node x to node y.

These two properties together ensure that both real packets reach the base station and also that the flow of real messages is hidden by fake messages since they are indistinguishable. An additional technical property ensures that the transmission of each pair of messages is sent to two different nodes. Formally:

Property 5.3: Exclusion. *Let m and m′ be a pair of messages and t be a particular transmission time. Let send(m, x, y, t) denote that x sends to y the message m at time t. The exclusion property states that*

$$\forall m, m', x, y, t \quad send(m, x, y, t) \wedge m \neq m' \Rightarrow \neg send(m', x, y, t)$$

The fulfillment of all these properties guarantee the usability of the system as well as the preservation of receiver-location privacy. Next, a data transmission protocol that is consistent with these properties is presented.

5.2.4 Transmission Protocol

The data transmission protocol implemented by HISP-NC is based on straight-forward operations that do not require a significant memory or computational overhead. In particular, this protocol only requires the introduction of a simple sorting operation to arrange the routing tables in the correct order and a pseudo-random number generator [74] to select combinations uniformly at random.

The provisions of Property 5.3 can be satisfied by means of a lightweight mechanism based on the combinations of two elements without repetition of the neighbors in the routing table of each node. The resulting combination do not have repeated elements; therefore, the two messages are sent to two different nodes. Moreover, if the routing tables are sorted incrementally in terms of the distance of the neighbors to the base station, as in Figure 5.2, Property 5.1 also holds since most of the combinations have a closer or equally distant neighbor in the first position. Finally,

---

Algorithm 5.1 Transmission Strategy

Input: *packet* ← *receive*()
Input: *combs* ← *combinations*({L^C, L^E, L^F}, 2)
Input: *FAKE_TTL*
  1: {$n1, n2$} ← *select_random*(*combs*)
  2: **if** *isreal*(*packet*) **then**
  3:   *send_random*($n1$, *packet*, $n2$, *fake*(*FAKE_TTL*))
  4: **else**
  5:   *TTL* ← *get_time_to_live*(*packet*) − 1
  6:   **if** *TTL* > 0 **then**
  7:     *send_random*($n1$, *fake*(*TTL*), $n2$, *fake*(*TTL*))
  8:   **end if**
  9: **end if**

---

the selection of combinations uniformly at random from the set of all possible combinations satisfy the remaining property, Property 5.2.

Upon the reception of a packet, a node* behaves as reflected in Algorithm 5.1. Together with the packet, the algorithm receives as input the combinations without repetition of two neighbors from the routing table of the node, and a network-wide parameter *FAKE_TTL* that can be established prior to the deployment of the network. The algorithm first decides which neighbors n_1 and n_2 will receive the two messages by selecting one combination uniformly at random (line 1). Then, if the packet received as input is real, the node forwards the message to n_1 and generates a fake message that is delivered to n_2. The fake message contains a time-to-live (TTL) argument that is set to *FAKE_TTL* (line 3). Also, note that the packets are sent in random order to prevent the adversary from trivially learning which is the real message. In case the packet received as input is fake, the node decrements by 1 the value of its time-to-live (line 5), and unless the TTL reaches 0, two fake packets with the current TTL value are sent to the corresponding neighbor nodes (line 7). Otherwise, the packet is simply discarded.

The *FAKE_TTL* parameter is dependent on the hearing range of the adversary and provides a trade-off between energy consumption and privacy protection. Since we consider adversaries with a hearing range similar to an ordinary sensor node (i.e., the family $\mathcal{ADV}_1$), fake messages might be forwarded only once but still exceed the reach of the adversary. This mechanism prevents fake messages from flooding the network and at the same time impedes adversaries from obtaining information from non-forwarded fake packets. Note that the value of *FAKE_TTL* could be tuned more efficiently by taking advantage of the context-aware capabilities of sensor nodes, as proposed in Chapter 4.

---

* The behavior is identical in the case the node is a source node or an intermediary.

5.3 Node Compromise Protection

This section describes the HISP-NC routing table perturbation scheme. Prior to describing the solution in detail, this section motivates the need for this type of protection mechanism and present some basic countermeasures that are not really useful to deal with node compromise attack. Also, some requirements to the perturbation scheme are established.

5.3.1 Overview

Almost any data transmission protocol depend on routing tables to make forwarding decisions. These tables usually contain information regarding the location or distance to the base station. For the operation of the data transmission protocol implemented by HISP-NC, it is only necessary that the neighbors of the node are sorted according to their distance to base station and not the distances themselves. The correct ordering of the table results in combinations of two neighbors that enable the delivery of data messages to the base station while preserving its location privacy.

However, if an adversary gains access to the routing tables, he would be able to trivially learn which nodes are closer to the base station without resorting to traffic analysis, thus, completely compromising location privacy despite the efforts done to obfuscate the traffic pattern at the routing layer.

The routing table perturbation scheme implemented by HISP-NC complements the data transmission protocol by introducing some noise to the routing tables of the sensor nodes in order to hinder the routing tables inspection attack. More precisely, the elements of the routing table are rearranged in such a way that neighbors closer to the base station are not necessarily at the top of the table, neighbors at the same distance are not compulsorily in the middle, and likewise neighbors further away are not always at the bottom. Notwithstanding, these modifications must not be in conflict with the properties defined in Section 5.2.3.

The devised perturbation algorithm is modeled as an optimization problem, and it is inspired on evolutionary strategies to find a solution. The algorithm is guided by a simple parameter, called the *bias*, which controls the degree of perturbation applied on the routing tables. This parameter balances between the efficiency and timeliness of the data transmission protocol and the resilience to routing table inspection attacks.

5.3.2 Basic Countermeasures

Due to the fact that HISP-NC requires the routing tables of the nodes to be sorted incrementally (i.e., $\{L^{\mathcal{C}}, L^{\mathcal{E}}, L^{\mathcal{F}}\}$), an attacker who gains access knows that the first element of the table leads him to the base station. Knowing this information, an attacker can eventually find this node and repeat the attack. After very few repetitions, the attacker has a very good estimation of the direction toward the base station without performing any type of traffic analysis attack. Therefore, it is necessary to introduce some uncertainty into the routing tables to prevent routing table inspection attacks from being a substantial threat to receiver-location privacy.

A possible countermeasure against routing table inspection attacks might be to modify the routing tables of only a subset of nodes in the network based on a particular probability distribution. Since the attacker does not know which nodes altered their routing tables, he cannot determine if the first element of an inspected table is certainly a node closer to the base station. However, this apparently effective countermeasure can be defeated by the adversary. The adversary could compromise a node and wait until the next discovery phase to check whether its routing table has changed. If so, the adversary only needs to wait for a sufficient number of updates until he discovers the pattern. In fact, the number of updates does not have to be necessarily high since observing the same routing table after a few discovery phases indicates a high probability that the original table is this one. To further increase the chances of correctly learning the real routing table, the adversary only needs to make more observations. In the long term, the original routing table stands out from the modified versions.

Another possible countermeasure is to store fake routing tables to provide some sort of routing tables k-anonymity. However, there are two main reasons why this does neither provide sufficient protection against inspection attacks. First, the sensor must somehow use some variable in its program to determine which is the real routing table and the attacker would also have access to it. Second, even if the memory and the programs are obfuscated to prevent the adversary from obtaining the variable or pointer to the real table, the attacker can identify which table is being used by observing the routing tables present in the node after various topology discovery phases. Assuming that the real routing table will be present in the node, the attacker can keep only those tables that remain after different topology discovery phases. In this way, the attacker reduces his uncertainty after each phase and eventually he only has the real routing table left. Finally, note that keeping all $k-1$ fake tables unaltered is also not an effective protection mechanism as the real routing table might change over time due to actual topology changes.

5.3.3 Perturbation Requirements

To prevent an attacker from easily gaining information about the location of the base station from the routing tables of the nodes, each and every sensor node must perturb its own table. After perturbing the routing tables, they must still enable the delivery of data packets at the base station while providing a sufficient level of uncertainty in the adversary.

A formal definition of a routing table is provided next. This definition will be later used to prove some desirable properties of the perturbation algorithm implemented by HISP-NC.

Table 5.2 Example of Routing Table and Positions

Position		Node
$N-1$	→	e_2
$N-2$	→	c_1
$N-3$	→	f_3
⋮		⋮
1	→	e_3
0	→	c_4

Definition 5.2 (Routing table).   *Let $L^* = L^C \cup L^{\mathcal{E}} \cup L^{\mathcal{F}}$ be the list of all the neighbors of a node n, where $L^C = \{c_1, c_2, c_3, \ldots\}$ are neighbors of level $n-1$, $L^{\mathcal{E}} = \{e_1, e_2, e_3, \ldots\}$ are neighbors of level n, and $L^{\mathcal{F}} = \{f_1, f_2, f_3, \ldots\}$ are neighbors of level $n+1$.*

A routing table is a bijection $r : \{N-1, \ldots, 0\} \to L^*$, being N the total number of neighbors.

Basically, this definition says that a routing table is just an ordering of all the neighbors of a particular node. Similarly, we can define $pos : L^* \to \{N-1, \ldots, 0\}$ as the inverse of r. Given a specific neighbor pos returns the position of this node in the table. An example is depicted in Table 5.2, where $pos(e_2) = N-1, pos(c_1) = N-2$, and so forth.

The previous definitions put us in a position to determine in which circumstances a routing table satisfies Property 5.1 and thus ensures the delivery of event messages to the base station. When this property is satisfied, we say that the routing table is correctly biased.

Theorem 5.1   *A routing table is correctly biased if $\sum_{n \in L^C} pos(n) > \sum_{n \in L^{\mathcal{F}}} pos(n),$*

In other words, a routing table is correctly biased if and only if the probability of choosing an element from L^C as the recipient of data packets is higher than the probability of choosing an element from $L^{\mathcal{F}}$.

Proof: Assume that we pick a random combination of neighbors (n_1, n_2), where $pos(n_1) > pos(n_2)$ as defined by our data transmission protocol. Given a subset $L \subseteq L^*$, we want to know what the probability is that the first node, n_1, is in L. This probability is given by the following expression:

$$\mathbb{P}(n_1 \in L) = \frac{1}{C} \sum_{n \in L} pos(n) \tag{5.1}$$

where $C = N * (N - 1)/2$ is the total number of combinations of two elements without repetition of L^*. Also note that $C = 1 + 2 + \cdots + (N - 1) = \sum_{n \in L^*} pos(n)$.

It is possible to write all possible combinations without repetitions of two nodes as a list of pairs, lexicographically ordered, from the routing table:

$$
\begin{array}{llllll}
(r(N-1), r(N-2)), & (r(N-1), r(N-3)), & (r(N-1), r(N-4)), & \ldots, & (r(N-1), r(0)) \\
 & (r(N-2), r(N-3)), & (r(N-2), r(N-4)), & \ldots, & (r(N-2), r(0)) \\
 & & (r(N-3), r(N-4)), & \ldots, & (r(N-3), r(0)) \\
 & & & & \vdots \\
 & & & & (r(1), r(0))
\end{array}
$$

Since the node $r(N - 1)$ appears in the first position of $N - 1$ pairs, the node $r(N - 2)$ in $N - 2$ pairs, and so on, they are exactly $(N - 1) + (N - 2) + (N - 3) + \cdots + 1$ pairs in the list, which is $N * (N - 1)/2 = C$.

Now, choosing a random pair (n_1, n_2) such that $pos(n_1) > pos(n_2)$ is equivalent to choosing any pair from the previous list. Thus, the probability that a certain node n_1 is chosen as the first entry is simply the number of elements in the routing table r whose position is below n_1, divided by the total number of pairs. This is precisely $pos(n_1)/C$ and Equation 5.1 follows directly. ■

The perturbation degree or bias of a routing table, $bias(r)$, is an important parameter to take into consideration. This parameter impacts on both the speed of convergence of data packets to the base station and the uncertainty level of the attacker. We define the bias of a routing table r, $bias(r) \in [-1, 1]$, as the probability of sending data packets in the direction of or in the opposite direction to the base station. This parameter compares the level or distance of the current node, $level(n_0)$, with the expected value of the level of the next node in the transmission path, that is, $E(level(n_1))$. The closer the bias is to 1, the greater the probability is that data packets are sent to nodes in L^C (i.e., the distance decreases). Likewise, a bias value close to -1 implies that it is highly likely that the first element of the resulting combination belongs to $L^{\mathcal{F}}$.

The bias of a routing table can be calculated as the weighted difference between number of combinations resulting from the neighbors in L^C and the number of combinations resulting from neighbors in $L^{\mathcal{F}}$. Formally,

$$bias(r) = \frac{1}{C} \left(\sum_{n \in L^C} pos(n) - \sum_{n \in L^{\mathcal{F}}} pos(n) \right) \tag{5.2}$$

Proof: By definition, we have that the bias of a routing table is

$$bias(r) := level(n_0) - E(level(n_1))$$

The level or distance of the next node n_1 is the same level as n_0, or this value decremented or incremented by 1. This is determined by the list of neighbors to which the node belongs, $L^{\mathcal{E}}$, $L^{\mathcal{C}}$, or $L^{\mathcal{F}}$, respectively. Thus,

$$
\begin{aligned}
E(level(n_1)) &= (level(n_0) - 1) * \mathbb{P}(n_1 \in L^{\mathcal{C}}) \\
&\quad + (level(n_0) + 1) * \mathbb{P}(n_1 \in L^{\mathcal{F}}) \\
&\quad + level(n_0) * \mathbb{P}(n_1 \in L^{\mathcal{E}}) \\
&= level(n_0) - [\mathbb{P}(n_1 \in L^{\mathcal{C}}) - \mathbb{P}(n_1 \in L^{\mathcal{F}})]
\end{aligned}
$$

and now the result follows directly from Equation 5.1. ■

As previously defined, the bias is a value in the $[-1, 1]$ interval, but not all values are eligible because the bias is dependent on the number of elements in $L^{\mathcal{C}}$ and $L^{\mathcal{F}}$. For example, $bias(r) = -1$ if and only if $L^* \equiv L^{\mathcal{F}}$, since $L^{\mathcal{C}} = \emptyset$ and $\sum_{n \in L^{\mathcal{F}}} pos(n) = C$.

Therefore, it is possible to calculate an upper and lower bound of the bias of a routing table based on the number of neighbors it has on each level. The maximum value, $bias_M(r)$, is reached when the elements in $L^{\mathcal{C}}$ are placed at the top of the routing table, the elements in $L^{\mathcal{F}}$ are placed at the bottom, and the elements in $L^{\mathcal{E}}$ are in between. Consequently, Equation 5.2 can be written in the following form:

$$bias_M(r) = \frac{1}{C} \left(\sum_{i=1}^{c} (N - i) - \sum_{i=1}^{f} (i - 1) \right) \tag{5.3}$$

where c, f, and N are the number of elements in $L^{\mathcal{C}}$, $L^{\mathcal{F}}$, and L^*, respectively.

Similarly, the minimum value, $bias_m(r)$, is reached when $L^{\mathcal{C}}$ is at the bottom, $L^{\mathcal{F}}$ at the top, and $L^{\mathcal{E}}$ in the middle. Then, we can define it as

$$bias_m(r) = \frac{1}{C} \left(\sum_{i=1}^{c} (i - 1) - \sum_{i=1}^{f} (N - i) \right) \tag{5.4}$$

After mathematical transformations, we have that the bias of a particular routing table r is bounded by the following equation:

$$\frac{c(c - 1) - 2f N + f(f + 1)}{N(N - 1)} \le bias(r) \le \frac{2cN - c(c + 1) - f(f - 1)}{N(N - 1)} \tag{5.5}$$

Note that this means that the bias value is within the interval, but, clearly, it cannot take all possible values within that interval. This mostly depends on the number of neighbors the node has of each level. More details are later provided in Section 5.4.2.

5.3.4 Perturbation Algorithm

The algorithm devised for perturbing the routing tables receives as input the original routing table and a desired bias value for the table. After manipulations of the routing table, the algorithm returns an ordering of the table that satisfies the desired bias to some degree since the desired value might not be reachable.

The perturbation must be implemented by all sensor nodes. This implies that the complexity of the algorithm in terms of memory and computational requirements should be as low as possible given the hardware-constrained devices where it must run. Therefore, it should not simply explore all possible solutions (i.e., orderings of the table) as this has a complexity of $\mathcal{O}(\mathcal{A}) = \frac{N!}{c!e!f!}$, where N is the total number of elements in the routing table and c, e, and f are the number of neighbors of the groups L^C, $L^{\mathcal{E}}$, and $L^{\mathcal{F}}$, respectively. This type of algorithm has the advantage of finding always the best solution, but the cost is determined by the total number of elements in L^C, $L^{\mathcal{E}}$, and $L^{\mathcal{F}}$. The higher the cardinality of each of these groups of neighbors, the larger the solution space. Therefore, a deterministic algorithm might be viable for sensor nodes when the value of N is low or when one of the groups is considerably larger than the rest (i.e., its cardinality is very close to N). Otherwise, the completion time and the memory requirements of the algorithm could be excessively high for tiny devices.

Alternatively, this problem can be modeled as an optimization algorithm where the objective function depends on the desired bias of the table and the positions of the nodes comprising it. More precisely, the devised perturbation algorithm is inspired by evolutionary strategies [48], where simple mutations are applied to the routing table in order to minimize the distance to the desired bias. In this case, the mutations consist of switching the positions of two elements in the routing table. This strategy is considerably more efficient than a deterministic approach as it can be observed in Figure 5.3a. This figure compares the order of complexity of both types of algorithms for different routing tables and desired bias value. The upper plane shows the number of iterations the deterministic algorithm needs to reach the solution. This value is noticeably larger in the deterministic case, and it increases linearly with the size of the routing table, while in the evolutionary algorithm (lower plane), it is hardly affected by this parameter. Actually, the results presented for the evolutionary algorithm do not represent the last iteration of the algorithm (i.e., *MAX_ITER* on the *y*-axis) but rather the last iteration when the value of the objective function was reduced, namely, the iteration when the algorithm reached the pseudo-optimal solution. This is used to estimate the average number of iterations that the evolutionary algorithm requires to find the solution.

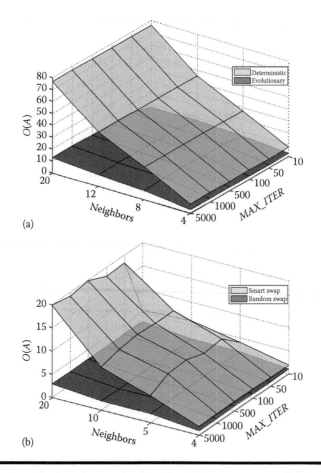

(a)

(b)

Figure 5.3 Complexity of perturbation algorithms. (a) Deterministic vs. evolutionary and (b) random swap vs. smart swap.

Algorithm 5.2 describes the devised routing tables perturbation algorithm. This algorithm is triggered immediately after the topology discovery phase and the nodes builds its real routing table, which is used as an input to the algorithm together with the desired bias and the maximum number of iterations to run. This last parameter is up to the network administrator and can be derived from simulations like the ones just described.

The algorithm first calculates the distance to the objective by means of the *energy* function (line 1). This energy function is defined as the distance between the desired bias and the bias of the current ordering of the table, and the operations performed from line 3 to line 11 are intended to reduce the aforementioned distance. Throughout this piece of code, a mutation is performed over the current routing table (line 4) and then its energy is calculated. The mutation consists of swapping two elements of

---

Algorithm 5.2   Perturbation Algorithm

Input: $br \leftarrow \{L^C, L^\mathcal{E}, L^\mathcal{F}\}$
Input: $bias, MAX\_ITER$
 1: $E \leftarrow energy(bias, br)$
 2: $i \leftarrow 0$
 3: **while** $(i < MAX\_ITER) \wedge (E \neq 0)$ **do**
 4:   $br' \leftarrow swap(br)$
 5:   $E' \leftarrow energy(bias, br')$
 6:   **if** $(E' < E)$ **then**
 7:     $br \leftarrow br'$
 8:     $E \leftarrow E'$
 9:   **end if**
10:   $i \leftarrow i + 1$
11: **end while**
12: **return** br

---

the table using a particular strategy. If the bias of the new version of the table is closer to the desired bias input to the algorithm, then the algorithm keeps this new version of the table and discards the previous one. The process is repeated for *MAX_ITER* iterations or until the desired bias is reached. At this point, the algorithm outputs the last version of the routing table that have been kept, which is the one with the lowest energy. Finally, the node must securely erase any data used during the operation of the algorithm.

As mentioned earlier, different strategies can be employed by the swapping function, and this will impact on the convergence speed to a solution. Figure 5.3b depicts the performance of our algorithm with two different *swap* functions. In particular, this figure represents a random and a smart swap function. In the former strategy (upper plane), the elements to be swapped are chosen uniformly at random. On the latter strategy (lower plane), the selection is guided by an heuristic, which consists of swapping the two elements that achieve the largest decrease on the value of energy function. As shown in the figure, the smart swapping converges faster than the random swapping on the solution, especially as the number of neighbors increases, but each swap is more computationally intensive.

Finally, observe that the perturbation algorithm might not reach the optimal solution but it converges to it. There are two potential reasons for this: either it is infeasible to achieve the expected solution for the given lists of neighbors (see Equation 5.5), or the number of iterations of the algorithm was insufficient for the swapping function to allow the convergence. Also note that given the nondeterministic nature of the solution, it may be that the result differs for two runs of the algorithm with the same input parameters. This provides an extra means of protection from reversing attacks.

5.4 Protocol Evaluation

This section presents a detailed analysis on the potential limitations that might hinder the successful operation of the HISP-NC protocol. First, we explore the impact of the network topology and the expected number of hops for real messages to reach the base station prior to and after the perturbation of the routing tables. Finally, we analyze the overhead introduced by our solution in terms of fake packet transmissions.

The simulation environment used to evaluate the HISP-NC scheme is based in MATLAB and is very similar to the one described in Section 4.4.1.

5.4.1 Network Topology

The distribution of real and fake messages is clearly impacted by the number of the neighbors in each of the groups of the routing table of the nodes. As stated in Section 5.3.3, the arrangement of the table and the size of each of the groups of neighbors determine the bias of the table. In other words, Property 5.1 could be unsatisfied if the number of neighbors in $L^{\mathcal{C}}$ is significantly lower than the number of neighbors in $L^{\mathcal{F}}$. This problem is dependent on the topology of the network and the hearing range of the nodes.

To have a clearer picture as to what extent this poses a real limitation to our data transmission protocol, we provide a numerical analysis on the number of elements in $L^{\mathcal{F}}$ that any sensor node can withstand without sacrificing the usability and privacy of the system. The present analysis considers the unperturbed version of the routing table, where the elements are arranged according to their distances to the base station.

Let N be the total number of neighbors of an arbitrary node such that $N = c + e + f$, where c, e, and f are the number of neighbors in $L^{\mathcal{C}}$, $L^{\mathcal{E}}$, and $L^{\mathcal{F}}$, respectively. The following theorem gives a sufficient condition on c, f, and N to ensure the desired property of data convergence.

Theorem 5.2 *Real messages follow a biased random walk converging to the base station iff $f < \sqrt{2c(N - c)}$ for any sensor node in the route.*

Proof: We want to show that if $f < \sqrt{2c(N - c)}$, then $\mathbb{P}(n_1 \in L^{\mathcal{C}}) > \mathbb{P}(n_1 \in L^{\mathcal{F}})$, which represent the probabilities of sending a data message to a node in $L^{\mathcal{C}}$ and $L^{\mathcal{F}}$, respectively.

The number of combinations of two neighbors where at least the first element belongs to $L^{\mathcal{F}}$ is

$$\binom{f}{2} = \frac{f(f - 1)}{2}$$

while the number of combinations of two neighbors where the first element of the duple is a node in $L^{\mathcal{C}}$ is

$$\binom{c}{2} + c(e+f)$$

Consequently, the probability of selecting a neighbor in $L^{\mathcal{C}}$ is higher than the probability of selecting a neighbor $L^{\mathcal{F}}$ if the number of combinations with a closer neighbor in the first position of the duple is larger than those with the first element being a further neighbor. Formally,

$$\mathbb{P}(n_1 \in L^{\mathcal{C}}) > \mathbb{P}(n_1 \in L^{\mathcal{F}}) \Leftrightarrow c(c-1) + 2c(e+f) > f(f-1)$$

In order to simplify the analysis, we make some generalizations that are less restrictive but still provide a sufficient condition for the proof:

$$2c(e+f) > f^2 \Rightarrow c(c-1) + 2c(e+f) > f(f-1)$$

Provided that $c + e + f = N$, the previous equation can be expressed as

$$f < \sqrt{2c(N-c)} \qquad (5.6)$$

Therefore, we might say that if Equation 5.6 is satisfied, then the following implication holds:

$$f < \sqrt{2c(N-c)} \Rightarrow \mathbb{P}(n_1 \in L^{\mathcal{C}}) > \mathbb{P}(n_1 \in L^{\mathcal{F}}) \qquad \blacksquare$$

Intuitively, the imposed restriction can be satisfied in manually deployed networks deployed following a particular topology (e.g., grid or mesh). Yet we deem it necessary to validate the feasibility of our restriction in randomly deployed networks by means of experimental simulations. In particular, Figure 5.4 depicts the average results over 50 repetitions of our network discovery protocol for various network sizes. We considered the following network parameters: (1) a square field area of side 1, (2) the transmission radius of the nodes that is set to 0.1, and (3) networks ranging in size from 100 to 700 randomly deployed nodes. In Figure 5.4a, we show that the probability of isolated nodes drops significantly when the network size is over 200 nodes. Moreover, Figure 5.4b presents the average number of neighbors closer, equal, and farther for any node in the network. In this figure, we also show that the restriction imposed by Equation 5.6 on the maximum number of further neighbors is satisfied at all times.

Note that the results shown in Figure 5.4b are average values, and there might be some nodes not satisfying the restriction. However, this would only pose some

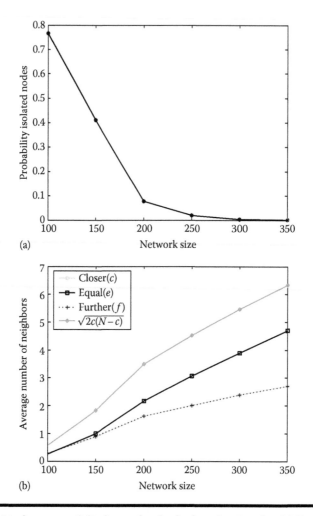

Figure 5.4 Node connectivity in randomly deployed networks. (a) Probability of isolated nodes and (b) neighbors restriction.

additional delay unless there are network regions with a high concentration of nodes unable to fulfill the imposed condition. This issue might cause network packets to continuously move back and forth impeding their progress toward the base station. This is not the case when the node density is sufficient. However, this is a problem that does not only affect our solution.

In general, we can state that when the density of a randomly deployed network is more than 350 nodes/km^2, there is a high probability of full connectivity, considering transmission ranges of 100 m. Also, the restriction on the number of neighbors is satisfied for such density.

5.4.2 Message Delivery Time

The probabilistic nature of our protocol introduces some uncertainty on the delivery of messages to the sink. This issue has some implications both on the reaction time of the network and the energy consumption of the nodes. Therefore, we provide some insights into the expected number of hops to reach the base station for a packet originated n hops away.

Let x_n be the expected number of hops for a packet originated at distance n. The proposed transmission protocol can be modeled by the following recurrence equation:

$$x_n = 1 + px_{n-1} + qx_n + rx_{n+1} \qquad (5.7)$$

This equation represents a biased random walk where the packet will be forwarded to a neighbor after increasing the number of hops by 1. At each hop, we have a probability p of delivering the packet to a node closer to the base station, a probability q of staying at the same distance, and a probability r of moving in the opposite direction. Therefore, the average speed toward the base station is $p - r$.

In general, this result is true for constant values of p and r but this is not always the case in sensor networks. The reason is that not all sensor nodes present the same distribution of neighbors. This depends on the hearing range of the nodes, the network topology, and their location in the field. In Figure 5.5, we present the performance of our protocol for WSNs deployed in a grid with equal transmission power for all nodes. We examine various configurations that are obtained by increasing the transmission power of the nodes, and this in turn changes the connectivity of the network. Each of these configurations presents, on average, 4, 8, 12, or 20 neighbors/node. Also, for each configuration, we place the source at various distances from the base station: 5, 10, 15, and 20 hops. Several source nodes are selected for each distance, and every single source node generates 500 data packets to be received by the base station.

The results show that the expected number of hops increases with the distance to the sink as well as with the connectivity of the nodes. As the number of neighbors available to a node increases, the more difficult it is for the adversary to make a decision on which of the recipients is actually closer to the base station. However, a significant increase in the number of neighbors also has implications on the delivery time because as the transmission range grows, more nodes are included in the group of equally distant neighbors (i.e., L^{ε}) of the node. This issue is shown in Figure 5.5b, where we provide a box plot representation of the number of neighbors closer (C), equal (E), and further (F) for the simulated network configurations. For example, C_4 indicates the number of closer neighbors in the 4neigh network configuration.

Additionally, note from Figure 5.5a that, for all the configurations, the average speed of the packets decreases when they are close to the sink. Consider, for example, the *4neigh* configuration. When the distance to the sink is 5, the expected

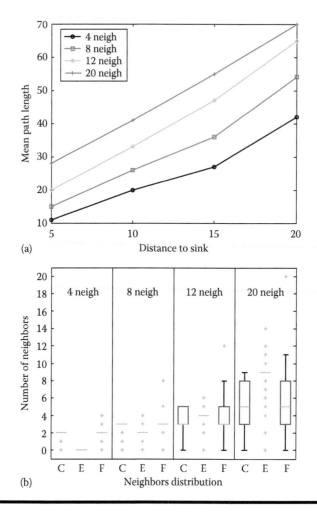

Figure 5.5 Protocol performance for various network configurations. (a) Expected number of hops and (b) distribution of neighbors.

delivery time is 11, while a packet at distance 20 will be delivered after 42 hops. This means that the time difference from distance 20 to 5 is 31, and thus, the average speed is $15/31 = 0.484$. However, in the proximities of the base station (from distance 5 to 0), the speed drops to $5/11 = 0.454$. The reason is that the distribution of neighbors for nodes around the base station is different from the distribution for distant nodes. More precisely, the nodes in close vicinity of the base station have very few nodes in the closer list, but the number of nodes at the same distance or further away is high. The imbalance between the lists of neighbors grows with the transmission range of the nodes, being more significant for the 20neigh configuration. In this case, the speed drops from 0.358 to 0.179 in the vicinity of the data sink.

As previously stated, the perturbation of the routing tables negatively impacts the efficiency of the data transmission protocol and thus affects the message delivery time.

We conducted a number of experiments for the same network configurations described before. We modified the routing tables of all the nodes using our perturbation algorithm, which is configured to perform at most 30 random swaps and uses input bias values between 0 and 1. For each simulation, we sent 500 messages from 10 random source nodes located at the edge of the network, which is 20 hops away from the base station. The results are presented in Figure 5.6a, where the mean

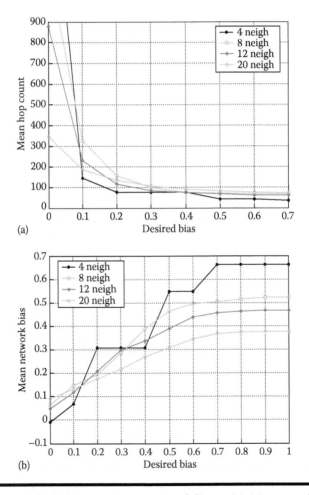

Figure 5.6 Perturbation impact on message delivery. (a) Mean number of hops and (b) mean network bias.

number of hops traveled by packets is depicted, and Figure 5.6b, which shows the relationship between the bias value used as input to the perturbation algorithm and the mean bias of the network after its application.

From Figure 5.6b, we can observe that for those configurations with a larger number of neighbors, the range of values defined for the bias is smaller. This is the reason why the mean number of hops increases more abruptly as the bias approaches zero in configurations with fewer neighbors. In particular, when the desired bias is exactly zero, the mean number of hops for the 4 neigh configuration is significantly high (over 1800 hops) because the mean network bias is slightly below zero (−0.0097). On the other hand, the mean hop count for the 20 neigh configuration is below 350 hops because the mean network bias is close to 0.1.

In general, setting the desired bias value over 0.2 ensures that the mean number of hops for any configuration is below 100 for a source node located at the edge of the network.

5.4.3 Fake Traffic Overhead

The injection of fake traffic is a fundamental feature of the HISP-NC data transmission protocol since it hides the flow of real messages. However, the amount of fake traffic must be kept as low as possible in order to extend the lifetime of the nodes. To control the propagation of fake messages, our protocol defines a system parameter, *FAKE_TTL*, which depends on the hearing range of the adversary in such a way that he is unable to observe the whole fake path. The idea is to prevent the adversary from controlling the transmissions of the node from which the first fake packet originated and the node that dropped the last fake packet, simultaneously. Otherwise, the attacker could learn information about the direction toward the base station.

Instead of injecting fake packets at regular intervals, which would provide the best privacy protection but would also deplete the sensors' batteries rapidly, the transmission of fake traffic is triggered by the presence of real packets. When the eavesdropping range of the adversary is large, the energy cost associated with fake transmissions would be similar to making sensor nodes inject fake traffic at regular intervals with the difference being that fake packets would be injected only in the presence of events.

In Figure 5.7, we illustrate the overhead imposed by HISP-NC for different time-to-live values. More precisely, we show the ratio of fake over real messages that are introduced to balance the transmissions in a band around the real path. When *FAKE_TTL* is set to zero, the ratio is 1 because each real packet is transmitted in conjunction with a single fake packet, which is no longer propagated. Note that the ratio is not affected by different network topologies since the number of transmissions performed by the protocol is independent of the connectivity of the sensor nodes. As the time-to-live grows, the ratio increase is in the order of $\mathcal{O}(2^{n+1})$

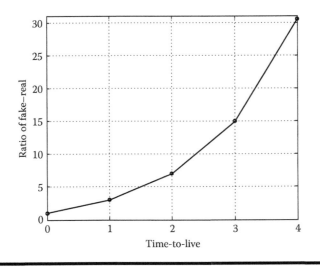

Figure 5.7 Overhead of fake messages.

where n is the hearing range of the adversary. In any case, given the adversarial model considered in this chapter, the overhead imposed by this approach is moderate.

Finally, note the overhead imposed by fake transmissions might be reduced by half if we introduce a slight modification. Instead of sending two packets upon the reception of traffic, we might send a single packet addressed to two node identifiers. In this way and assuming that the identifiers are hidden from potential observers, the two recipients receive the packet and continue with the forwarding process. The first identifier indicates the real recipient and the second indicates the fake recipient. This improvement is possible due to the broadcast nature of wireless transmissions, which allows all the neighbors of a node to overhear its messages.

5.4.4 Privacy Protection

The HISP-NC data transmission protocol aims to provide protection from local adversaries capable of performing various types of traffic analysis attacks. The strategy of the adversary is to repeatedly move to a node closer to the base station by observing the transmissions along the communication path. Starting at any point of the network he eventually finds a data sender. From this location, the adversary attempts to determine the direction to the base station by observing the communications of the data sender and its neighbors.

First, the adversary might perform a time-correlation attack and move in the direction of the neighbor forwarding the first message transmitted by the data sender. Given the features of our solution, several cases may occur depending on whether the packet is real or fake. If the packet is real, the adversary is highly likely to reduce by one, his distance to the base station. However, this is not necessarily the case because real traffic might also be forwarded in other directions. Moreover, the probability of following a real packet is lower than the probability of following a fake packet. The reason is that, as real messages move, they generate pairs of messages, one real and one fake, while fake messages trigger the transmission of pairs of fake messages. Also, note that the adversary can only be certain of whether he made the right choice when he follows a fake packet that is no longer propagated. This situation provides the adversary with no information about the direction to the base station because fake messages are forwarded in any direction. This is true unless the hearing range of the adversary allows him to observe both ends of the branch of fake messages. In that case, the adversary could determine that the root of the branch is closer to the base station with a high probability.

Alternatively, the adversary might choose to perform a sufficient number of observations before making a decision on the next move. In that case, the adversary will move toward the neighbor with the higher transmission rate. To reduce the success of this strategy, the HISP-NC transmission protocol makes nodes to evenly distribute messages among their neighbors, thus locally homogenizing the number of packets being observed by a potential adversary. Again, the adversary cannot distinguish real from fake packets unless he observes a node that, after receiving a packet, does not forward it. This implies that he is at the edge of the band of fake messages surrounding the path of real data. Being able to precisely determine the limits of the band of fake messages could provide the adversary with information on how to reach the base station. However, the number and behavior of events being reported by the sensor nodes may be extremely dynamic, which hinders the process of bounding the aforementioned band. Moreover, real packets are sent following a random walk that causes the band to be rather arbitrary. Consequently, even if the adversary was capable of delimiting the edges of the band at some point, this information does not necessarily lead him to the base station.

Notwithstanding, in an attempt to empirically demonstrate the validity of our privacy-preserving data transmission protocol, we have launched a number of simulations with different types of adversaries starting next to the data sources, located at various distances from the base station ranging from 5 to 20 hops. Each experiment was executed for 500 simulation steps, and we considered the same network configurations as in Section 5.4. First, we ran simulations under a random adversarial model that, for each simulation step, moves to a random neighbor regardless of the transmission of messages. Then, we run the experiments with attackers performing rate-monitoring and time-correlation attacks. The results are depicted in Figure 5.8a.

We observe that the success rate of a random adversary is significantly higher than for the other two types of adversaries, but still its success rate is close to or below 0.35. The random adversary is more effective for configurations where the average number of neighbors is smaller. Also note that in a quarter of the simulations, the adversary is placed only 5 hops away from the base station, which is when the adversary is more successful. Finally, it is worth noting that the success rate for the rate-monitoring

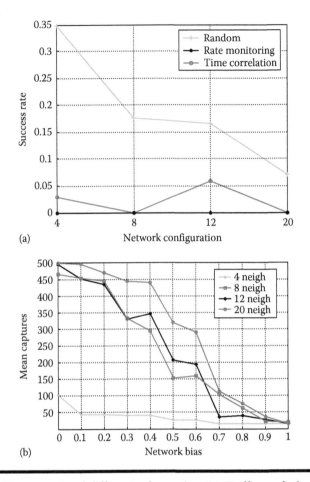

Figure 5.8 Success rate of different adversaries. (a) Traffic analysis attacks and (b) node capture attacks.

adversary is zero at all times; however, the time-correlation adversary reaches the base station occasionally, although the previous analysis suggests that this should not occur. The reason is that due to the nature of our simulator,* we were unable to precisely represent the behavior of a time-correlation adversary. Instead, the devised time-correlation adversary observes which messages are generated by the neighbors of the node, and from those neighbors, it randomly selects one as the next hop. The few times the adversary reaches the target is due to this random selection and because the initial position was only 5 hops away from the base station.

---

* It is not possible to obtain the exact time at which a message is transmitted and thus sort messages based on their creation time.

Additionally, we studied the success rate of an adversary performing node capture attacks. For each network configuration and bias value, we ran 10 simulations, where the adversary started at random positions from the border of the network (i.e., 20 hops away). Again, each simulation consisted of 500 simulation steps, and we assumed that the adversary was capable of capturing the routing tables of a node at each step. Also, we assumed that the adversary could move to the next node of interest to him by simply knowing its identifier, but in a real setting, the adversary might need to repeatedly capture neighbors until he eventually finds a particular node. Moreover, the adversary keeps track of the number of times he has visited each of the nodes in order to perform a more effective attack and prevent being trapped inside loops. Furthermore, the perturbation algorithm is configured to run during the deployment of the network for at most 30 iterations. Another parameter of the algorithm is the desired bias. However, if we used the same input bias for all nodes, provided that the distribution of the tables of the nodes might differ significantly, this would cause some nodes not to modify their routing tables at all and this issue could be exploited by the adversary. To prevent this, we adjusted the desired bias to the range of possible bias values of each particular node. In this way, the routing tables of all the nodes were perturbed to the same extent.

As expected, the number of captures an adversary needs to perform before reaching the base station increases as the bias of the network approaches zero (see Figure 5.8b). Clearly, the protection is more effective for configurations with a larger number of nodes* since the adversary keeps a record of already visited nodes and his strategy is to move to the first node in the routing table with the least number of visits. Although setting a very low bias is beneficial for protection against routing table inspection attacks, it also negatively affects the delivery time of packets to the base station. Additionally, the number of tables an adversary might capture is rather limited due to the complexity of performing node capture attacks and also because compromising many nodes might reveal that the network is being attacked. In particular, if we consider that an adversary could capture at most a 10th of the nodes in the field, it is safe to use a bias value less than or equal to 0.5. Consequently, the bias is an important parameter that should be carefully tuned in order to find the right balance between usability and protection, based on the likelihood of node capture attacks.

However, it is worth noting that any attacker that is able to capture a node can behave as the node. Such an adversary has access to the (perturbed) routing tables, and he can simulate the algorithm of the node, and by repeating this process all along the path, he will eventually reach the base station. This is true for any algorithm, not a problem solely of our solution, as long as the attacker can capture the routing tables and knows how the node works (i.e., he has all the secrets), he is able to simulate the nodes he is compromising. Still, implementing a perturbation algorithm is much

---

* The number of nodes are 400, 1600, 1600, and 3600 for the configurations of 4, 8, 12, and 20 neigh, respectively. Still, the distance from the edge to the base station is 20 hops in all cases.

better than not modifying the routing tables. In the latter case, the adversary simply needs to always move to the first neighbor in the routing table, and he will reach the base station with the minimum number of steps.

5.5 Summary and Improvements

This chapter has presented the HISP-NC scheme, a receiver-location privacy solution that aims to prevent both traffic analysis and routing table inspection attacks. The solution consists of a traffic normalization scheme, which relies on the injection of controlled amounts of fake traffic to hide the flow of real traffic, and a routing table perturbation scheme, which reorders the elements of the routing table according to a given bias in order to hinder inspection attacks while ensuring the delivery of data packets to the base station.

The feasibility of the HISP-NC scheme has been validated both analytically and experimentally through extensive simulations. In particular, we have analyzed the impact of the connectivity of the network on the convergence of the data packets and the privacy protection level. We have also investigated the expected convergence time of packets in order to gain insights into the expected delivery delay of our solution. Moreover, we have explored the overhead imposed in terms of fake traffic injection for adversaries with different eavesdropping capabilities. Finally, we have discussed and evaluated the privacy protection achieved against adversaries performing different types of traffic analysis and node capture attacks. The proposed solution has proven to be secure and efficient against local eavesdroppers and attackers capable of inspecting the routing tables of a limited number of nodes in the network.

The main drawback to this solution is that it introduces a significant overhead in order to provide a robust privacy protection level. The amount of fake traffic is moderate when the adversary has a limited hearing range, similar to that of an ordinary sensor, but the overhead increases exponentially with the hearing range of the adversary since fake traffic needs to extend beyond the area he or she controls. Therefore, an important improvement to this solution is to reduce the amount of fake traffic necessary to maintain a robust protection level in the presence of powerful adversaries with a larger hearing range.

Another interesting line of improvement is to protect the location of the base station not only during the data transmission phase but also during the topology discovery phase. The network is regularly flooded with a hop count message that allows each sensor node to determine the distance of its neighbors from the base station. This process is initiated by the base station, thus revealing its location to external observers. Incorporating an anonymous topology discovery protocol in the HISP-NC scheme would provide a complete solution to receiver-location privacy in WSNs.

Chapter 6

Conclusion

Privacy preservation has troubled society for centuries. Lately, this concern has grown due to the development and implementation of information and communication technologies capable of collecting, analyzing, and disseminating personal information automatically. These developments have drawn the attention of the research community, which has been challenged by a myriad of mechanisms capable of violating the right to individual privacy when performing online transactions. Although current data-harvesting systems are already incredibly powerful, their data collection capacities are being exceptionally extended, thanks to the integration of sensing technologies in computing systems, which provide them with the ability to gather information from the physical world directly. Therefore, the privacy problem can reach a whole new dimension with the deployment of ubiquitous technologies like sensor networks as they can collect personal information in places and situations hitherto unsuspected.

This chapter summarizes the contributions of this book and presents new areas of research that demand further attention from the privacy community in order to facilitate a seamless and privacy-aware integration of sensing technologies in our everyday lives.

6.1 Summary

Throughout this book, it has been proved that protecting privacy in scenarios involving the use of WSNs is an extremely complex and challenging task. This is mainly due to the features and requirements imposed by the sensor platforms as well as the environments where they are deployed. Indeed, there is a broad spectrum of privacy issues that may arise from the deployment and operation of these networks. These problems range from the exploitation of sensor networks as a tool for surreptitious

155

mass surveillance of individuals, corporations, and institutions to newer contextual privacy problems, which are caused by the particular mode of operation of these networks.

More precisely, the location privacy problem, which is the main focus of this book, is due to the communication pattern of sensor networks. The severe hardware limitation of sensor nodes profoundly affects the design of applications and protocols, which are guided by the simple and imperative need of saving energy. Since wireless communications are extremely costly, routing protocols tend to save as much energy as possible and this results in pronounced traffic patterns that allow an observer to trivially identify the nodes sending data and the nodes receiving it. This problem has been extensively studied in the realm of computer networks and has resulted in an amalgam of anonymous communications systems intended to counter traffic analysis attacks and thus prevent leaking sensitive information from the parties involved in online transactions. However, it has been shown in this book that computer-based anonymous communications systems are not suitable for sensor environments because they either pursue different anonymity properties, the attacker models have several differences, sensor nodes cannot perform costly operations or their application would limit the capabilities of the network.

The unsuitability of computer-based anonymity solutions has led to the development of a number of solutions specifically tailored for the location privacy problem in sensor networks. These solutions can be classified according to various criteria based on the information or resource to be protected and the capabilities of the attacker. Most solutions dealing with local attackers focus on the transmission of messages using random communication paths from the data sources to the base station. By doing this, the attacker cannot easily follow messages and thus reach either the data sender or the intended recipient. Whereas if the attacker has a global vision of the communications, most solutions concentrate on the generation of fake traffic either to hide the presence of events or to normalize the transmission rate across the network. Finally, very few studies have addressed the threat of an active attacker that disrupts the normal behavior of the network nodes or compromises them in order to access the memory contents of the nodes and the contents of data messages.

Despite the efforts of the research community, a problem present in all solutions developed to date is that the devised protection mechanisms are active all the time. This implies tremendous costs in terms of energy consumption but also from the viewpoint of the delay introduced in the signaling of messages to the base station. The context-aware location privacy (CALP) mechanism arises precisely from this idea, which seeks to benefit from one of the inherent mechanisms of sensor networks, that is their ability to sense their vicinity and activate the defense mechanism only when a real threat emerges. The devised scheme is able to influence on the routing protocol to dynamically readapt the communication paths in such a way that the ability of the attacker to trace messages in the field is significantly reduced. Furthermore, when combining the CALP mechanism with a shortest-path routing protocol, the result is a routing protocol in which packets deviate from the optimal communication path minimally, which occurs only when the attacker is within the communication range of messages. In this way, it is possible to drastically reduce the overhead caused by the application of a location privacy protocol in WSNs. Although the CALP mechanism has only been applied to protect the location of data sources, it seems reasonable to use the context-aware capabilities of the nodes for other privacy- or security-related mechanisms, such as protecting the location of the base station.

The protection of the base station is an even more complex problem since all the traffic generated by the network is addressed to this single point. Therefore, when the attacker has a local hearing range, devised solutions often rely on the randomization of routes, but it is often necessary to inject fake messages to other parts of the network, which inevitably increases energy consumption and do not always provide an adequate level of protection. Also, given the importance of the base station it is useful to consider other attack vectors not taken into account to date, such as the ability to capture nodes and retrieve information from them on how to reach the base station. A new and highly effective type of attack in this area is therefore the inspection of the routing tables of the nodes. These are precisely the issues addressed by HISP-NC, a protection mechanism capable of keeping hidden the position of the base station via two complementary protection mechanisms; one devoted to countering traffic analysis attacks and the other focused on protecting against attackers capable of capturing nodes and inspecting their routing tables. The first of these mechanisms is based on the transmission of packets to the base station using a biased random walk that is probabilistically hidden by means of fake traffic. The second mechanism consists of the perturbation of the routing tables in order to make it difficult for the attacker to determine which neighbors are closer to the base station while allowing the arrival of data packets at their destination.

6.2 Future Challenges

The number of research papers as well as the interest in source- and receiver-location privacy has increased notably in the last few years. The reason for this revolution is possibly due to the fact that WSNs are finally being integrated into real systems and also due to the growing interest in the development of new computing paradigms such as the Internet of Things, where sensor networks are a core technology. However, despite these advances, there is still ample room for improvement. In fact, there is an urgent need to address a number of research problems that are still open and will need to be resolved to achieve a privacy-preserving deployment of these technologies.

The following lists describe several challenges and areas of research that will demand further attention in the coming years. These challenges are focused on the location privacy problem, which is the main focus of this book, and they are presented according to their level of complexity and the effort required to make significant progress in this line of research.

6.2.1 Cost-Effective Location Privacy Solutions

Despite the number of solutions developed, so far most of them approach the problem in a similar way. Location privacy solutions either send packets on a (biased) random walk, introduce fake messages, or combine both strategies. These approaches present several downsides that include increased delivery delay, increased energy consumption, increased packet collisions, and so on. Moreover, the more powerful the adversary, the higher the overhead required to effectively counter him. As a result, location privacy solutions are generally too costly for hardware-constrained sensor networks, which are intended to provide real-time sensing capabilities with little or no maintenance on behalf of the network administrator.

Therefore, it is absolutely necessary to explore new mechanisms for deceiving the adversary. These mechanisms should avoid the use of fake traffic in favor of energy-efficient mechanisms. For example, an existing approach is to take advantage of already existing control traffic to convey data messages (i.e., cross-layer routing protocol) but it is also possible to take advantage of different mechanisms to hide the existence of transmissions from the adversary such as random frequency hopping. Also, the context-aware capabilities of the nodes can bring tremendous benefits to location privacy as the information collected by the sensors can be used by nodes to make informed decisions and decide on the most suitable protection mechanism at each particular moment. This information can also be used to determine when to activate or deactivate the protection mechanism depending on whether there is a threat to the network, thus reducing unnecessary costs to the network. Clearly, there is still room for original research to produce cost-effective location privacy solutions.

6.2.2 Complete Privacy Solutions

There is a large number of solutions in the literature but most of them concentrate on a single problem rather than tackling the privacy problem in a holistic way. These solutions either concentrate on protecting data sources or the base station but not both of them simultaneously even though the proposed techniques are similar and mostly depend on the hearing range of the adversary. The typical approach for countering local adversaries is to randomize the routing paths, but when the hearing range of the adversary grows, it is usually necessary to resort to the injection of fake traffic.

There are some subtleties that make solutions for source privacy ineffective for protecting receiver privacy and vice versa. This is particularly true when the adversary is a global eavesdropper. Data sources are concealed by making their transmissions independent of the presence of events, thus fake traffic is injected by nodes at regular intervals although they have no data to report to the base station. Conversely, to protect receiver-location privacy there must be areas in the network receiving at least the same amount of traffic as the base station. Although different, both problems can be resolved by a naive solution that consists of using a baseline flooding in conjunction with fake data sources. Again, the main drawback to this solution is its overhead. How to solve this problem in a cost-effective way demands further attention from the research community.

Although the focus here has been source- and receiver-location privacy in the presence of passive adversaries, for privacy solutions to be complete they should also consider other sorts of adversaries such as active adversaries capable of controlling a subset of nodes in the network. Also, it is important to consider not only the data transmission phase but the operation of the network as a whole. In fact, the topology discovery protocol, which is executed periodically to allow sensor nodes to detect topology changes in their vicinity caused by node mobility, node battery depletion or the presence of interferences disturbing the communication channel, leaks relevant information about the location of the base station to an observer. This process is always initiated by the base station and therefore can be easily spotted by a global adversary but even a local adversary can get a good idea as to the direction to the base station after several executions of the topology discovery protocol. As a result, an attacker can determine the location of the base station despite having a robust privacy-preserving data transmission protocol due to a leaking discovery protocol. In short, privacy preservation must be ensured against any type of attacker capable of obtaining sensitive information from different sources and throughout the operation of network.

6.2.3 Realistic Adversaries

The adversarial model considered in the literature is not formally defined and it is also quite unrealistic. The capabilities of the adversary and the actions he may be able to perform at all times must be consistent with the capabilities of a real attacker. The typical approach when defining the adversarial model is to establish a particular attack strategy, for example, a traceback attack, which remains unaltered for the duration of the attack. Instead of adapting the attack strategy to the current conditions of the scenario, in some papers the attacker sticks to the strategy even if he reaches a dead end point. At least, the adversary should be able to realize when he has been deceived by the protection mechanism and start over again. Therefore, it is necessary to formally define the capabilities of the adversary as well as the actions he may be able to perform at all times.

More realistic adversaries should also be able to reason about the current status of the network and infer new information from previous situations. They should also be able to access or use external sources of information. In general, research papers consider that the adversary has no prior knowledge about the network, the deployment area, or the elements being monitored. However, the adversary may have access to external information that he may use to defeat the privacy mechanism. For example, in an endangered animal monitoring scenario, the attacker may be aware of the habits and typical behavior of these particular animals. Also, the adversary may know the area where the sensor network is deployed and therefore he can be certain that it is impossible that a particular type of animal is present in certain areas at all or maybe not at that particular time of the day. Similarly, the attacker may be capable of determining which is the best location for the base station based on different circumstances such as the orography of the sensor field and the nature of the phenomenon being monitored. In general, an appropriate model for representing the knowledge of the adversary does not exist.

It is important to realize that the adversary will do anything in his power to achieve his goal. The attacker model considered in the literature is mostly passive and he limits his actions to observing the communications to derive location information. However, a determined adversary not only performs passive attacks but also interferes with the normal behavior of the network by injecting, blocking, or replaying legitimate traffic, compromising nodes, or even destroying them if necessary. The assumption of a passive adversary is very strong especially when the network is deployed in remote locations where the network is unattended most of the time and the adversary has enough time to tamper with sensor nodes. Therefore, it is essential to devise solutions capable of dealing with more realistic and determined adversaries.

6.2.4 Interoperable Evaluation Framework

Once the adversary has been formally defined, the challenge is to develop a solid evaluation framework that allows the efficiency of solutions to be accurately assessed and compare them in similar circumstances. The research community has struggled to develop solutions for the location privacy problem but there is no means to faithfully evaluate the acquired level of protection. In fact, different metrics are used to quantify location privacy in WSNs (e.g., safety period, entropy, and k-anonymity) but they are not always appropriate when dealing with different adversarial models or interoperable with each other thus impeding a complete and comprehensive comparison of existing and future solutions.

Currently, most of the devised solutions are evaluated by means of simulations but some effort has also been made to quantify location privacy in WSNs numerically. However, providing a formal model that accurately represents the behavior of the network and the adversary is an extremely challenging task, especially when the adversary has prior knowledge and is capable of following different strategies depending on the current status of the system, as previously noted. This is particularly difficult when the adversary has a local hearing range as he only has information about a portion of the network at any given time and this information is no longer current or valid when moving to another location. Whether past information is still useful in the future is not clear as the system is highly dynamic and past communications may not be currently relevant. Therefore, although it might be possible to determine the level of uncertainty of the adversary in one step, tracking the information gain of the adversary as he moves remains unmanageable.

Simulations present another important drawback that is reproducibility. Typically, there is a lack of homogeneity when evaluating the correctness of solutions through simulations. Some authors have turned to general-purpose simulators by adding some particular modules to consider the underlying network protocols in sensor networks such as IEEE 802.15.4. However, other authors have decided to simplify the process and ignore the subtleties and problems posed by considering lower layers of the protocol stack and focus on evaluating their solution against a particular attacker model. As a result, many authors have developed their own ad hoc simulator that in most cases is not made publicly available to the research community in order to verify the validity of the results or to test against new solutions. Moreover, there is no uniformity in the simulator parameters used when evaluating different solutions. Some relevant parameters to be homogenized are the density of the network and the average connectivity of the nodes, the number of simultaneous data sources, the number of simulation steps, and so on. Taking these features into account is essential to insightful analysis and comparison of results.

6.2.5 *Future Sensor Networks*

Location privacy has traditionally been tackled in sensor networks comprising a large number of equal sensor nodes that follow an event-driven data reporting method and communicate with a single base station. This setting is useful for large-scale unattended sensor networks deployed in remote locations for monitoring purposes. However, this is only one of many potential scenarios where sensor networks fit in and location privacy is relevant in most of them. New scenarios include, for example, those where sensor nodes communicate not only with the base station but also with other sensor nodes, or network deployments where a subset of sensor nodes have different roles or capabilities, say there are nodes with no battery restrictions because they are connected to the power grid or they are fitted with a directional antenna, a satellite connection, or similar. These new scenarios and communication models must be explored as they may bring about new privacy issues as well as new ways of improving privacy.

The dynamism of these networks is also a factor to take into great consideration. So far, location privacy solutions have considered static networks only, where sensor nodes remain in the same position they are deployed throughout the lifetime of the network. However, considering mobile sensor nodes or a mobile base station may introduce interesting challenges and opportunities from the perspective of location privacy. Moreover, introducing mobility models to sensor networks is consistent with the scenarios envisioned by the Internet of Things, where tiny computers with sensing capabilities are attached to everyday objects and people. This will result in one of the most promising areas for research and innovation as mobility will undoubtedly introduce new problems and attacker models. The interaction with possibly corrupted data relays will be increasingly common and there will be intermittent network connectivity problems, among many other. In short, there are countless variations of the original setting that need to be explored in order to protect location privacy in current and future scenarios.

The aforementioned challenges are mostly related to location privacy but there are several other privacy issues that may affect individuals and businesses if not taken into serious consideration when deploying sensor networks. Some of these challenges have already been described in Chapter 1, and they are also related to the exploitation of other types of metadata such as the time at which events are reported to the base station, the duration of transmissions, or the volume of traffic and the size of the packets being transmitted.

As sensor networks become an integral part of the Internet, query privacy will be increasingly important. Companies can offer sensor networks to consumers as a service. Service providers may deploy networks and allow clients to query data from them. Since sensor networks are no longer owned and used by the same entity some query privacy issues arise. The service provider may behave as an honest but curious adversary and try to learn the interests of its clients from the queries they issue or from the nodes that reply to the queries. At the same time the user may be willing to use the sensing platform but be reluctant to give away sensitive information.

Moreover, it will be necessary to establish limits to data collection and data sharing. Data collection will rise to exorbitant limits due to the integration of all sorts of sensors into all kinds of systems and places, even in the intimacy of our homes. Not only will temperature, humidity, and presence sensors be attached to tiny computers but also multimedia sensors such as microphones and videocameras. Sensor nodes will become a tool for an unprecedented large-scale surveillance network. Therefore, it is necessary to make legal and regulatory efforts to severely punish those entities misusing sensitive personal information. Another fundamental challenge here is the process of informing the user that he or she might be subject to data collection and asking for consent. Traditional computing devices have interfaces that allow the user to read and accept or decline privacy policies but sensor nodes do not have suitable interfaces for this purpose. It is important to avoid overwhelming the user with informed consent requests. In this respect, it might be useful to develop mechanisms to define privacy preferences in a simple way and to automatically negotiate with nearby devices whether the user is satisfied or not with the collection, processing, and dissemination of data about himself.

Limiting the access to the data collected by sensor nodes is also necessary as these data may be sensitive. The level of granularity of data being released by sensor nodes should depend on the entity requesting the data. This entails that the level of detail provided by a sensor upon a client request depends on its credentials and may range from providing no information at all to giving away raw data collected by the sensor. For example, a sensor node attached to a car may remain silent, declare being in a country, a particular city, or provide its exact GPS coordinates depending on who is requesting this information. This is important because once data have been released privacy cannot be recovered. Therefore, data must be processed before leaving the sphere of control of the node.

There is also room for innovation in the context of data-aggregation privacy and other similar secure multi-party computation performed by sensor nodes as they might want to combine or elaborate information based on the shares of possibly compromised sensor nodes. As sensor nodes are deployed in everyday contexts, they become more easily reachable by attackers especially when they are surrounded by devices that are unattended to and do not incorporate security modules and mechanism to hinder and alert to possible intrusions and tampering. In general, dealing with internal attackers will become a very interesting area of research.

A final and equally relevant point is raising user awareness on the problems derived from the deployment of sensing technologies in everyday objects. People need to react to the abuses of data-hungry businesses and organizations. This is extremely important since legislation is usually a response to the concerns of society and without reactive people legislation is bound to fall even further behind thus giving rise to an unprecedented privacy loss.

References

1. U. Acharya and M. Younis. Increasing base-station anonymity in wireless sensor networks. *Ad Hoc Networks*, 8(8):791–809, 2010.
2. I.F. Akyildiz, W. Su, Y. Sankarasubramaniam, and E. Cayirci. A survey on sensor networks. *IEEE Communications Magazine*, 40(8):102–114, 2002.
3. J.N. Al-Karaki and A.E. Kamal. Routing techniques in wireless sensor networks: A survey. *IEEE Wireless Communications*, 11(6):6–28, December 2004.
4. A.F. Westin. *Privacy and Freedom*, 1st edn. Atheneum, New York, 1967.
5. A. Alarifi and W. Du. Diversify sensor nodes to improve resilience against node compromise. In *Proceedings of the Fourth ACM workshop on Security of Ad Hoc and Sensor Networks, SASN'06*, New York, 2006. ACM, New York, pp. 101–112.
6. B. Alomair, A. Clark, J. Cuellar, and R. Poovendran. Statistical framework for source anonymity in sensor networks. In *IEEE Global Telecommunications Conference, GLOBECOM 2010*, Miami, FL, December 2010, pp. 1–6.
7. B. Alomair, A. Clark, J. Cuellar, and R. Poovendran. Towards a statistical framework for source anonymity in sensor networks. *IEEE Transactions on Mobile Computing*, 12(2):248–260, 2012.
8. N.A. Alrajeh, S. Khan, and B. Shams. Intrusion detection systems in wireless sensor networks: A review. *International Journal of Distributed Sensor Networks*, 2013(167575): 7, 2013, http://www.atmel.com/Images/2467s.pdf (accessed June 2016).
9. Anonymizer, Inc. Hide IP and anonymous web browsing software. May 2011, https://www.anonymizer.com/ (accessed June 2016).
10. C.A. Ardagna, M. Cremonini, S. De Capitani di Vimercati, and P. Samarati. An obfuscation-based approach for protecting location privacy. *IEEE Transactions on Dependable and Secure Computing*, 8(1):13–27, January 2011.
11. C.A. Ardagna, S. Jajodia, P. Samarati, and A. Stavrou. Providing users' anonymity in mobile hybrid networks. *ACM Transactions on Internet Technology*, 12(3):7:1–7:33, 2013.
12. Arduino. Lilypad arduino. Online. November 2014. https://www.arduino.cc/en/Main/ArduinoBoardLilyPad (accessed June 2016).
13. Atmel. ATmega128, ATmega128L datasheet. Online. Revised June 2011.
14. K. Bennett and C. Grothoff. GAP—Practical anonymous networking. In R. Dingledine, ed., *PET 2003*, vol. 2760 of Lecture Notes in Computer Science, pp. 141–160. Springer-Verlag, Dresden, Germany, March 26–28, 2003.

15. K. Bennett, C. Grothoff, T. Horozov, and J.T. Lindgren. An encoding for censorship-resistant sharing. 2003, https://gnunet.org/sites/default/files/ecrs.pdf (accessed June 2016).

16. A.R. Beresford and F. Stajano. Location privacy in pervasive computing. *IEEE Pervasive Computing*, 2(1):46–55, January 2003.

17. S. Biswas, S. Mukherjee, and K. Mukhopadhyaya. A countermeasure against traffic-analysis based base station detection in WSN. In *International Conference on High Performance Computing (HiPC 2007)*. Poster. http://hipc.org/hipc2007/posters/WSN.pdf (accessed June 2016).

18. A. Broder and M. Mitzenmacher. Network applications of bloom filters: A survey. *Internet Mathematics*, 1(4):485–509, 2004.

19. L. Buttyan, D. Gessner, A. Hessler, and P. Langendoerfer. Application of wireless sensor networks in critical infrastructure protection: Challenges and design options. *IEEE Wireless Communications*, 17(5):44–49, 2010.

20. J. Camenisch. Information privacy?! *Computer Networks*, 56:3834–3848, 2012.

21. R. Campbell, J. Al-Muhtadi, P. Naldurg, G. Sampemane, and M. Mickunas. Towards security and privacy for pervasive computing. In M. Okada, B.C. Pierce, A. Scedrov, H. Tokuda, and A. Yonezawa, eds., *Software Security Theories and Systems*, vol. 2609 of Lecture Notes in Computer Science, pp. 1–15. Springer, Berlin, Germany, 2003.

22. B. Carbunar, Y. Yu, W. Shi, M. Pearce, and V. Vasudevan. Query privacy in wireless sensor networks. *ACM Transactions on Sensor and Networks*, 6(2):14:1–14:34, March 2010.

23. C. Castelluccia, A.C.-F. Chan, E. Mykletun, and G. Tsudik. Efficient and provably secure aggregation of encrypted data in wireless sensor networks. *ACM Transactions on Sensor and Networks*, 5(3):20:1–20:36, June 2009.

24. M. Ceriotti, L. Mottola, G. Pietro Picco, A.L. Murphy, S. Guna, M. Corra, M. Pozzi, D. Zonta, and P. Zanon. Monitoring heritage buildings with wireless sensor networks: The Torre Aquila deployment. In *Proceedings of the 2009 International Conference on Information Processing in Sensor Networks, IPSN'09*, Washington, DC, 2009. IEEE Computer Society, Washington, DC, pp. 277–288.

25. G. Chai, M. Xu, W. Xu, and Z. Lin. Enhancing sink-location privacy in wireless sensor networks through *k*-anonymity. *International Journal of Distributed Sensor Networks*, 2012:16, 2012.

26. S. Chang, Y. Qi, H. Zhu, M. Dong, and K. Ota. Maelstrom: Receiver-location preserving in wireless sensor networks. In Y. Cheng, D.Y. Eun, Z. Qin, M. Song, and K. Xing, eds., *Wireless Algorithms, Systems, and Applications*, vol. 6843 of Lecture Notes in Computer Science, pp. 190–201. Springer, Berlin, Germany 2011.

27. D. Chaum. Untraceable electronic mail, return addresses, and digital pseudonyms. *Communications of the ACM*, 24(2):84–88, February 1981.

28. D. Chaum. The dining cryptographers problem: Unconditional sender and recipient untraceability. *Journal of Cryptology*, 1:65–75, 1988.

29. O. Cheikhrouhou, A. Koubaa, M. Boujelben, and M. Abid. A lightweight user authentication scheme for wireless sensor networks. In *Proceedings of the ACS/IEEE International Conference on Computer Systems and Applications*, Hammamet, Tunisia, May 16–19, 2010. IEEE Computer Society, Washington, DC, pp. 1–7.

30. H. Chen and W. Lou. From nowhere to somewhere: Protecting end-to-end location privacy in wireless sensor networks. In *29th International Performance Computing and Communications Conference, IPCCC'10*, Albuquerque, NM, 2010. IEEE, pp. 1–8.

31. J. Chen, X. Du, and B. Fang. An efficient anonymous communication protocol for wireless sensor networks. *Wireless Communications and Mobile Computing*, 12(14):1302–1312, October 2012.

32. J. Chen, H. Zhang, B. Fang, X. Du, L. Yin, and X. Yu. Towards efficient anonymous communications in sensor networks. In *IEEE Global Telecommunications Conference, GLOBECOM*, Houston, TX, 2011, pp. 1–5.

33. X. Chen, K. Makki, K. Yen, and N. Pissinou. Node compromise modeling and its applications in sensor networks. In *12th IEEE Symposium on Computers and Communications (ISCC 2007)*, July 2007, pp. 575–582.

34. O. Chipara, C. Lu, T.C. Bailey, and G.-C. Roman. Reliable clinical monitoring using wireless sensor networks: Experiences in a step-down hospital unit. In *Proceedings of the Eighth ACM Conference on Embedded Networked Sensor Systems, SenSys'10*, New York, 2010. ACM, New York, pp. 155–168.

35. C.-Y. Chow, M.F. Mokbel, and T. He. A privacy-preserving location monitoring system for wireless sensor networks. *IEEE Transactions on Mobile Computing*, 10(1):94–107, January 2011.

36. W. Conner, T. Abdelzaher, and K. Nahrstedt. Using data aggregation to prevent traffic analysis in wireless sensor networks. In *Distributed Computing in Sensor Systems*, vol. 4026 of Lecture Notes in Computer Science, pp. 202–217. Springer, Berlin, Germany, 2006.

37. Crossbow Technology, Inc. MICA2DOT—Wireless microsensor mote (datasheet). http://www.datasheetarchive.com/dl/Datasheet-026/DSA00462856.pdf (accessed June 2016).

38. J. Cuéllar, M. Ochoa, and R. Rios. Indistinguishable regions in geographic privacy. In *Proceedings of the 2012 ACM Symposium on Applied Computing (SAC'12)*, Riva del Garda (Trento), Italy, March 2012. ACM, Trento, Italy, pp. 1463–1469.

39. E. De Cristofaro, X. Ding, and G. Tsudik. Privacy-preserving querying in sensor networks. In *18th International Conference on Computer Communications and Networks, ICCCN'09*, San Francisco, CA, August 3–6, 2009. IEEE Computer Society, Washington, DC, pp. 1–6.

40. J. Deng, R. Han, and S. Mishra. Decorrelating wireless sensor network traffic to inhibit traffic analysis attacks. *Pervasive and Mobile Computing*, 2(2):159–186, 2006.

41. J. Deng, R. Han, and S. Mishra. Enhancing base station security in wireless sensor networks. Technical Report CU-CS-951-03. University of Colorado, Boulder, CO, 2003.

42. J. Deng, R. Han, and S. Mishra. Countermeasures against traffic analysis attacks in wireless sensor networks. In *International Conference on Security and Privacy for Emerging Areas in Communications Networks, SECURECOMM*, Washington, DC, 2005. IEEE Computer Society, Washington, DC, pp. 113–126.

43. R. Di Pietro, L.V. Mancini, C. Soriente, A. Spognardi, and G. Tsudik. Data security in unattended wireless sensor networks. *IEEE Transactions on Computers*, 58(11):1500–1511, November 2009.

44. R. Di Pietro and A. Viejo. Location privacy and resilience in wireless sensor networks querying. *Computer Communication*, 34(3):515–523, March 2011.

45. T. Dimitriou and A. Sabouri. Privacy preservation schemes for querying wireless sensor networks. In *IEEE International Conference on Pervasive Computing and Communications Workshops*, Seattle, WA, 2011, pp. 178–183.

46. R. Dingledine, N. Mathewson, and P. Syverson. Tor: The second-generation onion router. In *13th Conference on USENIX Security Symposium, SSYM'04*, San Diego, CA, August 9–13, 2004. USENIX Association, Berkeley, CA, pp. 21–21.

47. A. Dunkels, B. Gronvall, and T. Voigt. Contiki—A lightweight and flexible operating system for tiny networked sensors. In *29th Annual IEEE International Conference on Local Computer Networks*, November 2004, pp. 455–462.

48. A. Eiben and J. Smith. *Introduction to Evolutionary Computing*, 2nd edn. Natural Computing. Springer, New York, 2007.

49. A. El Kouche, L. Al-Awami, H. Hassanein, and K. Obaia. WSN application in the harsh industrial environment of the oil sands. In *Seventh International Wireless Communications and Mobile Computing Conference (IWCMC)*, Istanbul, Turkey, 2011, pp. 613–618.

50. H. Farhangi. The path of the smart grid. *IEEE Power and Energy Magazine*, 8(1):18–28, January–February 2010.

51. E. Fasolo, M. Rossi, J. Widmer, and M. Zorzi. In-network aggregation techniques for wireless sensor networks: A survey. *IEEE Wireless Communications*, 14(2):70–87, April 2007.

52. E. Felemban. Advanced border intrusion detection and surveillance using wireless sensor network technology. *International Journal of Communications, Network and System Sciences*, 6(5):251–259, 2013.

53. S. Goel, M. Robson, M. Polte, and E.G. Sirer. Herbivore: A scalable and efficient protocol for anonymous communication. Technical Report 2003-1890. Cornell University, Ithaca, NY, February 2003.

54. C. Gómez, J. Paradells, and J.E. Caballero. *Sensors Everywhere: Wireless Network Technologies and Solutions*. Fundación Vodafone España, Barcelona, Spain, 2010.

55. M. Gruteser, G. Schelle, A. Jain, R. Han, and D. Grunwald. Privacy-aware location sensor networks. In *Proceedings of the Ninth conference on Hot Topics in Operating Systems, HOTOS'03*, Berkeley, CA, 2003. USENIX Association, Berkeley, CA, p. 28.

56. K. Hayawi, A. Mortezaei, and M.V. Tripunitara. The limits of the trade-off between query-anonymity and communication-cost in wireless sensor networks. In *Proceedings of the Fifth ACM Conference on Data and Application Security and Privacy, CODASPY'15*, New York, 2015. ACM, New York, pp. 337–348.

57. T. He, S. Krishnamurthy, L. Luo, T. Yan, L. Gu, R. Stoleru, G. Zhou et al. VigilNet: An integrated sensor network system for energy efficient surveillance. *ACM Transactions on Sensor Networks*, 2(1):1–38, February 2006.

58. W. He, X. Liu, H. Nguyen, K. Nahrstedt, and T.T. Abdelzaher. PDA: Privacy-preserving data aggregation in wireless sensor networks. In *26th IEEE International Conference on Computer Communications*, Anchorage, Alaska, May 2007, pp. 2045–2053.

59. J. Holvast. History of privacy. In V. Matyás, S. Fischer-Hübner, D. Cvrcek, and P. Svenda, eds., *The Future of Identity in the Information Society*, vol. 298 of IFIP Advances in Information and Communication Technology, pp. 13–42. Springer, Berlin, Germany, 2009.

60. J. Horey, M.M. Groat, S. Forrest, and F. Esponda. Anonymous data collection in sensor networks. In *Proceedings of the 2007 Fourth Annual International Conference on Mobile and Ubiquitous Systems: Networking and Services (MobiQuitous)*, Philadelphia, PA, August 6–10, 2007. IEEE Computer Society, Washington, DC, pp. 1–8.

61. IEEE Smart Grid. Smart grid conceptual model. Online. September 2013, http://smartgrid.ieee.org/ieee-smart-grid/smart-grid-conceptual-model (accessed January 2016).

62. A. Jhumka, M. Leeke, and S. Shrestha. On the use of fake sources for source location privacy: Trade-offs between energy and privacy. *The Computer Journal*, 54(6):860–874, 2011.

63. Y. Jian, S. Chen, Z. Zhang, and L. Zhang. Protecting receiver-location privacy in wireless sensor networks. In *26th IEEE International Conference on Computer Communications, INFOCOM*, Anchorage, Alaska, May 2007, pp. 1955–1963.

64. Y. Jian, S. Chen, Z. Zhang, and L. Zhang. A novel scheme for protecting receiver's location privacy in wireless sensor networks. *IEEE Transactions on Wireless Communications*, 7(10):3769–3779, October 2008.

65. J.-R. Jiang, J.-P. Sheu, C. Tu, and J.-W. Wu. An anonymous path routing (APR) protocol for wireless sensor networks. *Journal of Information Science and Engineering*, 27(2):657–680, 2011.

66. P. Kamat, Y. Zhang, W. Trappe, and C. Ozturk. Enhancing source-location privacy in sensor network routing. In *25th IEEE International Conference on Distributed Computing Systems, ICDCS 2005*, Columbus, OH, June 2005, pp. 599–608.

67. P. Kamat, W. Xu, W. Trappe, and Y. Zhang. Temporal privacy in wireless sensor networks. In *27th International Conference on Distributed Computing Systems, ICDCS'07*, Washington, DC, 2007. IEEE Computer Society, Washington, DC, p. 23.

68. B. Karp and H.T. Kung. GPSR: Greedy perimeter stateless routing for wireless networks. In *Proceedings of the Sixth Annual International Conference on Mobile Computing and Networking*, Boston, MA, August 6–11, 2000. ACM, New York, pp. 243–254.

69. L. Kazatzopoulos, C. Delakouridis, G.F. Marias, and P. Georgiadis. iHIDE: Hiding sources of information in WSNS. In *International Workshop on Security, Privacy and Trust in Pervasive and Ubiquitous Computing, SecPerU'06*, Los Alamitos, CA, 2006. IEEE Computer Society, Los Alamitos, CA, pp. 41–48.

70. L. Kazatzopoulos, K. Delakouridis, and G.F. Marias. A privacy-aware overlay routing scheme in WSNS. *Security and Communication Networks*, 4(7):729–743, July 2011.

71. S. Kim, S. Pakzad, D. Culler, J. Demmel, G. Fenves, S. Glaser, and M. Turon. Health monitoring of civil infrastructures using wireless sensor networks. In *Proceedings of the Sixth International Conference on Information Processing in Sensor Networks, IPSN'07*, New York, 2007. ACM, New York, pp. 254–263.

72. K.H. Kwong, T.-T. Wu, H.G. Goh, K. Sasloglou, B. Stephen, I. Glover, C. Shen, W. Du, C. Michie, and I. Andonovic. Practical considerations for wireless sensor networks in cattle monitoring applications. *Computers and Electronics in Agriculture*, 81(0):33–44, 2012.

73. M. Langheinrich. A privacy awareness system for ubiquitous computing environments. In G. Borriello and L. Holmquist, eds., *UbiComp 2002: Ubiquitous Computing*, vol. 2498 of Lecture Notes in Computer Science, pp. 237–245. Springer, Berlin, Germany, 2002.

74. R. Latif and M. Hussain. Hardware-based random number generation in wireless sensor networks. In *Advances in Information Security and Assurance*, vol. 5576 of Lecture Notes in Computer Science, pp. 732–740. Springer, Berlin, Germany, 2009.

75. L. Lazos, R. Poovendran, and J.A. Ritcey. Analytic evaluation of target detection in heterogeneous wireless sensor networks. *ACM Transactions on Sensor Network*, 5(2):1–38, April 2009.

76. B.N. Levine and C. Shields. Hordes: A multicast based protocol for anonymity. *Journal of Computer Security*, 10(3):213–240, 2002.

77. P. Levis, S. Madden, J. Polastre, R. Szewczyk, K. Whitehouse, A. Woo, D. Gay et al. TinyOS: An operating system for sensor networks. In W. Weber, J.M. Rabaey, and E. Aarts, eds., *Ambient Intelligence*, pp. 115–148. Springer, Berlin, Germany, 2005.

78. Y. Li, L. Lightfoot, and J. Ren. Routing-based source-location privacy protection in wireless sensor networks. In *IEEE International Conference on Electro/Information Technology, EIT'09*, Windsor, Ontario, Canada, 2009, pp. 29–34.

79. Y. Li and J. Ren. Preserving source-location privacy in wireless sensor networks. In *Sixth Annual IEEE Communications Society Conference on Sensor, Mesh and Ad Hoc Communications and Networks, SECON'09*, Piscataway, NJ, 2009. IEEE Press, Piscataway, NJ, pp. 493–501.

80. Y. Li and J. Ren. Providing source-location privacy in wireless sensor networks. In *Fourth International Conference on Wireless Algorithms, Systems, and Applications, WASA'09*, Berlin, Germany, 2009. Springer-Verlag, Berlin, Germany, pp. 338–347.

81. Y. Li, J. Ren, and J. Wu. Quantitative measurement and design of source-location privacy schemes for wireless sensor networks. *IEEE Transactions on Parallel and Distributed Systems*, 23:1302–1311, July 2012.

82. Libelium. Libelium adds extreme range wireless connectivity to waspmote iot sensors. http://www.libelium.com/extreme-range-wireless-sensors-connectivity-through buildings-in-city-lora-868mhz-915mhz/, November 2014.

83. L. Lightfoot, Y. Li, and J. Ren. Preserving source-location privacy in wireless sensor network using STaR routing. In *IEEE Global Telecommunications Conference, GLOBECOM 2010*, Miami, FL, 2010, pp. 1–5.

84. L. Lightfoot, Y. Li, and J. Ren. STaR: Design and quantitative measurement of source-location privacy for wireless sensor networks. *Security and Communication Networks*, 9(3):220–228, March 2012.

85. B. Liu, O. Dousse, J. Wang, and A. Saipulla. Strong barrier coverage of wireless sensor networks. In *Proceedings of the Ninth ACM International Symposium on Mobile Ad Hoc Networking and Computing*, Hong Kong, People's Republic of China, May 27–30, 2008. ACM, New York, pp. 411–420.

86. G. Liu, R. Tan, R. Zhou, G. Xing, W.-Z. Song, and J.M. Lees. Volcanic earthquake timing using wireless sensor networks. In *Proceedings of the 12th International Conference on Information Processing in Sensor Networks, IPSN'13*, New York, 2013. ACM, New York, pp. 91–102.

87. G. Lo Re, F. Milazzo, and M. Ortolani. Secure random number generation in wireless sensor networks. In *Proceedings of the Fourth International Conference on Security of Information and Networks, SIN'11*, New York, 2011. ACM, New York, pp. 175–182.

88. J. Lopez, R. Roman, I. Agudo, and C. Fernandez-Gago. Trust management systems for wireless sensor networks: Best practices. *Computer Communications*, 33(9):140–3664, 2010.

89. B. Lynn, M. Prabhakaran, and A. Sahai. Positive results and techniques for obfuscation. In C. Cachin and J.L. Camenisch, eds., *Advances in Cryptology—EUROCRYPT 2004*, vol. 3027 of Lecture Notes in Computer Science. Springer, Berlin, Germany, 2004, pp. 20–39.

90. M. Mafuta, M. Zennaro, A. Bagula, G. Ault, H. Gombachika, and T. Chadza. Successful deployment of a wireless sensor network for precision agriculture in Malawi. *International Journal of Distributed Sensor Networks*, 2013(150703):13, 2013.

91. M. Mahmoud and X. Shen. A cloud-based scheme for protecting source-location privacy against hotspot-locating attack in wireless sensor networks. *IEEE Transactions on Parallel and Distributed Systems*, 23(10):1805–1818, 2012.

92. M.E. Mahmoud and X. Shen. Secure and efficient source location privacy-preserving scheme for wireless sensor networks. In *Proceedings of the IEEE International Conference on Communications, ICC'12*, Ottawa, Ontario, Canada, June 10–15, 2012. IEEE Communications Society, Ottawa, Ontario, Canada, pp. 1123–1127.

93. A. Mainwaring, D. Culler, J. Polastre, R. Szewczyk, and J. Anderson. Wireless sensor networks for habitat monitoring. In *Proceedings of the First ACM International Workshop on Wireless Sensor Networks and Applications, WSNA'02*, New York, 2002. ACM, New York, pp. 88–97.

94. G. Mao, B. Fidan, and B.D.O. Anderson. Wireless sensor network localization techniques. *Computer Networks*, 51(10):2529–2553, 2007.

95. K. Martinez and J.K. Hart. Glacier monitoring: Deploying custom hardware in harsh environments. In E. Gaura, M. Allen, L. Girod, J. Brusey, and G. Challen, eds., *Wireless Sensor Networks*, pp. 245–258. Springer, New York, 2010.

96. E. McCallister, T. Grance, and K. Scarfone. *Guide to Protecting the Confidentiality of Personally Identifiable Information (PII)*. Special publication 800-122. National Institute of Standards and Technology (NIST), Gaithersburg, MD, 2010.

97. K. Mehta, D. Liu, and M. Wright. Location privacy in sensor networks against a global eavesdropper. In *IEEE International Conference on Network Protocols, ICNP 2007*, Beijing, People's Republic of China, October 16–19, 2007. IEEE, Piscataway, NJ, pp. 314–323.

98. K. Mehta, D. Liu, and M. Wright. Protecting location privacy in sensor networks against a global eavesdropper. *IEEE Transactions on Mobile Computing*, 11(2):320–336, 2012.

99. MEMSIC. TelosB platform. Online. http://www.memsic.com/wireless-sensor-networks/TPR2420. November 2014.

100. S. Misra and G. Xue. Efficient anonymity schemes for clustered wireless sensor networks. *International Journal of Sensor Networks*, 1(1):50–63, 2006.

101. A.A. Nezhad, D. Makrakis, and A. Miri. Anonymous topology discovery for multihop wireless sensor networks. In *Third ACM Workshop on QoS and Security for Wireless and Mobile Networks, Q2SWinet'07*, New York, 2007. ACM, New York, pp. 78–85.

102. A.A. Nezhad, A. Miri, and D. Makrakis. Location privacy and anonymity preserving routing for wireless sensor networks. *Computer Networks*, 52(18):3433–3452, December 2008.

103. D. Niculescu and B. Nath. Trajectory based forwarding and its applications. In *Proceedings of the Ninth Annual International Conference on Mobile Computing and Networking*, San Diego, CA, September 14–19, 2003. ACM, New York, pp. 260–272.

104. Oracle Labs. Sun spot world. Online, November 2014. http://www.sunspotworld.com/.

105. S. Ortolani, M. Conti, B. Crispo, and R. Di Pietro. Events privacy in WSNs: A new model and its applications. In *IEEE International Symposium on a World of Wireless, Mobile and Multimedia Networks (WoWMoM)*, Lucca, Italy, June 2011, pp. 1–9.

106. Y. Ouyang, Z. Le, G. Chen, J. Ford, and F. Makedon. Entrapping adversaries for source protection in sensor networks. In *2006 International Symposium on World of Wireless, Mobile and Multimedia Networks, WOWMOM'06*, Washington, DC, 2006. IEEE Computer Society, Los Alamitos, CA, pp. 23–34.

107. Y. Ouyang, Z. Le, Y. Xu, N. Triandopoulos, S. Zhang, J. Ford, and F. Makedon. Providing anonymity in wireless sensor networks. In *IEEE International Conference on Pervasive Services*, Istanbul, Turkey, July 2007, pp. 145–148.

108. C. Ozturk, Y. Zhang, and W. Trappe. Source-location privacy in energy-constrained sensor network routing. In *Second ACM Workshop on Security of Ad Hoc and Sensor Networks, SASN'04*, Washington, DC, 2004. ACM, New York, pp. 88–93.

109. S. Pai, S. Bermudez, S.B. Wicker, M. Meingast, T. Roosta, S. Sastry, and D.K. Mulligan. Transactional confidentiality in sensor networks. *IEEE Security and Privacy*, 6(4):28–35, July–August 2008.

110. A. Pfitzmann and M. Hansen. A terminology for talking about privacy by data minimization: Anonymity, unlinkability, undetectability, unobservability, pseudonymity, and identity management. August 2010. v0.34, http://dud.inf.tu-dresden.de/literatur/Anon_Terminology_v0.34.pdf (accessed June 2016).

111. K. Pongaliur and L. Xiao. Maintaining source privacy under eavesdropping and node compromise attacks. In *IEEE International Conference on Computer Communications, INFOCOM*, Shanghai, China, April 2011, pp. 1656–1664.

112. K. Pongaliur and L. Xiao. Sensor node source privacy and packet recovery under eavesdropping and node compromise attacks. *ACM Transactions on Sensor Networks*, 9(4):50:1–50:26, July 2013.

113. A. Proano and L. Lazos. Hiding contextual information in WSNs. In *IEEE International Symposium on a World of Wireless, Mobile and Multimedia Networks, WoWMoM*, San Francisco, CA, June 2012, pp. 1–6.

114. A. Proano and L. Lazos. Perfect contextual information privacy in WSNs under colluding eavesdroppers. In *Sixth ACM Conference on Security and Privacy in Wireless and Mobile Networks, WiSec'13*, Budapest, Hungary, April 17–19, 2013. ACM, New York.

115. J.-F. Raymond. Traffic analysis: Protocols, attacks, design issues, and open problems. In H. Federrath, ed., *Proceedings of Designing Privacy Enhancing Technologies: Workshop on Design Issues in Anonymity and Unobservability*, Lecture Notes in Computer Science 2009. Springer-Verlag, Berlin, Germany, July 2000, pp. 10–29.

116. M.G. Reed, P.F. Syverson, and D.M. Goldschlag. Anonymous connections and onion routing. *IEEE Journal on Selected Areas in Communications*, 16(4):482–494, May 1998.

117. M.K. Reiter and A.D. Rubin. Crowds: Anonymity for web transactions. *ACM Transactions on Information and System Security*, 1(1):66–92, 1998.

118. J. Ren, Y. Li, and T. Li. Routing-based source-location privacy in wireless sensor networks. In *IEEE International Conference on Communications, ICC'09*, Piscataway, NJ, 2009. IEEE Press, New York, pp. 620–624.

119. R. Roman. Application-driven security in wireless sensor networks. PhD thesis, University of Malaga, Málaga, Spain, 2008.

120. P. Samarati. Protecting respondents' identities in microdata release. *IEEE Transactions on Knowledge and Data Engineering*, 13(6):1010–1027, November 2001.

121. R.A. Shaikh, H. Jameel, B.J. d'Auriol, S. Lee, Y.-J. Song, and H. Lee. Network level privacy for wireless sensor networks. In *Fourth International Conference on Information Assurance and Security, ISIAS'08*, Napoli, Italy, September 2008, pp. 261–266.

122. S. Shakkottai. Asymptotics of query strategies over a sensor network. In *23rd Annual Joint Conference of the IEEE Computer and Communications Societies*, Hong Kong, China, vol. 1 of INFOCOM 2004, 2004, pp. 548–557.

123. E.M. Shakshuki, T.R. Sheltami, N. Kang, and X. Xing. Tracking anonymous sinks in wireless sensor networks. In *International Conference on Advanced Information Networking and Applications, AINA*, Bradford, U.K., May 2009. IEEE Computer Society, Los Alamitos, CA, pp. 510–516.

124. C.E. Shannon. Communication theory of secrecy systems. *Bell System Technical Journal*, 28:656–715, 1949.

125. M. Shao, W. Hu, S. Zhu, G. Cao, S. Krishnamurthy, and T. La Porta. Cross-layer enhanced source location privacy in sensor networks. In *IEEE Conference on Sensor, Mesh, and Ad Hoc Communications and Networks, SECON'09*, Rome, Italy, June 2009. IEEE Communications Society, pp. 1–9.

126. M. Shao, Y. Yang, S. Zhu, and G. Cao. Towards statistically strong source anonymity for sensor networks. In *27th IEEE Conference on Computer Communications, INFOCOM 2008*, Phoenix, AZ, April 2008, pp. 466–474.

127. M. Shao, S. Zhu, W. Zhang, G. Cao, and Y. Yang. pdcs: Security and privacy support for data-centric sensor networks. *IEEE Transactions on Mobile Computing*, 8(8):1023–1038, August 2009.

128. J.-P. Sheu, J.-R. Jiang, and C. Tu. Anonymous path routing in wireless sensor networks. In *IEEE International Conference on Communications, ICC'08*, Beijing, China, May 2008, pp. 2728–2734.

129. V. Shnayder, M. Hempstead, B. Chen, G.W. Allen, and M. Welsh. Simulating the power consumption of large-scale sensor network applications. In *Proceedings of the Second International Conference on Embedded Networked Sensor Systems, SenSys'04*, New York, 2004. ACM, New York, pp. 188–200.

130. R. Shokri, G. Theodorakopoulos, P. Papadimitratos, E. Kazemi, and J.-P. Hubaux. Hiding in the mobile crowd: Location privacy through collaboration. *IEEE Transactions on Dependable and Secure Computing*, 11(3):266–279, May 2014.

131. S. Spiekermann and L.F. Cranor. Engineering privacy. *IEEE Transactions on Software Engineering*, 35(1):67–82, January 2009.

132. Texas Instruments. Datasheet MSP430F15x, MSP430F16x, MSP430F161x mixed signal microcontroller (rev. G). Online, October 2002. Revised March 2011, http://www.ti.com/lit/ds/symlink/msp430f1611.pdf (accessed June 2016).

133. The Institute of Electrical and Electronics Engineers (IEEE). IEEE Standard for Information technology—Telecommunications and information exchange between systems—Local and metropolitan area networks—Specific requirements. Part 15.4: Wireless medium access control (MAC) and physical layer (PHY) specifications for low-rate wireless personal area networks (LR-WPANs), 2003, http://standards.ieee.org/getieee802/download/802.15.4-2003.pdf (accessed June 2016).

134. The MathWorks, Inc. MATLAB—The language of technical computing. Online. http://www.mathworks.com/products/matlab/ (accessed June 2016).

135. C. Tunca, S. Isik, M.Y. Donmez, and C. Ersoy. Distributed mobile sink routing for wireless sensor networks: A survey. *IEEE Communications Surveys Tutorials*, 16(2): 877–897, 2014.

136. B. Vaidya, M. Chen, and J.J.P.C. Rodrigues. Improved robust user authentication scheme for wireless sensor networks. In *IEEE Conference on Wireless Communication and Sensor Networks*, Allahabad, India, December 15–19, 2009. IEEE Xplore, Piscataway, NJ, pp. 1–6.

137. T.M. Vu, R. Safavi-Naini, and C. Williamson. Securing wireless sensor networks against large-scale node capture attacks. In *Proceedings of the Fifth ACM Symposium on Information, Computer and Communications Security, ASIACCS'10*, New York, 2010. ACM, New York, pp. 112–123.

138. J.P. Walters, Z. Liang, W. Shi, and V. Chaudhary. Wireless sensor network security: A survey. In Y. Xiao, ed., *Security in Distributed, Grid, and Pervasive Computing*. Auerbach Publications, Boca Raton, FL, 2007, pp. 367–409.

139. H. Wang, B. Sheng, and Q. Li. Privacy-aware routing in sensor networks. *Computer Networks*, 53(9):1512–1529, 2009.

140. H.-J. Wang and T.-R. Hsiang. Defending traffic analysis with communication cycles in wireless sensor networks. In *10th International Symposium on Pervasive Systems, Algorithms, and Networks, ISPAN,* Kaohsiung, Taiwan, 2009, pp. 166–171.

141. Y. Wang, G. Attebury, and B. Ramamurthy. A survey of security issues in wireless sensor networks. *IEEE Communications Surveys Tutorials,* 8(2):2–23, 2006.

142. S. Warren and L. Brandeis. The right to privacy. *Harvard Law Review,* IV(5), 198, December 1890.

143. W. Wei-Ping, C. Liang, and W. Jian-Xin. A source-location privacy protocol in WSN based on locational angle. In *IEEE International Conference on Communications, ICC'08,* Beijing, People's Republic of China, May 19–23, 2008. IEEE Communications Society, pp. 1630–1634.

144. M. Weiser. The computer for the 21st century. *Scientific American,* 265:94–104, 1991.

145. J. Wilson and N. Patwari. Radio tomographic imaging with wireless networks. *IEEE Transactions on Mobile Computing,* 9(5):621–632, May 2010.

146. A. Wood, J.A. Stankovic, G. Virone, L. Selavo, Z. He, Q. Cao, T. Doan, Y. Wu, L. Fang, and R. Stoleru. Context-aware wireless sensor networks for assisted living and residential monitoring. *IEEE Network,* 22(4):26–33, 2008.

147. Y. Xi, L. Schwiebert, and W. Shi. Preserving source location privacy in monitoring-based wireless sensor networks. In *20th International Parallel and Distributed Processing Symposium, IPDPS 2006,* Rhodes Island, Greece, April 2006, p. 8.

148. Y. Yang, M. Shao, S. Zhu, B. Urgaonkar, and G. Cao. Towards event source unobservability with minimum network traffic in sensor networks. In *First ACM Conference on Wireless Network Security, WiSec'08,* New York, 2008. ACM, New York, pp. 77–88.

149. Y. Yang, S. Zhu, G. Cao, and T. LaPorta. An active global attack model for sensor source location privacy: Analysis and countermeasures. In *Security and Privacy in Communication Networks,* vol. 19 of Lecture Notes of the Institute for Computer Sciences, Social Informatics and Telecommunications Engineering. Springer, Berlin, Germany, 2009, pp. 373–393.

150. J. Yao. Source-location privacy based on directed greedy walk in wireless sensor networks. In *Sixth International Conference on Wireless Communications Networking and Mobile Computing (WiCOM),* September 2010, pp. 1–4.

151. J. Yao and G. Wen. Preserving source-location privacy in energy-constrained wireless sensor networks. In *Proceedings of the 28th International Conference on Distributed Computing Systems Workshops, ICDCSW'08,* Washington, DC, 2008. IEEE Computer Society, Los Alamitos, CA, pp. 412–416.

152. L. Yao, L. Kang, F. Deng, J. Deng, and G. Wu. Protecting source–location privacy based on multirings in wireless sensor networks. *Concurrency and Computation: Practice and Experience,* 27(15):3863–3876, 2015.

153. L. Yao, L. Kang, P. Shang, and G. Wu. Protecting the sink location privacy in wireless sensor networks. *Personal and Ubiquitous Computing,* 17(5):883–893, 2013.

154. B. Ying, J.R. Gallardo, D. Makrakis, and H.T. Mouftah. Concealing of the sink location in WSNs by artificially homogenizing traffic intensity. In *The First International Workshop on Security in Computers, Networking and Communications* (*INFOCOM Workshops*), April 2011, pp. 988–993.

155. B. Ying, D. Makrakis, and H.T. Mouftah. A protocol for sink location privacy protection in wireless sensor networks. In *IEEE Global Telecommunications Conference, GLOBECOM*, Houston, TX, December 5–9, 2011. IEEE Communications Society, Piscataway, NJ, pp. 1–5.

156. D. Zhang, J. Ma, Q. Chen, and L.M. Ni. An RF-based system for tracking transceiver-free objects. In *Fifth Annual IEEE International Conference on Pervasive Computing and Communications*, White Plains, New York, March 19–23, 2007. IEEE Computer Society, Washington, DC, pp. 135–144.

157. J. Zhang and V. Varadharajan. Wireless sensor network key management survey and taxonomy. *Journal of Network and Computer Applications*, 33(2):63–75, 2010.

158. L. Zhang, H. Zhang, M. Conti, R. Di Pietro, S. Jajodia, and L.V. Mancini. Preserving privacy against external and internal threats in WSN data aggregation. *Telecommunication Systems*, 52(4):2163–2176, 2013.

159. W. Zhang, C. Wang, and T. Feng. GP2S: Generic privacy-preservation solutions for approximate aggregation of sensor datas. In *Sixth Annual IEEE International Conference on Pervasive Computing and Communications, PerCom'08*, Hong Kong, People's Republic of China, March 17–21, 2008. IEEE Computer Society, Washington, DC, pp. 179–184.

Index

A

Adversaries, WSN security
 internal *vs.* external attacks, 6
 mote class *vs.* laptop class adversaries, 6–7
 passive *vs.* active attacks, 6
Angle-based privacy solutions, 64–65
Anonymity networks, 25
Anonymous path routing (APR) protocol, 58
Attacker model, 125–126
Authenticated Diffie–Hellman key exchange, 38

B

Backbone flooding, 90–91
Baseline flooding, 60
Biased random walk protocol, 129
Bidirectional tree (BT) scheme, 71–72, 88
 DBT scheme, 72–73
 ZBT scheme, 72–73

C

CALP, *see* Context-aware location privacy
CEM, *see* Cyclic entrapment method
Centralized anonymous communications
 systems, 31
 black box devices, 48
 entry and exit points, 49
 local and internal adversaries, 48
 mixes
  computational overhead, 36–37, 49
  free-route selection, 49
  internal adversaries, 37, 49
  layered encryption, 38, 49
  limitations, 37
  message delays, 49
  mix cascade, 36

 network topology, global knowledge
  of, 36
 packets are padded (PAD), 36
 public-key decryption, 36, 49
 store-and-forward device, 35
 temporal storage and decryption, 35
 unlinkability, 35
 onion routing
  architecture and transmission process,
   38–39
  computational and memory demands, 39
  data transmission period, 39–40
  disadvantage, 40
  extra terminology, 40
  layered cryptography, 49
  link-key encrypted connection, 40
  low-latency anonymous communication
   system, 38
  onion, public-key layered data
   structure, 38
  path setup process, 39–40
  session keys, 49
  symmetric-key encryption, 38
  Tor, 38–40
 single-proxy solutions
  end-to-end encryption, 34
  ephemeral routes, 35
  internal adversaries, 35
  network nodes, 34–35
  operation, 34
  payload encryption, 49
  renaming process, 34
  source anonymity, 33
  trace-back attack, 49
  tracking and profiling, 33
Computer-based anonymous communications
  systems
  anonymity properties

177

location protection, data sources and base
station, 29
many-to-one communication model,
30, 51
message unlinkability, 30
pseudonyms, nodes' IDs, 29
relationship unlinkability, 30
sender anonymity, 29
source anonymity, 29–30
unobservability, 30
centralized schemes, 31
black box devices, 48
entry and exit points, 49
local and internal adversaries, 48
mix-based solution, 35–38
onion routing and Tor, 38–40
single-proxy solutions, 33–35
classification of solutions
centralized solutions, 31
decentralized solutions, 31
features, 31–32
high-latency solutions, 33
low-latency solutions, 33
communications setting, 26–27
cryptographic primitives, 26
decentralized schemes, 31
Crowds, 41–43
DC-nets and Herbivore, 45–48
GAP, 43–45
Hordes, 41–43
semitrusted network core elimination, 41
terminology
action, 28
anonymity, 27–28
privacy, 27
undetectability, 28
unlinkability, 28
unobservability, 28–29
traditional system suitability, 50
traffic analysis attacks, 26
Concealing sink location (CSL), 90
Context-aware location privacy (CALP)
advantage, 99
adversary detection, 103–104
attacker movements anticipation, 102
data forwarding process
network topology discovery protocol, 107
permissive data forwarding, 107–108
plug-in component, 107
routing protocol, 106–107
strict data forwarding, 107

internal adversaries, 122
mechanism, 156–157
network model, 100
route updating process, 105–106
shortest-path routing
data relays, 108
energy-efficient routing protocols,
108, 121
greedy forwarding decisions, 108–109
hardware-constrained devices, 112
initialization phase, 108
locally optimal neighbor selection,
108–109
path adaptation, 109–110
permissive CALP routing, 110–111
protocol evaluation, 112–121
routing table of node N, 112
strict minimum safety distance, 109, 111
topology discovery protocol, 108
software integration, 102–103
threat model, 101–102
undetectability, 121
Crowds
blender, 41
communications, 41
computational operations and memory
consumption, 42–43
dummy packet injection, 50
global adversaries, 50
internal adversaries, 43, 50
local adversaries, 43, 50
random node selections, 42
sender ID renaming, 42
symmetric-key packet reencryption, 42
time-correlation attacks, 43
Cryptographic pseudonyms
anonymous one-hop communication
scheme, 58
EAC protocol, 58
HIR scheme, 57–58
keyed hash function, 56–57
node revocation mechanism, 59
pseudo-random function, 56
RHIR, 58
secret key, 56
Cyclic entrapment method (CEM), 68–69

D

Data-centric sensor (DCS) networks, 82, 98
Data forwarding process

network topology discovery protocol, 107
permissive data forwarding, 107–108
plug-in component, 107
routing protocol, 106–107
strict data forwarding, 107
Decentralized anonymous communications
systems, 31
Crowds
blender, 41
communications, 41
computational operations and memory
consumption, 42–43
dummy packet injection, 50
global adversaries, 50
internal adversaries, 43, 50
local adversaries, 43, 50
random node selections, 42
sender ID renaming, 42
symmetric-key packet reencryption, 42
time-correlation attacks, 43
DC-nets and Herbivore, 50
computational overhead, 47–48
impediments, 46–47
memory requirements, 47
operation, 45–46
ring topology, 47
round, 46
senders and recipients unobservability, 46
slot reservation protocol, 47
source node collude, 48
XOR performance, 46
GAP, 50
anonymous file sharing, peer-to-peer
networks, 43
baseline fake traffic, 45
hardware-constrained nodes, 44
internal adversaries, 44
local and global adversaries, 45
message forwarding, 44
node operation, 43–44
overhead, 44–45
public keys, 44
queries and data traversing, 44
Hordes
computational operations and memory
consumption, 43
multicast messages, 42
public-key cryptography, 42
public keys and session keys storage, 43
signed list of members, 42
semitrusted network core elimination, 41

Decoy sink protocol, 95–96
Denial of service (DoS) attacks, 7, 9
Destination Controlled Anonymous Routing
Protocol for Sensornets (DCARPS),
55–56
Differential enforced fractal propagation
(DEFP), 89
Differential fractal propagation (DFP), 87
Dining cryptographers (DC)-nets, 50
computational overhead, 47–48
impediments, 46–47
memory requirements, 47
operation, 45–46
ring topology, 47
round, 46
senders and recipients unobservability, 46
slot reservation protocol, 47
source node collude, 48
XOR performance, 46
Directed random paths
Random Parallel routing scheme, 65–66
RRIN, 66–68
STaR protocol, 68
walking phase, guide mechanism
DROW, 64
PRLA, 64–65
WRS, 66
Directed random walk (DROW), 64
Dual cross-layer approach, 62–63
Dynamic bidirectional tree (DBT) scheme,
72–73

E

Efficient Anonymous Communication (EAC)
protocol, 58
Energy-aware approaches, global adversaries
bogus traffic filtering scheme, 77
cross-layer scheme, 75–76
dynamic programming algorithm, 79
greedy algorithm, 79
intermessage delays, 78
MCDS, 78–79
source simulation, 75, 80
statistically strong source unobservability,
77–78, 80
UHT, 76–77
Euclidean minimum-spanning tree (EMST), 93
Event-driven data reporting method, 161
Extremely constrained sensor nodes, 3

F

Fair information practices (FIPs), 11
Fake data sources
    baseline flooding protocol, 71
    BT scheme, 71–73
    persistent fake source, 71
    short-lived fake source, 71
FAKE_TTL parameter, 133
Fractal propagation (FP), 86–87, 89

G

GAP, *see* GNUnet Anonymity Protocol
Global adversaries
    Crowds, 50
    GAP, 45
    receiver-location privacy problem
        bogus traffic injection, 89
        relocation and disguise, 94–96
        sink simulation, 92–94
        traffic homogenization, 90–92
    sink simulation
        artificial hotspots creation, 93–94
        Chai et al.'s approach, 92–93
        Mehta et al.'s approach, 92–93
    source-location privacy problem
        dummy traffic injection, 74–75
        energy-aware approaches, 75–80
        topological, functional, or hardware
            constraints, 73
GNUnet Anonymity Protocol (GAP), 50
    anonymous file sharing, peer-to-peer
        networks, 43
    baseline fake traffic, 45
    hardware-constrained nodes, 44
    internal adversaries, 44
    local and global adversaries, 45
    message forwarding, 44
    node operation, 43–44
    overhead, 44–45
    public keys, 44
    queries and data traversing, 44

H

Hashing-based ID randomization (HIR) scheme,
    57–58
High-performance sensor nodes, 3
HISP-NC routing table perturbation scheme

basic countermeasures, 134–135
bias of routing table, 137–138
complementing data transmission
    protocol, 134
definition, 135–136
perturbation algorithm, 134
    cardinality, 139
    completion time and memory
        requirements, 139
    complexity, 139–140
    deterministic *vs.* evolutionary, 139–140
    energy function, 140–141
    optimization algorithm, 139
    random *vs.* smart swap function,
        140–141
    perturbation degree/bias, 136–137
Homogeneous injection for sink privacy with
    node compromise protection
    (HISP-NC) scheme
    biased random walk protocol, 129
    data transmission protocol, 132–133
    disadvantage, 153
    hiding real messages flow, 128
    improvement, 153
    network model, 124–125
    properties
        convergence, 131–132
        exclusion, 132
        homogeneity, 132
    protocol evaluation
        fake traffic overhead, 148–149
        message delivery time, 145–148
        network topology, 142–144
        privacy protection, 149–153
    routing table
        creation, 130–131
        of node x, 129–130
        perturbation scheme, 134–141
    threat model
        definition, 125
        routing table inspection attack,
        127–128
        traffic analysis attacks, 125–127
    time-to-live parameter, 130
Hordes
    computational operations and memory
        consumption, 43
    multicast messages, 42
    public-key cryptography, 42
    public keys and session keys storage, 43
    signed list of members, 42

I

ID confusion technique, 84
Identity attacks, 8–9
Identity, route, and location (IRL) privacy
        algorithm, 80–81
Information flow attacks, 7, 9
Information Hiding in Distributed
        Environments (iHIDE) scheme, 69
Inquisitive adversary, 101–102
    mean path length, 115–116
    number of captured sources, 114–115
Internal adversaries, 48
    CALP, 122
    Crowds, 43, 50
    GAP, 44
    mixes, 37, 49
    single-proxy solutions, 35
    source-location privacy problem
        compromised nodes, 80
        DCS networks, 82
        IRL privacy algorithm, 80–81
        location decoupling, 80
        packet transformation approach, 81
        SPENA, 81–82
        trust-based routing scheme, 80
Internet of Things, 1; *see also* Wireless sensor
        network

L

Local adversaries, 48
    Crowds, 43, 50
    receiver-location privacy problem
        basic countermeasures, 84–85
        biased random walks, 85–86
        content analysis attack, 83
        fake traffic injection, 86–87
        rate-monitoring attack, 84
        sink simulation, 87–89
        time correlation attack, 83–84
    sink simulation
        BT scheme, 88
        decentralized hotspot generation, 89
        DEFP, 89
        fake packet injection scheme, 87–88
        fake traffic generation, 87
        hotspots, 87
        maelstrom, 88
    source-location privacy problem
        directed random paths, 64–68
        fake data sources, 71–73

mote-class attackers, 59
    network loop methods, 68–70
    route randomization protocols, 59
    safety period, 59
    traceback attack, 59
    undirected random paths, 60–64
Location privacy problems
    definition, 16
    motivating scenario, 17–18
    receiver-location privacy problem, 20–22
    source-location privacy problem, 18–20
Location privacy routing, 86
Location privacy solutions
    node identity protection
        cryptographic pseudonyms, 56–59,
            96–97
        IEEE 802.15.4 MAC frame format, 54
        network map, 54
        node anonymity, 54–55
        packet headers, 54
        payload protection, 54
        pool of pseudonyms, 55–56, 96
    receiver-location privacy
        baseline flooding protocol, 83
        definition, 83
        global adversaries, 89–96
        hiding base station location, 83
        local adversaries, 83–89
        multihop routing protocol, 83
    source-location privacy
        definition, 59
        global adversaries, 73–80
        internal adversaries, 80–82
        local adversary, 59–73
        passive adversaries, 59
    taxonomy of solutions, 96

M

Maelstrom, 88
MCDS, *see* Minimum connected dominating set
Mean path length, 115–116
Message delivery time, HISP-NC protocol
    mean network bias, 147–148
    mean number of hops, 147–148
    network configurations, protocol
        performance
        distribution of neighbors, 145–146
        expected number of hops, 145–147
    recurrence equation, 145

Minimum connected dominating set (MCDS), 78–79
Mobile sensor nodes, 161
Multiparent routing (MPR), 85–86

N

Network-centric privacy problems
  content-oriented privacy
    end-to-end encryption, 13
    homomorphic encryption schemes, 13
    internal attacker, 13
    query privacy, 14
    secure encryption schemes, 12–13
    Smart Grid scenario, 12–13
  context-oriented privacy
    communication pattern, 16
    frequency spectrum, 15
    message size, 15–16
    metadata, 15
    network operation, 15
    temporal privacy, 16
    traffic analysis, 15
    transmission rate, 15
  privacy perpetrator, 12
Network loop methods
  CEM, 68–69
  distance-based RRIN approach, 70
  energy imbalance problem, 70
  fake packet injection, 70
  iHIDE scheme, 69
  initialization, 70
  NMR scheme, 69–70
  path diversification, 70
Network mixing ring (NMR) scheme, 69–70
Network topology discovery protocol, 124
Node compromise protection, *see* HISP-NC
      routing table perturbation scheme
Node identity protection
  cryptographic pseudonyms, 96–97
    anonymous one-hop communication scheme, 58
    EAC protocol, 58
    HIR scheme, 57–58
    keyed hash function, 56–57
    node revocation mechanism, 59
    pseudo-random function, 56
    RHIR, 58
    secret key, 56
  IEEE 802.15.4 MAC frame format, 54

  network map, 54
  node anonymity, 54–55
  packet headers, 54
  payload protection, 54
  pool of pseudonyms, 55–56, 96

O

Obfuscating partial hash (OPH), 82
Onion routers (ORs), 38–40
Onion routing
  architecture and transmission process, 38–39
  computational and memory demands, 39
  data transmission period, 39–40
  disadvantage, 40
  extra terminology, 40
  link-key encrypted connection, 40
  low-latency anonymous communication system, 38
  onion, public-key layered data structure, 38
  path setup process, 39–40
  symmetric-key encryption, 38
  Tor, 38–40

P

Path length distribution, 117–118
Patient adversary, 101
  mean path length, 116
  number of captured sources, 115
Phantom Routing
  flooding phase
    baseline flooding, 60
    probabilistic flooding, 60
  phantom single-path routing protocol, 60–61
  Random Parallel routing scheme, 65–66
  RRIN, 66–68
  STaR protocol, 68
  walking phase
    beacon frames, 62–63
    cloud-based approach, 63–64
    cross-layer routing protocol, 61–62
    DROW, 64
    energy waste, 61
    fake source nodes, 63
    five-step random walk, 61
    GROW, 61–62
    phantom source, 60
    PRLA, 64–65
    safety periods, 60–61
  WRS, 66

Phantom source, 60
Physical attacks, 7–9
Privacy protection, HISP-NC protocol
   base station direction, 149
   node capture attacks, 151–152
   real *vs.* fake packet probability, 150
   time-correlation attack, 149
   traffic analysis attacks, 150–151
Probabilistic flooding, 60
Probabilistic receiver-location privacy
   anti-traffic analysis techniques, 123
   HISP-NC scheme
      biased random walk protocol, 129
      data transmission protocol, 132–133
      hiding real messages flow, 128
      network model, 124–125
      node compromise protection, 134–140
      properties, 131–132
      protocol evaluation, 141–153
      routing table creation, 130–131
      routing table of node x, 129–130
      threat model, 125–128
      time-to-live parameter, 130
   randomizing and normalizing traffic
      pattern, 123
   routing tables, 123
Protocol attacks, 8–9
Proxy-based filtering scheme (PFS), 77

Q

Query privacy, 162

R

Random Parallel routing scheme, 65–66
Rate-monitoring attack, 127
Receiver anonymity, 28
Receiver-location privacy problem, 20–22
   baseline flooding protocol, 83
   definition, 83
   global adversaries
      bogus traffic injection, 89
      relocation and disguise, 94–96
      sink simulation, 92–94
      traffic homogenization, 90–92
   hiding base station location, 83
   local adversaries
      basic countermeasures, 84–85
      biased random walks, 85–86

      content analysis attack, 83
      fake traffic injection, 86–87
      rate-monitoring attack, 84
      sink simulation, 87–89
      time correlation attack, 83–84
   multihop routing protocol, 83
Relationship unlinkability, 28
Relocation for increased anonymity (RIA)
      scheme, 94–95
Reverse HIR (RHIR), 58
Route updating process, 105–106
Routing through random selected intermediate
      node (RRIN), 66–68

S

SAS, *see* Simple anonymity scheme
Sender anonymity, 28
Shortest-path CALP routing
   data relays, 108
   energy-efficient routing protocols, 108, 121
   greedy forwarding decisions, 108–109
   hardware-constrained devices, 112
   initialization phase, 108
   locally optimal neighbor selection, 108–109
   path adaptation, 109–110
   permissive CALP routing, 110–111
   protocol evaluation
      privacy protection level, 113–115
      protocol overhead, 115–118
      safety distance impact, 118–121
      simulation scenario, 112–113
   routing table of node N, 112
   strict minimum safety distance, 109, 111
   topology discovery protocol, 108
Simple anonymity scheme (SAS), 55–56
Single cross-layer approach, 62–63
Sinkhole attack, 8
Sink simulation
   global adversaries
      artificial hotspots creation, 93–94
      Chai et al.'s approach, 92–93
      Mehta et al.'s approach, 92–93
   local adversaries
      BT scheme, 88
      decentralized hotspot generation, 89
      DEFP, 89
      fake packet injection scheme, 87–88
      fake traffic generation, 87
      hotspots, 87
      maelstrom, 88

Sink Toroidal Routing (STaR) protocol, 68
Source-location privacy problem, 18–20
  definition, 59
  global adversaries
    dummy traffic injection, 74–75
    energy-aware approaches, 75–80
    topological, functional, or hardware
      constraints, 73
  internal adversaries
    compromised nodes, 80
    DCS networks, 82
    IRL privacy algorithm, 80–81
    location decoupling, 80
    packet transformation approach, 81
    SPENA, 81–82
    trust-based routing scheme, 80
  local adversary
    directed random paths, 64–68
    fake data sources, 71–73
    mote-class attackers, 59
    network loop methods, 68–70
    route randomization protocols, 59
    safety period, 59
    traceback attack, 59
    undirected random paths, 60–64
Source Privacy under Eavesdropping and Node
    compromise Attacks (SPENA), 81
Sybil attack, 8

T

Time correlation attacks, 20, 127
Tor, 38–40
Traceback attack, *see* Source-location privacy
    problem
Traffic rate monitoring, 21
Tree-based filtering scheme (TFS), 77
Typical sensor nodes, 3

U

Undirected random paths, *see* Phantom Routing
Unobservable handoff trajectory (UHT), 76–77
User-centric privacy problems
  FIPs, 11
  large-scale surveillance networks, 10
  privacy-by-architecture principle, 11–12
  privacy-by-policy approach, 11

W

Weighted random stride (WRS), 66
Wireless sensor network (WSN)
  base stations/sink, 2
  communication model, 4
  data aggregation, 5–6
  data collection capacities, 155
  data-harvesting systems, 155
  event-driven model, data reporting
    method, 4
  flooding-based routing protocols, 5
  future sensor networks
    compromised sensor nodes, 163
    data-aggregation privacy, 162
    data collection and data sharing, 162
    data-hungry businesses and organizations,
      163
    event-driven data reporting
      method, 161
    internal attackers, 163
    mobile sensor nodes, 161
    multi-party computation, 162
    service providers, 162
  individual privacy, online transactions, 155
  location privacy problem, 2
    anonymous communications
      systems, 156
    base station protection, 157
    CALP mechanism, 156–157
    communication pattern, 156
    complete privacy solutions, 158–159
    cost-effective location privacy
      solutions, 158
    hardware limitation of sensor
      nodes, 156
    HISP-NC, 157
    interoperable evaluation framework,
      160–161
    realistic adversaries, 159–160
  networks deployment and operation, 155
  privacy problems
    classification, 9–10
    location privacy, 16–22
    network-centric privacy, 12–16
    user-centric privacy, 10–12
  security
    adversaries, 6–7
    confidentiality and integrity attacks, 7
    intrusion detection systems, 8
    key management schemes, 8

network availability, 7
potential threats, 7–9
trust management systems, 8
sensor nodes/motes
applications, 2
classification, 3
hardware limitation, 6
power unit, 3–4
processing unit, 3

radio interface/transceiver, 3–4
sensing unit, 2–3
single-/shortest-path routing protocol, 5
Wormhole attack, 8
WSN, *see* Wireless sensor network

Z

Zigzag bidirectional tree (ZBT) scheme, 72–73